Practical Playwright Test

Next-Generation Web Testing and Automation

Jean-François Greffier

Apress®

Practical Playwright Test: Next-Generation Web Testing and Automation

Jean-François Greffier
Rennes, France

ISBN-13 (pbk): 979-8-8688-2159-2 ISBN-13 (electronic): 979-8-8688-2160-8
https://doi.org/10.1007/979-8-8688-2160-8

Copyright © 2026 by Jean-François Greffier

This work is subject to copyright. All rights are reserved by the Publisher, whether the whole or part of the material is concerned, specifically the rights of translation, reprinting, reuse of illustrations, recitation, broadcasting, reproduction on microfilms or in any other physical way, and transmission or information storage and retrieval, electronic adaptation, computer software, or by similar or dissimilar methodology now known or hereafter developed.

Trademarked names, logos, and images may appear in this book. Rather than use a trademark symbol with every occurrence of a trademarked name, logo, or image we use the names, logos, and images only in an editorial fashion and to the benefit of the trademark owner, with no intention of infringement of the trademark.

The use in this publication of trade names, trademarks, service marks, and similar terms, even if they are not identified as such, is not to be taken as an expression of opinion as to whether or not they are subject to proprietary rights.

While the advice and information in this book are believed to be true and accurate at the date of publication, neither the authors nor the editors nor the publisher can accept any legal responsibility for any errors or omissions that may be made. The publisher makes no warranty, express or implied, with respect to the material contained herein.

Managing Director, Apress Media LLC: Welmoed Spahr
Acquisitions Editor: Anandadeep Roy
Project Manager: Jessica Vakili

Cover designed by eStudioCalamar

Cover image designed by Holger Langmaier on pixabay

Distributed to the book trade worldwide by Springer Science+Business Media New York, 1 New York Plaza, New York, NY 10004. Phone 1-800-SPRINGER, fax (201) 348-4505, e-mail orders-ny@springer-sbm.com, or visit www.springeronline.com. Apress Media, LLC is a Delaware LLC and the sole member (owner) is Springer Science + Business Media Finance Inc (SSBM Finance Inc). SSBM Finance Inc is a **Delaware** corporation.

For information on translations, please e-mail booktranslations@springernature.com; for reprint, paperback, or audio rights, please e-mail bookpermissions@springernature.com.

Apress titles may be purchased in bulk for academic, corporate, or promotional use. eBook versions and licenses are also available for most titles. For more information, reference our Print and eBook Bulk Sales web page at http://www.apress.com/bulk-sales.

Any source code or other supplementary material referenced by the author in this book is available to readers on GitHub. For more detailed information, please visit https://www.apress.com/gp/services/source-code.

If disposing of this product, please recycle the paper

Life is a series of obstacles and challenges best engaged through assiduous study and frequent jumps into uncertainty. Anything else is boring.

—*American McGee*

Table of Contents

About the Author .... **xiii**

About the Technical Reviewer .... **xv**

Acknowledgments .... **xvii**

Introduction .... **xix**

Chapter 1: Getting Started **1**

   Introducing Playwright 1

      Why Choose Playwright 1

      Architecture 3

      Browsers 3

   Prepare Your Environment 5

      Prerequisites 5

      TL;DR 8

      npm, yarn, pnpm 8

      Check the Prerequisites 9

   Your First Test 9

   Develop Faster with Your Favorite IDE 12

      Playwright Test for VS Code 12

      JetBrains Test Automation Plugin 13

      Using Another IDE? 13

   Useful Resources to Get You Started 14

TABLE OF CONTENTS

Chapter 2: Write Tests Efficiently 17
Playwright Test Building Blocks 17
Common Built-In Fixtures 18
Organizing Your Tests 20
Actions 26
Basic Interactions 27
Forms 28
Advanced Actions 31
Get Rid of Overlays 33
Assertions 34
Generic Assertions 34
Web-First Assertions 36
Snapshots 38
Visual Regression Testing 38
Aria Snapshots 40
Write Better Assertions 43
async/await and Promise 44
Common Pitfalls 45
Advanced Patterns with Promises 46
Configure Playwright Test 47
Configuration File 47
Using Environment Variables for More Flexibility 51
Overrides in Test Files 52
Command Line Interface 52
Write Tests Efficiently 53
Codegen 54
UI Mode 56
A Great Workflow to Write and Debug Tests 56
Summary 58

Chapter 3: Locators 59

CSS and XPath 59
CSS 59
XPath 61
Legacy and Experimental Locators 61
Testing Library Queries 62
getByText 64
getByRole 65
getByLabel 68
getByTestId 69
Advanced Patterns 71
Working with iframes 71
Filtering Locators 72
Chaining Locators 74
Craft Better Apps with Semantic HTML 75
Locators Good Practices 77
Locators Tier List 77
Dos and Don'ts 78
Summary 80

Chapter 4: Continuous Integration 81

Why Adding Playwright to Your CI? 81
Our Pipeline with Playwright Test and GitHub 82
Prerequisites 82
Install Dependencies 83
Install Playwright Browsers 84
Run the Tests 85
Run GitHub Actions Locally with act 86
Other CI Solutions 88
Docker and Playwright 89
Docker 89

vii

TABLE OF CONTENTS

- Use Official Docker Image with GitHub Actions 90
- Taylor Your Own Docker Image 91
- Gotcha: Visual Regression Testing and CI 92
- Advanced Pipeline 94
  - Adjusting Parallelism and Timeout 94
  - Retrieve Reports As Artifacts 95
- Reporting 96
- Debugging Afterward with Logs, Reports, and Traces 98
  - Make Sense of Logs 98
  - HTML Report 100
  - Time-Travel with Traces 102
  - Run It on Your Machine 105
- Summary 106

Chapter 5: Make It Fast 107

- Parallelism 108
  - How Many Workers Should You Use? 108
  - Your Machine vs. a CI Agent 111
  - Understand the Different Parallelism Options 112
- Sharding 114
  - Set It Up with GitHub 116
  - Reconstruct Reports 117
- Save Time and Money in CI 120
  - Optimize Your Application and Environment 120
  - Authentication 121
  - Leverage --only-changed Option 123
  - Pushing the Envelope 124
- Tests at Scale with Testing Services 127
  - Microsoft Playwright Testing 128
  - Endform 128
- Summary 129

TABLE OF CONTENTS

Chapter 6: Extending Playwright Test 131

Custom expect 131
Custom expect Message 131
Extend expect 132
Make Your Own CSS Matcher 133
Compose Your Matchers Collection 135

Reporters 137
Add Extra Information 137
Third-Party Reporters 141
Write Your Own 142

Test Data 145
Faker for Inclusive, Realistic Data 145
Define Test Cases in JSON or CSV 148
Parametrize Tests 149
Parametrize Projects with Test Options 150

Summary 152

Chapter 7: Fixtures Deep Dive 153

Improve Your Tests with Fixtures 154
Your First Fixture 157
Decoupling Setup and Test 159
Composition 163
Wrap-Up 164

Page Object Model 164
POM Class 165
POM with Fixture 167

More Fixtures Usages 168
Injecting Test Data 168
Automatic Fixtures 170
Test Options 171

Create Your Fixture Collection 173
Keep One Custom Test 173

ix

TABLE OF CONTENTS

Mix It with Third-Party 174

Organize Fixtures and Helpers 174

DRY vs. WET 175

Summary 176

Chapter 8: Mocking and Emulation 177

Device Emulation 177

userAgent 178

screen, viewport, deviceScaleFactor 179

Is This a Mobile? 180

Usage 180

Mobile Testing 182

Space and time 182

Locale 183

Timezone 183

Clock API 184

Permissions 187

Geolocation 188

Network 189

Route 189

Emulating a Slow Network 191

Record and Replay HAR 193

Injecting JavaScript 194

Chrome DevTools Protocol 195

Using CDP to Slow Down the CPU 196

Summary 197

Chapter 9: Gain Confidence Thanks to Reliable Tests 199

Built-In Reliability: Auto-Waiting, Retries, and Timeouts 199

Understanding Actions Auto-Waiting 200

Web-First Assertions 202

Fine-Tune Your Timeouts 203

Test Retry 204

TABLE OF CONTENTS

 Flakiness 206
  How to Detect Flaky Tests 207
  Strategies to Fix Flaky Tests 212
 Summary 221

Chapter 10: Automation and More with Playwright 223
 Playwright Library 223
 Web Scraping 225
 Generating Artifacts: Screenshots, PDFs, Videos 228
  Screenshots for Your Documentation 228
  Recording Videos 229
  PDF Generation 230
 Monitoring with Playwright and Checkly 232
  Peace of Mind 232
  Use with Playwright 233
  Benefits 234
 Summary 235

Chapter 11: Beyond End-to-End Testing 237
 Behavior-Driven Development 237
  Playwright-BDD 238
  Alternative: Approval Testing 239
 REST API Testing 240
  Your First GET 241
  Simple Data Validation 242
  Context Request 245
  Why Playwright for API Testing? 245
 Component Testing 245
  …with Playwright 247
  …with Playwright and Storybook 252
 Summary 255

TABLE OF CONTENTS

Chapter 12: Solving the Test Frameworks Puzzle 257
The Test Pyramid Is a Wrong Model 258
State of JavaScript Testing 260
Frameworks 261
JS Runtimes 261
End-to-End 261
Mocking 262
And More 262
A Homogenous Testing Stack 262
Static – Prettier, ESLint, Stylelint, TypeScript 264
Unit – Vitest 264
Integration – Testing Library 265
End-to-End – Playwright Test 266
Conclusion 267

Index 269

About the Author

Jean-François Greffier is an experienced front-end engineer. His main interests are software craft and testing. Recently awarded Microsoft MVP, he is a Playwright ambassador. He is not only an advocate, but also an open source contributor to Playwright on documentation, bug fixes, and features. He is also the maintainer of the Playwright Angular Schematic.

About the Technical Reviewer

Simon Knott is a Senior Software Engineer on the Playwright Core Team at Microsoft. Before joining Microsoft, he worked on the Content Delivery Networks and Functions infrastructure at Netlify and founded Quirrel, an open source job queueing solution acquired by Netlify. Simon holds a bachelor's degree in Computer Science from Hasso Plattner Institute near Berlin.

Simon is the creator of SuperJSON, a widely adopted JSON serialization library, was part of the React 18 Working group, and has contributed to projects like Chromium, VS Code, Next.js, Apache Traffic Server, and Pandas. Simon has presented at the BeJS conference, local Typescript meet-ups, and the FSJam Podcast and served as the technical reviewer for this very book!

Simon is passionate about making modern web development more productive. When he doesn't, you'll usually find him cooking, woodworking, or cycling around Berlin.

Acknowledgments

First, thanks to Anandadeep Roy for trusting me with this project and for his enthusiasm. Many thanks to everyone at Apress for helping me to focus on actually writing the book.

Thanks to my family for their patience and ongoing support.

Simon Knott helped to make the book not only technically correct but also much better. He made this the best version of the book it could be. Simon, I do hope we can grab a coffee someday.

Thanks to the beta readers Tanguy Michel and Ronan Barbot, who gave me a welcome different perspective. Thanks to Butch Mayhew, who gave me feedback in the early process of laying down my plan. Thanks to Tanguy Michel and Nica Mellifera for agreeing to be interviewed.

Many thanks to Debbie O'Brien for welcoming me among the Playwright Ambassadors.

If it takes a village to raise a child, it certainly takes a tech community to create a book. RennesJS, Snowcamp, Slickteam, Conserto Explos, Playwright Ambassadors – these meetups, conferences, and communities helped me to grow. Thank you.

Introduction

Who Is This Book For?

For a long time, programming was a complicated craft. It had to address almost impossible technical challenges: How do I race against the beam and create a video game out of a few transistors? How can I make great software with a few bytes of RAM? It also needed to be correct and reliable, with legal requirements like calculating taxes accurately.

Software is everywhere: in our pockets, our cars, our several microcomputers. We didn't quite reach the ubiquitous computing the engineers dreamed of in the 1980s, but the closest thing we have are web apps. You can access your favorite applications, with your profile and data, from pretty much any devices that hold a web browser. Our smartphones are multiple times more powerful than the ancient machines that started personal computing.

Now as developers we have to deal with several languages, frameworks, dependencies, but we also need to care about deployment, security, accessibility, design, multi-platform… I believe that today, writing software is complex. To paraphrase the Manifesto for Agile Software Development, we are still uncovering better ways of developing software. To help us to make great software, we need great tooling. Microsoft Playwright is an awesome end-to-end testing solution that I discovered a few years ago. It's a great piece of tooling that can help you craft better software and untangle its complexity.

This book is primarily meant for front-end or full-stack developers that want to further progress by mastering end-to-end testing with Playwright Test. Quality Assurance professionals should also find value in this work, as it goes in-depth with Playwright Test techniques, automation, and testing strategy. Actually, this book is for any individual contributors that care deeply about high-quality software.

You don't have to be an expert front-end developer, but some knowledge of HTML, CSS, and TypeScript is needed. A curiosity toward testing principles is a plus. Being familiar with unit test frameworks like Jest or Vitest is helpful, but experience with end-to-end testing tools is not necessary.

INTRODUCTION

Playwright officially supports TypeScript, Python, Java, and .Net. However, I chose to focus on the TypeScript flavor and its test runner: Playwright Test.

The first chapters will help you get started with Playwright Test and give you great basics. The second part details advanced concepts and will hopefully be a resource while you practice what you've learned. Finally, the last part focuses on what's beyond end-to-end testing and how to use Playwright Test in your testing strategy.

CHAPTER 1

Getting Started

In this chapter, you'll get an overview of what Playwright Test is about and its advantages and inconveniences, so you can decide when to use it. You'll learn how to set up your environment and run your first test. Look for useful online resources at the end to complement this book.

Introducing Playwright

Playwright is an open source project sponsored and primarily maintained by Microsoft. It automates the web by driving three browsers: Chromium, Firefox, and WebKit (the tech behind Safari). This means that you can automate and test your web applications on all three major browser families.

Moreover, Playwright is an automation solution geared toward end-to-end testing. It provides assertions adapted to web testing, its own Playwright Test runner, as well as a Codegen generator, and a trace recorder.

With its Developer eXperience, speed of execution, availability for different languages and test reliability, Microsoft Playwright quickly gained in popularity. In this chapter, we'll look at how to prepare your environment, install Playwright, and create your first testing project.

Why Choose Playwright

Testing is sometimes seen as too complex, difficult to implement in the customer or technical context, time-consuming, useless, and so on. Fortunately, unit and integration tests are becoming increasingly accepted practices, but end-to-end tests are not. They are rarely used, as they are considered slow, fragile, and difficult to write and maintain. End-to-end testing reputation is so bad among developers that many relegate these tests to specialized automation engineers.

CHAPTER 1   GETTING STARTED

Playwright is significantly faster than competing end-to-end testing solutions. In fact, as demonstrated in the article "Cypress vs Selenium vs Playwright vs Puppeteer speed comparison,"[1] the tool is fast, even for large test suites. Furthermore, it's easy to parallelize test execution via vertical scaling (more CPUs) or horizontal scaling (more machines). These parallelization features are built-in and do not rely on third-party plugins.

Tests on browsers are often fragile, typically "working on my machine" but failing in continuous integration. This phenomenon, known as flakiness, is well known to end-to-end testers. Depending on network conditions and the target machine, it's sometimes tempting to wait a second or two "just in case." Or wait until something is eventually present.

Fortunately, Playwright takes care of all this automatically with **auto-wait**. Before performing an action, the test framework will ensure that the criteria are met. For example, before clicking on an element, it must be enabled, visible, not moving, and have a listener for the click.

What also happens is that a change in the application breaks the tests: the DOM structure has changed, or the CSS classes. These tests that break at the slightest change are too closely linked to implementation: use CSS or XPath selectors to find the elements to be tested.

Playwright offers numerous types of selectors: text, accessibility attributes, CSS, or even positional. Above all, you can combine selectors to find what's both relevant and robust. Playwright's generator, Codegen, generates the most robust selector possible.

Playwright tests are easier to write thanks to Codegen. It opens a browser window in which you interact with the web application you want to test, and a second window with the Playwright inspector. Your actions are recorded and create code in the language of your choice. This tool also enables you to test and design more readable and robust selectors.

Tests are also easy to debug. Step-by-step tests can be run using either the VS Code extension or Codegen. Best of all, Playwright's trace viewer provides a history of Playwright calls, browser console, and network traces and allows you to inspect the browser page at any point in time, even if the test ran on a different machine, like your Continuous Integration.

---

[1] https://blog.checklyhq.com/cypress-vs-selenium-vs-playwright-vs-puppeteer-speed-comparison

Architecture

I've often been asked what are Playwright, Playwright Test, and why it's only available in TypeScript when you can test in other languages.

Playwright is actually made up of several tools:

- **Playwright Library:** This is the heart of Playwright, enabling it to talk to different browsers. It can be used in several languages: TypeScript, Python, Java, .Net officially, but also Go, Ruby, and more thanks to open source language bindings. This library is used by many projects in different contexts because it only does browser automation, and does it well. No tests here.

- **Playwright Expect:** These are the famous web-first assertions that help you to assert conditions linked with the DOM. Available in all supported languages, it can be used with different test frameworks. The TypeScript version is compatible with the expect library and usable with your preferred test runner: Jest, Vitest, Mocha, ...

- **Playwright Test:** This is Playwright's test runner, which fetches and executes tests, creates reports, and handles parallelization and sharding. It's a great, modern test runner that is tailored for Playwright. This component is only available for TypeScript. For other languages, it's up to you to use a suitable test runner: JUnit, Pytest, MSTest, etc.

- **Codegen:** The code generator that lets you record a user path and generate the corresponding code for several languages, whether for Playwright Library or Playwright Test.

- **Trace Viewer:** It allows you to visualize the traces of an automation or a test. The tool is also available online.

Browsers

One important point to bear in mind is the browsers supported by Playwright. In fact, Playwright's core principle is to test the web, on the major browser families.

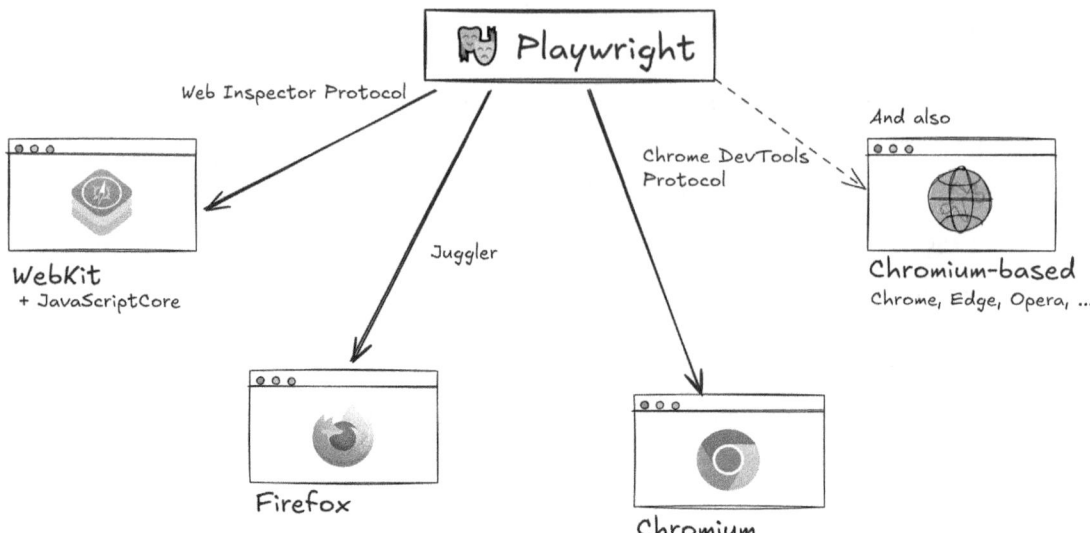

Figure 1-1. *Playwright communicates via browser debug protocol*

As shown in Figure 1-1, Playwright supports three major browsers:

- **Chromium:** Playwright supports Chromium, and browsers based on it: Chrome, Brave, Opera, Edge, ... This is made possible because Playwright uses the Chromium DevTools Protocol.[2]

- **Firefox** is supported via a patched build and the Juggler protocol.

- **WebKit** is a special case, which is here for a very specific reason. Apple Safari is only available on iPhone, iPad, and macOS. To run macOS, you need to run it on a Mac. What's more, it's not legally possible to virtualize macOS by yourself.

  So to have a browser that works on your machine (macOS, Linux, or Windows) and on your Continuous Integration, we're going to use the best alternative: a browser made with the same building bricks as Safari.

> **Note** Playwright's build of WebKit can be used in other contexts where you need a Safari-like browser. For instance, Cypress uses it for WebKit support (experimental).

---

[2] Fun trivia: This very CDP protocol was developed by the same people as Playwright.

Thanks to its approach, Playwright can automate the three main browser engines. The main drawback is that the browsers are bound to the version of Playwright you are installing. For example, it is impossible to test an older version of Firefox with the latest Playwright.

Prepare Your Environment

Playwright is a Node.js application that comes with its own web browsers for automation. Remember, in this book, we talk about Playwright Test which means exclusively the TypeScript flavor of Playwright. It is also available for other languages: Python, Java, .Net, but this is not the subject of this book.

Prerequisites

You'll need an up-to-date version of Node.js, and the main operating systems are supported. Here are the requirements as of today:[3]

- Node.js 20+
- Windows 10+, Windows Server 2016+, or Windows Subsystem for Linux (WSL)
- macOS 14 Ventura, or later
- Debian 12+, Ubuntu 22.04, Ubuntu 24.04, on x86-64 and arm64 architecture

I suggest you recommend the Long-Term Support version of Node.js (LTS). If you are doing frontend or backend in JavaScript, that's probably already the version you are using: the LTS version is the main version of Node.js, providing fixes to critical bugs for up to 30 months.

I highly recommend using nvm[4] to install Node.js. It will allow you to install automatically Node.js and npm, update them, and switch versions on the fly to suit your needs.

---

[3] See https://playwright.dev/docs/intro#system-requirements for up-to-date information
[4] nvm https://github.com/nvm-sh/nvm, or NVM for Windows https://github.com/coreybutler/nvm-windows which offers similar functionalities

CHAPTER 1   GETTING STARTED

> **Note**   Only Debian 12 and 13 and Ubuntu 22.04 and 24.04 are officially supported.
>
> However, derivatives of those distros such as Raspbian, KDE Neon, Linux Mint… are fine. If you are using something else, you still can resort to Docker.

Depending on your operating system, you'll probably need a number of dependencies in order to run the browsers for our tests. Playwright downloads and installs for you its own browsers: Chromium, Firefox, and WebKit (like Safari).

On a fresh Debian image (Bookworm Slim), here's what you get if you don't install these dependencies but try to install the Playwright browsers.

Playwright Host validation warning:

```
Host system is missing dependencies to run browsers.
Missing libraries:
    libglib-2.0.so.0
    libgobject-2.0.so.0
    libnss3.so
    libnssutil3.so
    libsmime3.so
    libnspr4.so
    libdbus-1.so.3
    libatk-1.0.so.0
    libatk-bridge-2.0.so.0
    libcups.so.2
    libgio-2.0.so.0
    libdrm.so.2
    libexpat.so.1
    libxcb.so.1
    libxkbcommon.so.0
    libatspi.so.0
    libX11.so.6
    libXcomposite.so.1
    libXdamage.so.1
    libXext.so.6
```

```
    libXfixes.so.3
    libXrandr.so.2
    libgbm.so.1
    libpango-1.0.so.0
    libcairo.so.2
    libasound.so.2
```

Fortunately, there's a command that will check these dependencies and install them if necessary. Note that this will ask for root access if needed.

```
npx playwright install-deps
```

If you don't want Playwright to install the dependencies automatically for you, you can make a dry run. In this way, you can inspect what will be installed, copy-paste, modify, and adapt the command to manage it yourself.

```
$ npx playwright install-deps --dry-run
sh -c "apt-get update&& apt-get install -y --no-install-recommends
libasound2 libatk-bridge2.0-0 libatk1.0-0 libatspi2.0-0 libcairo2 libcups2
libdbus-1-3 libdrm2 libgbm1 libglib2.0-0 libnspr4 libnss3 libpango-1.0-0
libx11-6 libxcb1 libxcomposite1 libxdamage1 libxext6 libxfixes3
libxkbcommon0 libxrandr2 xvfb fonts-noto-color-emoji fonts-unifont
libfontconfig1 libfreetype6 xfonts-scalable fonts-liberation fonts-ipafont-
gothic fonts-wqy-zenhei fonts-tlwg-loma-otf fonts-freefont-ttf libcairo-
gobject2 libdbus-glib-1-2 libgdk-pixbuf-2.0-0 libgtk-3-0 libharfbuzz0b
libpangocairo-1.0-0 libx11-xcb1 libxcb-shm0 libxcursor1 libxi6 libxrender1
libxtst6 libsoup-3.0-0 gstreamer1.0-libav gstreamer1.0-plugins-bad
gstreamer1.0-plugins-base gstreamer1.0-plugins-good libegl1 libenchant-2-2
libepoxy0 libevdev2 libgles2 libglx0 libgstreamer-gl1.0-0 libgstreamer-
plugins-base1.0-0 libgstreamer1.0-0 libgudev-1.0-0 libharfbuzz-icu0
libhyphen0 libicu72 libjpeg62-turbo liblcms2-2 libmanette-0.2-0 libnotify4
libopengl0 libopenjp2-7 libopus0 libpng16-16 libproxy1v5 libsecret-1-0
libwayland-client0 libwayland-egl1 libwayland-server0 libwebp7
libwebpdemux2 libwoff1 libxml2 libxslt1.1 libatomic1 libevent-2.1-7"
```

CHAPTER 1   GETTING STARTED

TL;DR

Prepare your Linux environment with this:

```
sudo apt update
sudo apt install curl
curl -o- https://raw.githubusercontent.com/nvm-sh/nvm/v0.40.3/install.sh | bash
nvm install --lts
nvm use --lts
npx playwright install-deps
```

npm, yarn, pnpm...

Quick reminder that the example scripts use npm, the node package manager that comes with Node.js. You can use others; the examples are all written with npm so as not to clutter the text.

A few equivalents of common package manager usage:

```
# init
npm init playwright
yarn create playwright
pnpm create playwright

# run a script that is defined by package.json
npm run hello
yarn hello
pnpm run hello

# run a binary from a package
npx playwright test
yarn playwright test
pnpm exec playwright test
```

Bun is an alternative runtime that is compatible with Node.js and does many more things. Playwright doesn't officially support bun, but the growing popularity of both solutions means that bun has made quite an effort to be able to run Playwright Test. Check their website to know more: https://bun.sh.

Here are a few hints for you to try bun for yourself:

```
# init
# npm init something == npx create-something
bunx create-playwright
# run a script that is defined by package.json
bun run hello
# run a binary from a package
bunx playwright test

# not working at the time of writing
bunx --bun playwright test
```

Check the Prerequisites

Now we can verify that we have everything set up: Node.js must return the current version, dependencies are installed.

```
node -v
npx playwright install-deps
```

We are now ready to initiate our first Playwright Test project.

Your First Test

Let's start by creating a new project:

```
mkdir playwright-example
cd playwright-example
npm init -y
```

We've just initialized an empty Node.js project; now let's install Playwright Test.

```
npm init playwright
```

`npm init playwright` will use another package behind the scenes, `create-playwright`, which is a wizard that will ask you a few questions to help you set up your test project. It's pretty straightforward, but two questions might puzzle you: which language to use and whether to install browsers.

CHAPTER 1   GETTING STARTED

At the question on using TypeScript or JavaScript, I advise selecting TypeScript. First, your tests don't have to be in the same language as the app being under tests. So, if your app is not using TypeScript, it's not a problem. Second, TypeScript is pretty awesome at catching issues while you write tests. If you are not familiar with it, I promise it's not too scary.

The wizard asks you if it should download browsers for you; you should always say yes as it will download browsers only if needed. Even better, Playwright will keep track of the browsers usage and will clean up browsers that are unused. For example, this happens when you update a Playwright Test installation and the browser version is not used by another project.

OK, let's take a look at what files the initialization script has added (Table 1-1).

Table 1-1. *Files added by initialization script*

File	
tests/example.spec.ts	Test file, which will be run with through Playwright Test
tests-examples/demo-todo-app.spec.ts	Example of a much more complete test on a TODO list application. Move this file to the tests folder or change the config to run it.
playwright.config.ts	Playwright Test's configuration file
package.json	
.gitignore	

Also note that the `@playwright/test` package is installed as a dev dependency and that the `.gitignore` file is updated.

> **Note**   If you're working with Angular, there is a schematic for Playwright.
>
> This community Playwright Test integration with Angular is the one featured when you run `ng e2e` and select Playwright.
>
> In addition to initializing Playwright Test, it will configure your project to run an Angular development server. Note that you can also use `npm init playwright` without any drawbacks.[5]

---

[5] Trust me, I'm the author of Playwright Angular Schematic.

We'll now check the installation and run the tests:

```
npx playwright test
```

Let's take a look at the test file we just ran.

Listing 1-1. example.spec.ts

```
import { test, expect } from "@playwright/test"; //1

test("has title", async ({ page }) => { //2
  await page.goto("https://playwright.dev/");

  // Expect a title "to contain" a substring.
  await expect(page).toHaveTitle(/Playwright/);
});
test("get started link", async ({ page }) => {
  await page.goto("https://playwright.dev/");

  // Click the get started link.
  await page.getByRole("link", { name: "Get started" }).click(); // 3

  // Expects page to have a heading with the name of Installation.
  await expect(
    page.getByRole("heading", { name: "Installation" })
  ).toBeVisible(); // 4
});
```

Some important points (see inline comments in Listing 1-1):

1. The test functions must be explicitly imported. `test` or `expect` are not global.

2. The test syntax is fairly close to other popular test frameworks, such as Jest.

3. The API allows you to perform actions.

4. And assertions.

CHAPTER 1   GETTING STARTED

Finally, let's open the HTML test report as the Command Line Interface suggests:

`npx playwright show-report`

The test runner opens the HTML report automatically if a test failed. This behavior can be changed with the configuration file.

You probably noticed that six tests passed. Actually the test file has two tests, that will run on three different browsers (Chromium, Firefox, WebKit).

Our project is set up, but one last thing remains to install and configure before you can write tests efficiently.

Develop Faster with Your Favorite IDE

Having the right tooling is important, and Playwright Test can easily be integrated to your daily development routine.

Playwright Test for VS Code

If you are using Visual Studio Code, I highly recommend the official extension by the Playwright team (Figure 1-2). It is called Playwright Test for VS Code" and is published by Microsoft.

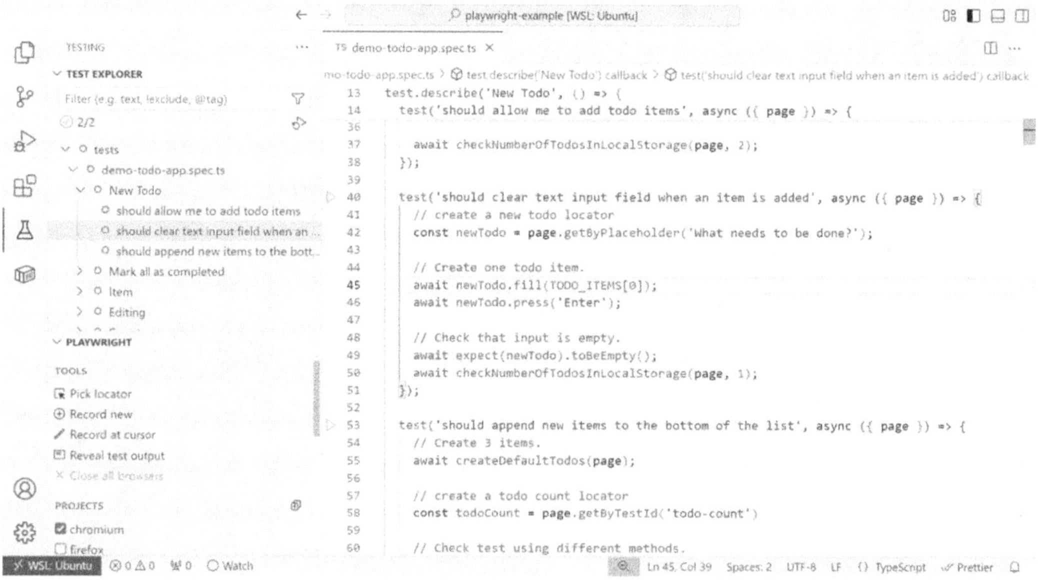

Figure 1-2. Playwright VS Code Extension

With this extension, you can

- Run and debug tests directly from the editor.
- Have a view of all tests.
- Run tests with a watch mode.
- Run the test and display the browser.
- Record tests.
- Record at cursor: Record actions and assertions in an existing test. That's my personal favorite.
- ...and more.

JetBrains Test Automation Plugin

JetBrains edits a popular family of IDE such as WebStorm, PhpStorm, or IntelliJ.

All these products support Playwright Test with no problem. You'll have the ability to list, run, and debug tests.

You can also install JetBrains' new Test Automation plugin. It adds better code completion and a Web inspector. The Web inspector is a browser conveniently displayed to the side of your code, with a Locator selector.

Alas, the Locator selector does not automatically choose the best locator for you, and it is up to you to decide what kind of Locator to generate. Also, it's a pity that it is not possible to record a test from the IDE.

Again, WebStorm and alike can run and debug Playwright test without any plugin.

Using Another IDE?

Are you using Vim? Or something else?

My favorite solution is VS Code, but you don't have to change your habits: Playwright Test can be used without a dedicated IDE or extension. We will see that the built-in tools such as Codegen or the UI Mode can help you in your daily developments. The CLI test runner offers a good experience as well. (Actually, for Vim, you should try vim-test, which is compatible with Playwright.)

CHAPTER 1   GETTING STARTED

Useful Resources to Get You Started

The goal of this book is to explain in-depth key principles of Playwright and testing, in a simple way. I encourage you to consult the official documentation to get an exhaustive reference. In addition, here are some online resources that complement this book.

- **The official Playwright documentation**: Not only is it a complete reference on Playwright Library and Playwright Test, but it is also packed with guides that will help you on a daily basis.

    https://playwright.dev/docs/intro

- **Playwright Solutions** is like a giant FAQ on Playwright, packed with guides and solutions to common problems or questions. This blog is written by Butch Mayhew, a fellow Playwright Ambassador.

    https://playwrightsolutions.com

- **QA tips by Abi**: Abigail Armijo is an experienced QA. In her blog, she shares articles related to automated testing in general. Check out her Playwright Sample GitHub repo, full of various usage examples.

    https://abigailarmijo.substack.com

    https://github.com/effiziente1/playwrightSample

- **Awesome Playwright** is a curated list of awesome tools, utils, and projects using Playwright.

    https://github.com/mxschmitt/awesome-playwright

- **Get started with end-to-end testing: Playwright** has a great YouTube playlist to get you started, by Debbie O'Brien.

    https://www.youtube.com/playlist?list=PLQ6Buerc008ed-F9OksF7ek37wR3y916p

- **The Discord community**: I recommend the official Discord community, where you'll find myself online with thousands of Playwright enthusiasts. It's a great place to get help and find out about the latest releases.

    `https://aka.ms/playwright/discord`

CHAPTER 2

Write Tests Efficiently

You'll learn in this chapter how to create end-to-end tests with the introduction of basic notions: Locators, Actions, and Assertions. We will see how to interact with web pages, including the most challenging use cases. I will detail the different kinds of assertions, and not only how to write tests, but how to do it efficiently.

Playwright Test Building Blocks

Playwright is not only a browser automation solution, but one that was made for end-to-end testing. For that, the framework gives us some building blocks:

- Locators to find HTML Elements
- Actions to interact with them
- Assertions to perform checks

Locators are one of the key parts of Playwright; that's why I dedicated an entire chapter. For now, just remember that they are ways to locate an Element, usually from the page Object. The most common methods to get a Locator are the getBy* methods.

Actions are interactions with the DOM: fill a text input, select options, checkboxes, click and navigate among others.

Inspired by Jest's expect library,[1] Playwright provides basic assertions and Web-first assertions. The latter are aware of how elements are rendered in the DOM. For example, it verifies if a checkbox is checked, if an element is visible, if it is in the viewport, if it holds a specific HTML attribute…

```
// Locator
const closeButton = page.getByRole('button', { name: 'close' })
```

---

[1] Jest is actually a test framework's framework: it's highly modulable, and expect can be used outside of Jest – https://www.npmjs.com/package/expect.

```
// Action
await closeButton.click();
// Assertion
await expect(page.getByText("Bye !")).toBeVisible()
```

All are offered by Playwright and an assertion library that you can use with various test runners. In TypeScript, it can be easily used with Jest or Vitest. The same assertions are available for other supported languages and testing frameworks: PyTest, JUnit, NUnit, …

Playwright Test is a test runner specifically tailored for end-to-end testing with Playwright. Like most testing frameworks, it allows test generation, reports, and parallelization out of the box. Because it is dedicated to Playwright, it is adapted to the specificity of end-to-end testing. Also, the reporting is better integrated. Here too, it has some similarities with the popular Jest framework, so you might be familiar with some structure and notions.

Common Built-In Fixtures

One specificity of Playwright Test is that it is based on fixtures. You can see them as a kind of dependency injection that also takes care of the test lifecycle. We'll develop more on that later in a later chapter, which details how to use fixtures and also write your own.

We perform tests or automation on a `page`, that comes from an isolated context from a `browser`.

Another way to put it:

- `Browser` is Chromium, Firefox, WebKit…
- `Context` is an incognito session
- `Page` is a tab in this session

Without fixtures, you'll have to create a `page` (with its isolated `context`) on each test. We can keep the `browser` for the whole test suite.

Listing 2-1. example-no-fixtures.spec.ts

```
import { test, expect, chromium } from "@playwright/test";

test.describe("example", () => {
  // Test setup
```

```
  let browser, context, page;
  test.beforeAll(async () => {
    browser = await chromium.launch();
  });
  test.afterAll(async () => {
    await browser.close();
  });
  test.beforeEach(async () => {
    context = await browser.newContext();
    page = await context.newPage();
  });
  test.afterEach(async () => {
    await context.close();
  });

  test("has title", async () => {
    await page.goto("https://playwright.dev/");

    // Expect a title "to contain" a substring.
    await expect(page).toHaveTitle(/Playwright/);
  });

  test("get started link", async () => {
    await page.goto("https://playwright.dev/");

    // Click the get started link.
    await page.getByRole("link", { name: "Get started" }).click();

    // Expects page to have a heading with the name of Installation.
    await expect(
      page.getByRole("heading", { name: "Installation" })
    ).toBeVisible();
  });
});
```

Listing 2-2. example-fixtures.spec.ts

```ts
import { test, expect } from '@playwright/test';

test.describe('example', () => {
  test('has title', async ({ page }) => {
    await page.goto('https://playwright.dev/');

    // Expect a title "to contain" a substring.
    await expect(page).toHaveTitle(/Playwright/);
  });

  test('get started link', async ({ page }) => {
    await page.goto('https://playwright.dev/');

    // Click the get started link.
    await page.getByRole('link', { name: 'Get started' }).click();

    // Expects page to have a heading with the name of Installation.
    await expect(
      page.getByRole('heading', { name: 'Installation' }),
    ).toBeVisible();
  });
});
```

Without Playwright Test's fixtures, you have to manage this lifecycle by yourself. Cumbersome. With fixtures, the highlighted test setup code in Listing 2-1 is not needed! It is replaced by the page fixture that has been passed by Playwright Test. That's much clearer.

If you need to manage context yourself in a test, you still can. Simply use { page, context } in your test function parameter. You can also use page.context(), very handy when your app opens a new page as it will in the same context.

Organizing Your Tests

From describe block to projects, here are different solutions to organize even the biggest test suites.

Inside a Test File

The first way to have a clean and flexible organization of tests is to have simple and readable test files. I personally use the Arrange Act Assert pattern to keep test cases easy to read.

As the name suggests, it means separating your code into three steps:

- **Arrange:** You may need some environment setup; go to the page to test, login. This is only preparation work for the test case.
- **Act:** You perform an action that will create a change.
- **Assert:** You can then assert that the state of the web app is as expected.

You can either add comments to make the usage of the pattern explicit or simply add newlines to separate the steps.

Listing 2-3. Arrange Act Assert

```
test('get started link', async ({ page }) => {
  await page.goto('https://playwright.dev/');

  await page.getByRole('link', { name: 'Get started' }).click();

  await expect(page.getByRole('heading', { name: 'Installation' })).toBeVisible();
});
```

End-to-end tests can become verbose as they usually have a lot of actions, compared to unit tests that have a much smaller perimeter. Playwright Test offers `step` to organize the insides of your tests. It is not only useful in the test code, but the reports will also display the steps name.

```
test("test", async ({ page }) => {
  await test.step("Log in", async () => {
    // ...
  });
  // ...
});
```

Like other popular test frameworks, `describe` helps you to group related tests together. We also have `beforeAll`, `afterAll`, `beforeEach`, `afterEach` hooks for set up and teardown respectively for all, and for each test of a describe.[2]

Listing 2-4. describe and hooks

```
test.describe("a well organized test suite", () => {
  test.describe("logged in", () => {
    test.beforeEach(async () => {
      await test.step("login", async () => {
        // ...
      });
    })
    test("test 1", async () => {
      // ...
    });
    test("test 2", async () => {
      // ...
    });
  });
  test("logged out", async () => {
    // ...
  });
});
```

Files and Folders

An obvious way to organize tests is to do so by file names and folders.

By default, Playwright Test will run files with the name of the form `*.spec.ts` in the `testDir`. This can be configured in `playwright.config.ts` as in Listing 2-5.

---

[2] You can use beforeAll/afterAll without describe, but I don't advise it.

Listing 2-5. playwright.config.ts

```ts
import { defineConfig } from '@playwright/test';

export default defineConfig({
  testDir: './e2e',
  testMatch: '*todo-tests/*.spec.ts',
  testIgnore: '*test-assets',
});
```

This can also be done with the Command Line Interface

```
# run a file
npx playwright test my.spec.ts
# a folder
npx playwright test folder/
# pattern that does a partial match
npx playwright test mobile
# regex
npx playwright test "example.*spec"
```

Tip To verify your pattern and rules without running the tests, you can simply use the `--list` option.

```
npx playwright test --list
```

Fine-Grained Rules with Tags

Sometimes, the different case combinations are more complex, and organizing tests by folder is just not enough. I develop applications that will run on different sets of devices: TV, desktop, and mobile. Some of my tests must run only on TV, some never on TV, and the other tests on every platform.

For that, we'll use a combination of tags and grep. First, we need to add tags to our tests. Tags must start with @. It can be done at the `test` level, but I found doing it on `describe` is clearer.

Then you can use the `--grep` option to do the filtering.

```
# one tag
npx playwright test --grep @a
# OR
npx playwright test --grep "@a|@b"
# AND
npx playwright test --grep "(?=.*@a)(?=.*@b)"
```

`--grep-invert` is to exclude a tag

```
# exclude a tag
npx playwright test --grep-invert @a
# OR
npx playwright test --grep-invert "@a|@b"
```

You can use them together

```
# can use both
npx playwright test --grep @a --grep-invert @b
```

Projects

You can use test folder, pattern, and tags in Playwright configuration file, but there is more: you can group together browser configuration with complex test matching in a coherent project. A project is a group of tests with the same configuration. All the tag and folder filters we just saw are available in projects, making them the ultimate way to organize your tests.

Consider Listing 2-6.

- Checkout project will override the test directory.
- TV excludes tests that can't run on TV, with a custom device setup.
- Mobile uses the Pixel 5 device definition.

Then you can either run all or select a specific project. For example, checkout tests with `npx playwright test --project=checkout`.

Listing 2-6. playwright.config.ts

```ts
import { defineConfig, devices } from "@playwright/test";

export default defineConfig({
  testDir: "./e2e",
  projects: [
    {
      name: "checkout",
      testDir: "./e2e/checkout",
      use: { ...devices["Desktop Chrome"] },
    },
    {
      name: "TV",
      use: {
        userAgent:
          "Mozilla/5.0 (SMART-TV; LINUX; Tizen 8.0) AppleWebKit/537.36 (KHTML, like Gecko) 108.0.5359.1/8.0 TV Safari/537.36",
        viewport: {
          width: 1920,
          height: 1080,
        },
        defaultBrowserType: "chromium",
      },
      grepInvert: /@noTV/,
    },
    {
      name: "mobile",
      use: { ...devices["Pixel 5"] },
      grep: /@mobile/,
    },
  ],
});
```

CHAPTER 2 WRITE TESTS EFFICIENTLY

There is one last practice to help you organize your tests. If you have many tests with different goals and setup, you might want to consider having multiple `playwright.config.ts` files.

Actions

Playwright can interact with a vast range of HTML Elements with different actions like click, fill inputs, upload file, navigate...

One of the mechanisms that makes Playwright Test very reliable is auto-waiting by checking actionability before performing an action. For example, Playwright checks that the Locator resolves, the Element is visible, enabled, not blocked by other Elements... before interacting with it. You can refer to the Playwright documentation for the full list of actionability, but honestly, it's a mechanism that is useful precisely because you can just forget it.

Action	Attached	Visible	Stable	Receives Events	Enabled	Editable
check	Yes	Yes	Yes	Yes	Yes	-
click	Yes	Yes	Yes	Yes	Yes	-
dblclick	Yes	Yes	Yes	Yes	Yes	-
tap	Yes	Yes	Yes	Yes	Yes	-
uncheck	Yes	Yes	Yes	Yes	Yes	-
hover	Yes	Yes	Yes	Yes	-	-
scrollIntoViewIfNeeded	Yes	Yes	Yes	-	-	-
screenshot	Yes	Yes	Yes	-	-	-
fill	Yes	Yes	-	-	Yes	Yes
selectText	Yes	Yes	-	-	-	-
dispatchEvent	Yes	-	-	-	-	-

Figure 2-1. *Playwright Documentation lists all the actionability checks*

Basic Interactions

Those are the simplest but also the most used actions.

goto

This is usually the action that starts it all: to test a page, we have to open it first. Unlike many other actions, this one is only available on page and not on Locator.

To assert that this action worked as expected, you have different choices:

- Just go on with your end-to-end test; auto-waiting of your next actions or assertions will take care of it for you.

- Checking the current URL is especially useful when you are testing routing and redirections.

    ```
    await expect(page).toHaveURL(expectedURL);
    ```

- You can inspect the response and check the HTTP status:

    ```
    expect(response?.status()).toBe(200);
    // ok() means HTTP 2xx
    expect(response?.ok()).toBeTruthy();
    ```

click, dblclick, tap, hover

Clicking an Element, being a link, a button, a menu, is one of the fundamental interactions with a web application. It is simply done by calling click() on a Locator, and most of the time this is all you need. You can also perform a right-click, or add a keyboard key modifier.

Other mouse and touch interactions are double-click – dblclick, tap gesture – tap, and mouse hover – hover.

It is possible to dispatch a click event, but Playwright will not perform actionability checks. With dispatch, you may trigger standard events like MouseEvent, TouchEvent, DeviceOrientationEvent, or your own. Some web applications use custom events, e.g., to signal that a specific action happened.

```
await locator.dispatchEvent("click");

await locator.dispatchEvent("wheel", { deltaY: 1664 });
// custom event, specific to app
await locator.dispatchEvent("myEvent", {});
```

Forms

Apart from links, forms are the most common way to interact with a web application – text input and button to log in, text inputs, checkbox, select, and so on to subscribe to a service or order a product. Forms are also some of the complex workflows to test.

fill, clear

`fill` sets the value of an input. It works with a wide variety of `<input>` types: text, color, date, email, password, range... This should be your go-to method to fill an input.

`clear` clears the input; it is a convenient alias for `fill("")`. More than that, it's a more expressive method name.

You can assert the value of such inputs with toHaveValue.

press, pressSequentially

`press` and `pressSequentially` simulate key presses. It's tempting to use it on an input as it will focus the Element and perform key presses on it, but `fill` is usually sufficient, and faster. `press` can be useful outside of forms to test keyboard interactions. Think web apps with keyboard shortcuts, for example.

`pressSequentially` will simulate key presses of the characters constituent of a string.

```
await locator.pressSequentially("Hello");
await locator.pressSequentially("World", { delay: 100 });
```

If you want to press special keys, you need to use `press`:

```
await locator.press("ArrowUp");
await locator.press("ArrowUp");
await locator.press("ArrowDown");
await locator.press("ArrowDown");
```

```
await locator.press("ArrowLeft");
await locator.press("ArrowRight");
await locator.press("ArrowLeft");
await locator.press("ArrowRight");
await locator.pressSequentially("BA");
```

If you need even more control, you should use the keyboard API which allows performing key up, key down, holding a key, repeat.

check, uncheck

Checkboxes are another common Element in a form. It is either checked or unchecked. check and uncheck will not only click on the Element, but will also ensure that it actually changed.

Because checkboxes are often grouped logically together, it is common to put them into a `<fieldset>`. This makes the modification of several checkboxes easy. Consider the following example where we have a group of checkboxes that we want to check.

Listing 2-7. HTML

```html
<fieldset>
  <legend>Choose your monster's features:</legend>

  <div>
    <input type="checkbox" id="scales" name="scales" checked />
    <label for="scales">Scales</label>
  </div>

  <div>
    <input type="checkbox" id="horns" name="horns" />
    <label for="horns">Horns</label>
  </div>
</fieldset>
```

Here in Listing 2-7a test, we look for the checkboxes within the group (the fieldset). Don't worry, Locator chaining is described in more detail in the Locators chapter. Then we use .all() to get all the corresponding Locators and iterate on them.

CHAPTER 2   WRITE TESTS EFFICIENTLY

Listing 2-7a. form.spec.ts

```
test("check all from a fieldset", async ({ page }) => {
  const group = page.getByRole("group", { name: "Choose your monster's" });
  for (const checkbox of await group.getByRole("checkbox").all()) {
    await checkbox.check();
  }
});
```

This is one of the rare cases where you want a Locator to select multiple Elements. You can assert the value of such inputs with toBeChecked.

Radio Buttons

Radio buttons are very similar to checkboxes, but when you select a radio button of a group, the others are unselected. Trying to uncheck a radio button with Playwright will result in an error.

You can assert the value of such inputs with toBeChecked.

selectOption

The <select> HTML element can either represent a combobox or a listbox. A combobox, or drop-down list, allows you to select just one option. With Playwright, you can select it with the value or the label of this option.

```
// By value or label
await locator.selectOption('blue');

// By value
await locator.selectOption({ value: 'blue' });

// By label
await locator.selectOption({ label: 'Blue' });
```

The listbox allows you to make a multiple selection, often by Ctrl-clicking the options. The only difference in HTML is by adding a multiple attribute.

```
<select multiple>
  <option value="red">Red</option>
```

```
  <option value="green">Green</option>
  <option value="blue">Blue</option>
</select>
```

Bear in mind that every time you select an option, it unselects the others. If you want to select several options, you have to do it in one call.

```
await page.getByRole("listbox").selectOption(["blue", "red"]);
```

You can assert the value of such inputs with `toHaveValue()` and `toHaveValues()`. Beware, the order of multiple values is taken into account for the comparison.

blur, focus, and Low-Level Actions

All the methods we've seen perform actionability check and focus the input. Here are some ways to have more control:

- Actionability check can be bypassed with the `force` option.
- `blur` and `focus` can be called manually.
- `page.mouse` can move the mouse, click, perform mouse down and up, trigger scroll wheel.
- `page.keyboard` gives you access to the keyboard. You can press a key, repeat, key down and up.
- `dispatchEvent` is available to send a standard or custom event.

These are low-level and are usually not necessarily, so I advise using them sparingly.

Advanced Actions

These actions are often cumbersome to achieve with an automation or test framework, yet they are really easy with Playwright.

Drag and Drop

Thanks to the low-level Locator and mouse API, you could hover an element, click down the mouse button, move the mouse, and release the button on a destination Element to perform drag and drop. It works, but it's complicated.

Instead, consider the simplicity of the method dragTo:

```
await page.locator('#item-to-be-dragged').dragTo(page.locator('#item-to-drop-at'));
```

There are a few cases where the manual method is needed, but it's rare. And painful.

Upload a File

The <input type="file"> HTML Element allows selecting a file to be uploaded from your computer or smartphone. It usually renders as a button showing "Browse..." or the Label attached to the input.

To interact with such input, you can use the following.

Listing 2-8. setInputFiles

```
await fileInput.setInputFiles('assets/myfile.pdf');
```

Note that Codegen can record a file input action. Neat, except that it will only record the file name and not its path (absolute or relative).

If you use a relative path, then it is resolved relative to the current working directory (i.e., from where Playwright is run).

Like <select>, you can add the multiple attribute to allow a multiple selection.

```
<input id="uploadInput" type="file" multiple />
```

In this case, simply add an array of filepath to setInputFiles. Interestingly, you can also create a file programmatically from a Buffer (Listing 2-9).

Listing 2-9. upload a Buffer

```
await fileInput.setInputFiles({
  name: "file.txt",
  mimeType: "text/plain",
  buffer: Buffer.from("this is test"),
});
```

For some reason, you **cannot** mix filename string and buffer. But since we are using Node.js, it's fairly easy to read a file and convert it to a Buffer.

Get Rid of Overlays

"We value your privacy", "Subscribe to our newsletter!", "We like cookies 😊", "Check our new 72-pages terms of use", "This is probably illegal in the European Union" – these annoying messages are now everywhere. They are not only annoying, but they hurt accessibility and testability.

If you are developing a website or an application, my first advice is to do less of those dialogs and popups. For example, you do not need a cookie banner if you don't collect cookies. You can have usage statistics without collecting personal information.

The next best thing is to block these annoyances if they perturb your test.

1. If its behavior is consistent, like a one-time cookie banner at the start of a new session, you should dismiss it as part of your test. Click on the "OK" button from the overlay, and carry on with the rest of the test.

2. You may not have to do anything: maybe it is not blocking for the test. Or performing an action on another element will make it disappear.

3. If it's random or appears on several occasions during the test, you should consider `addLocatorHandler`.

As the name suggests, this is to add a function that will handle the overlay if the designated Locator appears. We accept cookies in the following example.

Listing 2-10. addLocatorHandler

```
const overlay = page.getByTitle("Consent window");
await page.addLocatorHandler(overlay, async () => {
  await overlay
    .contentFrame()
    .getByRole("button", { name: "Accept all" })
    .click();
});

// test starts
// ...
```

A more radical way is to remove the Element from the DOM by executing JavaScript from within the tested page.

```
const overlay = page.getByTitle("Consent window");
await page.addLocatorHandler(overlay, async () => {
  await overlay.evaluate((el) => el.remove());
});

// test starts
// ...
```

As for `window.alert()`, `confirm()`, or `prompt()` dialogs, they are automatically dismissed by Playwright. If you want to manage them, you'll have to do it through `page.on('dialog')` event.

Assertions

So far we have clicked around, filled forms, or more thanks to actions. While these implicitly check that the Elements are present and actionable, we will need to verify various things to write tests. For that, we will use explicit assertions.

Generic Assertions

Playwright offers assertions as `expect`. If you ever used the popular testing framework Jest, this should be familiar. Playwright took inspiration from Jest's assertion library. In fact, it used to be literally based on the `expect` library. Now it is an in-house implementation that is largely compatible. It means that the basic assertions are the same, and it can usually be extended with libraries meant for Jest expect.

The generic assertions do not need to be awaited, since they don't need to wait on anything and don't depend on interaction with the browser. Here in Listing 2-11 are some useful, everyday generic assertions.[3]

---

[3] Full list here: `https://playwright.dev/docs/test-assertions#non-retrying-assertions`. Jest's expect documentation is full of great examples: `https://jestjs.io/docs/expect`.

Listing 2-11. Generic assertions

```
// Same value, same Object instance
expect(value).toBe(expectedValue);
// Deep-equality
expect(value).toEqual(expectedValue);
// For numbers
expect(value).toBeGreaterThan(expectedValue);
expect(value).toBeLessThan(expectedValue);
```

You'll also find advanced patterns, like object matching and asymmetric matchers. This is really useful to perform assertions on complex API responses, for example. You can find details on this usage in Chapter 11.

```
const value = {
  a: true,
  b: 4,
  c: {
    values: ["one", "two", "three"],
    anything: 21,
    color: "red",
    prop: 2
  },
};
const expectedValue = {
  a: true,
  c: {
    values: ["one", "two", "three"],
    anything: expect.anything(),
    color: expect.stringMatching(/red|blue/),
    prop: expect.any(Number),
  },
};
expect(value).toMatchObject(expectedValue);
```

Web-First Assertions

Playwright is meant for end-to-end testing on browsers, so for that it provides web-first assertions, i.e., assertions that are based on the DOM, HTML, and CSS and make sense for a web page.

```
// text and visibility
await expect(locator).toContainText(text)
await expect(locator).toHaveText(expected)
await expect(locator).toBeVisible()
await expect(locator).toBeHidden()
await expect(locator).toBeInViewport()
// page
await expect(page).toHaveTitle(title)
await expect(page).toHaveURL(url)
// input
await expect(locator).toBeChecked()
await expect(locator).toHaveValue(value)
await expect(locator).toHaveValues(values)
// attribute and CSS
await expect(locator).toHaveAttribute(name, value)
await expect(locator).toHaveClass(expected)
await expect(locator).toHaveCSS(name, value)
await expect(locator).toHaveId(id)
await expect(locator).toHaveJSProperty(name, value)
await expect(locator).toHaveRole(role)
// accessibility
await expect(locator).toHaveAccessibleDescription(description)
await expect(locator).toHaveAccessibleName(name)
// visual regression
await expect(locator).toHaveScreenshot(name)

await expect(locator).toBeAttached()
await expect(locator).toBeDisabled()
await expect(locator).toBeEditable()
await expect(locator).toBeEmpty()
await expect(locator).toBeEnabled()
```

```
await expect(locator).toBeFocused()
await expect(locator).toHaveCount(count)
```

Is a checkbox checked? Is it visible (in the DOM)? In the viewport? Does it hold a specific HTML attribute or a CSS class?... These assertions are crucial for testing on a browser, since they will help you to make sense of and verify things on the web.

Web-first assertions are also called auto-retrying assertions. I prefer the first one, as it conveys the meaning that it is based on the DOM. One interesting thing to note is that these assertions are asynchronous for two reasons:

- Playwright drives browsers via their debug protocol in a client–server manner; between the test runner and the browser. This client–server architecture is asynchronous by nature. If you forget to `await` your actions and assertions, you are just doing "fire and forget" and your tests will be unstable.

- Playwright will retry automatically web-first assertions until they are satisfied as part of its auto-waiting mechanism. This tackles flakiness by introducing waiting if necessary.

  For example, if you expect an element to be visible at a given time you might have issues. It might work most of the time on your machine. But you may have overlooked that the component needs hydration from network, or make calculation, or reads the local storage. These time-consuming actions may be extremely fast on your machine, but might be a tad slower on the Continuous Integration, or on a computer with less horsepower than yours, or on a low-end mobile with a 3G network...

Warning   Don't forget to `await` your web-first assertions! If you think Playwright auto-waiting is too long, you can adjust the retry `timeout` per expect or in the configuration file.

Snapshots

Snapshot testing is a common practice that consists of taking a snapshot of something, an Object, DOM, an image, and comparing it to a reference file previously saved. The assertion fails if the two snapshots do not match.

In the case of Playwright, it can be useful to assert API response. We will see later that it can also be handy for approval testing.

```
expect(JSON.stringify(json.data)).toMatchSnapshot();
```

Note that because `toMatchSnapshot()` does not depend on the DOM or browser, it is not asynchronous and does not need to be awaited.

The first time you run this method, the test will fail because there is no snapshot file yet. Playwright will create it automatically for you, and consequent runs will pass. To update the snapshot, you should use the option `--update-snapshots`, shortcut `-u`.

Snapshot files are code, or at least you should treat them as such. It means that they should be checked-in into your version control system (e.g., git), you should do peer-review on the snapshots when there is a change, and you might have to manage merge conflicts.

Warning   Be careful to not over-rely on snapshot tests. They are convenient and fast, but don't overlook changes and update snapshots files without review. By doing so, your tests lose value as you may easily let bugs slip.

`toMatchSnapshot()` makes comparison on strings. It can also compare images, but this is not encouraged anymore. Instead, you should use the dedicated `toHaveScreenshot()` for visual regression tests.

Visual Regression Testing

`toHaveScreenshot()` will make a screenshot and compare it to a reference snapshot file. We'll see that this is easy to use, but difficult to maintain.

```
// Visible page screenshot
await expect(page).toHaveScreenshot();
// Full page screenshot
```

```
await expect(page).toHaveScreenshot({ fullPage: true });

// Locator screenshot
await expect(locator).toHaveScreenshot();
```

Similarly to other snapshot assertions, you'll have to run the test once to generate reference snapshot files. Use `--update-snapshots` (shortcut `-u`) to update the snapshot.

Screenshot comparison is brittle; here are points of attention:

- Testing a full page or a big area may not be a good idea. If you make a snapshot of a full page, many contents may change, intended or not. So try to focus on a part (i.e., a Locator) where the rendering is important to check eventual regressions.

- Luckily, Playwright got our back on some undesired changes: It will deactivate the cursor (it's blinking), and disable CSS animations.

- For some areas that are unwanted, you may need to add a mask. For example, maybe you have an advertisement that changes all the time, or an animated GIF. For that, there is `mask`:

```
const stargazers = page.getByRole("link", {
  name: "stargazers on GitHub",
});
await expect(locator).toHaveScreenshot({ mask: [stargazers] });
```

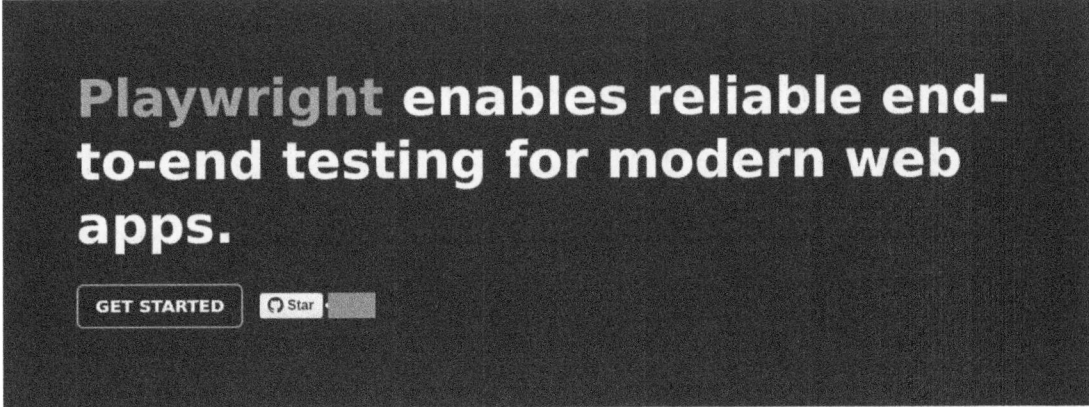

Figure 2-2. Notice the stargazers number was masked

Image snapshots files should be committed, which can be an issue as Git was not originally designed for that. Git is primarily made to store code (as text), not binary files. If you have several screenshot files, you should consider Git LFS.

Git Large File Storage (LFS) is an extension that replaces large files with text pointer in Git, and stores the actual binary files content on a remote service, like GitHub. This will keep your Git repo small, improving clone and fetch times.

My suggestion would be to not over rely on visual regression testing. It takes significant efforts to maintain them. The error messages are not clear: instead of having a log showing the snapshot diff, or an explicit error, you'll have "failed". Depending on your needs, the cost-benefit balance may be in favor of the Aria snapshots.

Aria Snapshots

This is the latest addition to Playwright snapshots, and probably the most useful of the three. Let's explore this assertion in detail.

You already know the DOM, the Document Object Model, maybe the CSSOM, its CSS counterpart. But do you know the AOM? The Accessibility Object Model is an API to access the accessibility tree, which describes a web page for assistive technologies. The accessibility tree will concentrate on the content and structure of the document, making it readable and easy to navigate. The AOM is part of WAI-ARIA. The Web Accessibility Initiative – Accessible Rich Internet Applications (WAI-ARIA) specifies how to increase the accessibility of web pages and web applications. The great thing about accessibility is that it is both friendly to humans and machines. This is not surprising: If you think about it, there are some commons between assistive technology like a screen reader and an automation framework like Playwright.

Listing 2-12 is an Aria snapshot that represents the accessibility tree of an Element. Can you make sense of it?

Listing 2-12. Aria snapshot

```
- banner:
  - heading "Playwright enables reliable end-to-end testing for modern web
    apps." [level=1]
  - link "Get started":
    - /url: /docs/intro
  - link "Star microsoft/playwright on GitHub":
```

```
    - /url: https://github.com/microsoft/playwright
  - link "72k+ stargazers on GitHub":
    - /url: https://github.com/microsoft/playwright/stargazers
```

The Element is a banner that contains a heading (a `<h1>`), and three links. I find this snapshot very descriptive and easy to read. The nice thing about ARIA snapshot is that they will only take into account meaningful information from your HTML, and will ignore the implementation details.

These different HTML snippets (Listing 2-13) will yield the same accessibility ARIA snapshot.

Listing 2-13. HTML snippets

```
<a
  class="gh-count"
  href="https://github.com/microsoft/playwright/stargazers"
  rel="noopener noreferrer"
  target="_blank"
  aria-label="72k+ stargazers on GitHub"
  style="display: block"
>
  72k+
</a>

<a href="https://github.com/microsoft/playwright/stargazers">
  72k+ stargazers on GitHub
</a>
```

`class`, `rel`, and `style` are all implementation details that will not affect the basic functionalities of this link.

You can pass the expected snapshot as an argument. Otherwise, the snapshot file will be written to the disk.

```
// Should match expected
await expect(locator).toMatchAriaSnapshot(`
- link "72k+ stargazers on GitHub":
  - /url: https://github.com/microsoft/playwright/stargazers`);

// Should match *.aria.yml file
```

```
await expect(locator).toMatchAriaSnapshot();
```

Similarly to other snapshot assertions, you'll have to run the test once to generate the reference files. Use --update-snapshots (shortcut -u) to update the snapshot.

ARIA snapshots are very flexible: you can match the accessibility exactly, or just partially; ignore some Elements, use regular expressions.

```
# You can match all attributes
- heading "Title" [level=1]

# Or omit some
- heading "Title"
- heading [level=1]
- heading

# Use Regex
- heading /Issues \d+/

# But you can't match string partially without Regex
- heading "Playwright enables reliable end-to-end testing for modern
  web apps."
# This will not work
- heading "Playwright enables"
```

The same goes for Elements, you don't have to list all of them.

```
- banner:
  - heading "Playwright enables reliable end-to-end testing for modern web
    apps." [level=1]
  - link "Get started":
    - /url: /docs/intro
# Still work if this link is commented out
#  - link "Star microsoft/playwright on GitHub":
#    - /url: https://github.com/microsoft/playwright
  - link "72k+ stargazers on GitHub":
    - /url: https://github.com/microsoft/playwright/stargazers
```

Or on the contrary, you can be strict:

```
- banner:
  - /children: equal
  - heading "Playwright enables reliable end-to-end testing for modern web
    apps." [level=1]
  - link "Get started":
    - /url: /docs/intro
# Snapshot will not match because of this part
#  - link "Star microsoft/playwright on GitHub":
#    - /url: https://github.com/microsoft/playwright
  - link "72k+ stargazers on GitHub":
    - /url: https://github.com/microsoft/playwright/stargazers
```

The /children can be set to

- contain (default): Matches if all specified children are present in order
- equal: Matches if the children exactly match the specified list in order
- deep-equal: Matches if the children exactly match the specified list in order, including nested children

I personally love ARIA snapshot because it focuses on what is important. First, they break when they should: meaningful content changed, or content structure was affected. Second, they don't break on unimportant changes: a CSS class changed, a developer did some refactoring, and a <span> was introduced. ARIA snapshots are ideal to quickly look for regression by having some check that nothing broke.

Write Better Assertions

The first advice for better assertions is to favor web-first assertions over generic assertions whenever possible, e.g., toBeChecked(), toBeVisible(), toContainText(), toHaveCount().

```
// ✘ Incorrect
expect(await locator.textContent()).toBe("Action");

// ☑ Will auto-retry
await expect(locator).toHaveText("Action");
```

> **Remember** Web-first assertions will auto-wait for the Locator and retry automatically the assertion, while the generic assertion will check at that point of time only. This also means that you should remember to `await` web-first assertions.

```
// ✗ Incorrect
expect(locator).toHaveText("Action");
```

```
// ☑ Correct
await expect(locator).toHaveText("Action");
```

A very useful ESLint rule of that is `@typescript-eslint/no-floating-promises`. It will ensure that you don't forget to add `await` when needed. In addition, the ESLint Plugin Playwright can find wrong usage of generic assertions.

Don't hesitate to add `test.step` to group together logical steps of your tests.

async/await and Promise

JavaScript in a browser or Node.js is single-threaded: it means that the code is executed line after line, in a serial way. However, it can defer things outside the event loop such as disk read and write, network request, database access, ... One way to manage the asynchronous nature of those is to use callback functions. Once we have progress, or completion, a function will be called back.

Callbacks can be confusing, and cause what is called "callback hell" when you need to have a callback into a callback into callback. That's why we have the Promise object. Promise is used to give the status of an asynchronous call, and its result.

A `Promise` has three states: pending, fulfilled, and rejected.

- Pending is the default state.

- Fulfilled means it is done; it can also hold the result value.

- Rejected is the error state; it can hold the error reason.

You can use `.then()` to execute a function when a Promise resolves, but then we'll be back to callback hell as we nest calls within each other. A great syntax to improve that is `await`:

```
await page.goto("https://www.example.com");
```

On the other side, to notify that a function is asynchronous and returns a Promise, we can use the keyword `async`:

```
test('get started link', async ({ page }) => {
});
```

Common Pitfalls

The most common mistake I see is to don't wait for asynchronous code when needed.

Mainly two things are asynchronous in Playwright Tests: actions and assertions. Actions like `goto()` or `click()` will happen in the browser land. It means that Playwright will send a request to the browser through CDP, Juggler, or WebKit protocol. So, just like a network request, it is asynchronous. Some assertions `expect().to...()` will be asynchronous too. The web-first assertions are asynchronous because they depend on the browser, and they benefit from the auto-retry mechanism.

The functions I mentioned all return a `Promise`. First, you can check the Playwright documentation; you also probably have a hint of the returned type in your IDE. Second, because the type is set in TypeScript, we can use ESLint to ensure there are no dangling Promises.

You can use the `typescript-eslint` rule `no-floating-promises`. I usually add `eslint-plugin-playwright` as well because it will catch many more things.

Another common mistake is to wait for synchronous code when it is not needed.

```
const banner = await page.locator('#promotional-banner')
```

This function doesn't return a `Promise`, and your IDE will probably emit a warning. Note that adding extra `await` will not have impact, but it is still a bad practice since it clutters your code unnecessarily.

CHAPTER 2   WRITE TESTS EFFICIENTLY

Advanced Patterns with Promises

Sometimes we need to do some fancy things with Promise: wait for any of them to finish, wait for all of them to finish; with or without error. I advise you to take a look at the MDN page on Promise.[4]

- *knock knock*

- *An async function*

- *Who's there?*

Playwright documentation has a great example of such advanced usage: you click on a button that will open a page in a new tab.

The problem is, you are locked if you wait for the new tab before clicking. If you do it at the same time without waiting, you have a race condition. The solution is to wait for both and continue when both Promise are fulfilled.

```
// wait for popup AND click
const [newPage] = await Promise.all([
  page.waitForEvent('popup'),
  page.getByText('open the popup').click();,
]);
// Interact with the new popup normally.
await newPage.getByRole('button').click();
console.log(await newPage.title());
```

Here is another way to write it.[5] It is actually what Codegen will create when dealing with multiple tabs.

Listing 2-14. Delayed await

```
// Start waiting for popup before clicking. Note no await.
const popupPromise = page.waitForEvent('popup');
await page.getByText('open the popup').click();
const newPage = await popupPromise;
```

---

[4] https://developer.mozilla.org/en-US/docs/Web/JavaScript/Reference/Global_Objects/Promise

[5] Adapted from Playwright official documentation https://playwright.dev/docs/api/class-page#page-event-popup

```
// Interact with the new popup normally.
await newPage.getByRole('button').click();
console.log(await newPage.title());
```

In Listing 2-14, we can notice

- line 2: How we call page.waitForEvent() before the click() that will trigger the event
- line 4: We await the popupPromise after the click, but before using the new page

Configure Playwright Test

Playwright Test can be configured at many different levels; let's untangle this.

Configuration File

playwright.config.ts centralizes Playwright Test settings and project configuration. We'll list some interesting configuration points in this part, but there are many more. I advise you to play with it while reading this part; you can't go wrong as TypeScript will help us find typos and provides auto-completion.

Keep in mind that playwright.config.ts will affect Playwright Test, and tooling such as the UI mode or Playwright Test for VS Code as well.

Top-Level Options

These options are global configuration, for example, for the test runner.

There are a bunch of settings linked with parallelism and the test runner: fullyParallel, retries, workers. We will see them in detail later on; let's say for now that the default settings are reasonable. You will need to adjust them for Continuous Integration.

reporter allows selecting one or more test reports to generate. I find the syntax for reporter really odd. You can set one reporter as a string, or reporters as an Array of … Arrays.

```
// Single reporter
reporter: 'html',
reporter: [['html']],
// Single reporter with options
reporter: [['html', { open: 'always' }]],
// Multiple reporters
reporter: [['list'], ['json', { outputFile: 'test-results.json' }]],
```

webServer is a great configuration point. It will start for you a local test server via a shell command. I recommend adding the URL of the server; it should be the same value as use.baseURL as seen in Listing 2-15.

Listing 2-15. playwright.config.ts

```
webServer: {
  command: "npm run start",
  url: "http://127.0.0.1:3000",
  reuseExistingServer: !process.env.CI,
  timeout: 10_000,
},
use {
  baseURL: "http://127.0.0.1:3000",
}
```

If url is specified, Playwright Test will wait for it to be ready (i.e., return an HTTP code 2xx, 3xx, 400-403). This ensures two things:

- Tests will start after the script is run, without using clunky scripting that may not be cross-platform, or a third-party solution.

- The server is up and running. If it's not, Playwright will stop here even before trying to run tests. I find the default timeout of 60 seconds to be excessive, so adjusting it seems fitting. reuseExistingServer allows running your dev server locally when you are developing an application, and reuse it with Playwright. It has no benefit in Continuous Integration, hence the reuseExistingServer: !process.env.CI

Test Use

The options under use are linked to the test environment: browser, user agent, emulation, recording...

`baseURL` is an important option that tells Playwright what is under test. Once it is set up, you can then use paths in your tests.

```
// Goes to baseURL
await page.goto('/');
// or to a sub path
await page.goto('/products/1664?preview=true');
```

It means that the test URL is not hard-coded in your test anymore, but programmatically configured. You can easily run your test suite against different environments' URLs without code changes. You can also set the `baseURL` per project.

You can record screenshot, video, or traces for each test. I usually only need `trace`.

```
use: {
  trace: 'on-first-retry',
},
```

Tracing slows down execution, so Playwright's team recommends the setting `on-first-retry`. With this setting, failed tests will run again, this time with tracing on. You can then retrieve the trace file and consult it with the Trace Viewer.

The use Object holds the configuration for emulation, network, locale... I personally advise adding them to projects as you usually need to emulate several different environments...

Projects

A project is a group of tests with the same configuration.

Projects can either be used to run all tests with different configurations, or a set of tests per project. Projects can have the settings of use and some of the top-levels. Again, don't hesitate to experiment.

Listing 2-16. playwright.config.ts

```ts
import { defineConfig, devices } from '@playwright/test';

export default defineConfig({
  testDir: './e2e',
  projects: [
    {
      name: 'checkout',
      testDir: './e2e/chekout',
      use: { ...devices['Desktop Chrome'] },
    },
    {
      name: 'chromium',
      use: { ...devices['Desktop Chrome'] },
    },
    {
      name: 'firefox',
      use: { ...devices['Desktop Firefox'] },
      testIgnore: /snapshot/,
    },
    // ...
  ],
});
```

In Listing 2-16, the checkout tests will only run tests in the `./e2e/checkout` folder, and all test files will be run with the other projects.

The most common usages for projects are

- A specific set of tests with one configuration. Like the checkout tests that we can run with `npx playwright test --project=checkout`
- Different device configurations to run tests against.

A device is defined as follows; you may set one or more of these settings:

- `viewport`: The pages' width and height

CHAPTER 2   WRITE TESTS EFFICIENTLY

- `userAgent`: Many systems rely on user agent to identify a device
- `deviceScaleFactor`: Linked to the Device Pixel Ratio, we'll see more on that in the emulation chapter
- `isMobile`: Indication for the tests; it will be available as a fixture
- `hasTouch`
- `defaultBrowserType`: Can be either `chromium`, `firefox`, or `webkit`

You've probably noticed the usage of `devices`, imported from Playwright Test. They are device definition for your convenience. You can use JavaScript's spread syntax on a device definition to use it.

```
...devices['Desktop Firefox']
```

Available devices go from desktop browser, recent iPhone to Blackberry devices (!). You can create your own set of devices to reuse.

Using Environment Variables for More Flexibility

Maybe you've noticed the usage of the env variable `process.env.CI` in the configuration file created by Playwright. Most Continuous Integration providers will set a CI env variable to true. By using this, you can have different settings on your local machine or on your pipeline.

Because `playwright.conf.ts` and test files are, well, TypeScript, they are particularly flexible. To go further, you can use dotenv. It's a Node.js module that loads environment variables from a `.env` file.

```typescript
import { defineConfig, devices } from '@playwright/test';
import dotenv from 'dotenv';

dotenv.config({ path: '.env' });

export default defineConfig({
  use: {
    baseURL: process.env.FRONT_URL,
  },
  // ...
});
```

It's really handy to switch between environments. In Listing 2-17, dotenv will attempt to load the `.env.production` file according to NODE_ENV. It will fall back to `.env` if needed.

Listing 2-17. Using different .env files

```
import { defineConfig, devices } from '@playwright/test';
import dotenv from 'dotenv';

- dotenv.config({ path: '.env' });
+ dotenv.config({ path: [`.env.${process.env.NODE_ENV}`, '.env'] });
```

Listing 2-17a. Using different .env files

```
NODE_ENV=production npx playwright test
```

Overrides in Test Files

Sometimes you need to adjust the test settings for a specific file, or a group of tests, without changing the global Playwright Test configuration.

You can call `test.use()` at the top of a file or inside a `describe` block. For example, to force every test in a file to run with a French locale:

```
test.use({ locale: 'fr-FR' });
```

You can also override some settings of an individual assertion. The most common is changing the timeout of a single check. Here we unset the timeout with a value of 0.

```
await expect(locator).toBeVisible({ timeout: 0 });
```

Command Line Interface

Playwright Test CLI options are perfect to temporary override settings while developing. It has a lot of useful options; run `npx playwright test --help` to get a comprehensive list of commands. Below are my favorite commands. Should it be a cheat sheet?

Listing 2-18. Filtering tests

```
# All
npx playwright test
```

```
# By name
npx playwright test test.spec.ts
# By tag
npx playwright test --grep=@tag
npx playwright test --grep-invert=@tag
# By project
npx playwright test --project=chromium
npx playwright test --project=chromium --project=firefox
# Dry run
npx playwright test --list
```

Listing 2-19. Execution

```
# Run tests according to their status
npx playwright test --last-failed
npx playwright test --only-changed
npx playwright test --only-changed=origin/main
# Update snapshots
npx playwright test -u
# Workers for parallelization
npx playwright test --workers=1
npx playwright test --workers=99%
```

Listing 2-20. UI mode and debugging

```
# UI mode
npx playwright test --ui
# Force the trace mode
npx playwright test --trace=on
# Undocumented and experimental CLI watch mode
PWTEST_WATCH=1 npx playwright test
```

Write Tests Efficiently

Being efficient often means using the right tool for your needs. Let's see how Playwright can make your life easier.

CHAPTER 2   WRITE TESTS EFFICIENTLY

Codegen

Playwright is certainly not the first web automation solution to propose a recording tool, but Playwright's take on it is brilliant. Codegen is a very capable tool that will record and generate a test or automation code for you. It's a great starting point for your tests, that will be better after some cleaning and refactor.

If you haven't yet, start it up now!

`npx playwright codegen`

This command will display two things:

- The browser under test, where you can open an URL and interact with the pages and tabs. You'll notice that the Elements are highlighted when hovered, showing the suggested Locator. There is also a small toolbar.

- The Playwright Inspector shows many information like the generated code, the same toolbar as in the browser, copy, debugger commands, ...

Figure 2-3. *Codegen toolbar*

"Record" allows generating test code from your actions. It can be paused and unpaused at any time.

"Pick Locator" allows getting a Locator and seeing it in the Playwright Inspector. The other buttons will generate assertions:

- `toBeVisible()`
- `toContainText()`
- `toHaveValue()`
- `toMatchAriaSnapshot()`

When you pick a Locator, it will appear in the Locator text area of the inspector. You can then write your own Locator in this area to try it out and see highlighted the corresponding Elements.

CHAPTER 2   WRITE TESTS EFFICIENTLY

Figure 2-4. *Playwright Inspector*

If you are recording, Codegen will create the corresponding code in the selected language. Here we want "Test Runner" for Playwright Test, but it can also generate Python, Java, or C#. Note that Codegen can only record some actions: click, doubleclick, navigation (goto), fill, select. Say, if you want to make drag and drop, you'll have to pick the Locators. What I do is that I click on the Elements (if it has no side effect), and then I rework the generated code to perform the intended action.

Locators' best practice rules come built-in in Codegen; so it will create for you the best Locator it can. Sometimes, it needs advanced techniques to have readable and maintainable Locators. We'll see how to do that in the next chapter.

55

CHAPTER 2   WRITE TESTS EFFICIENTLY

UI Mode

Similarly to the VS Code extension, the UI mode lists and allows you to filter all your Playwright tests. When you run them, they will actually be executed against a headless browser and display the result on the right.

You have there a time-travel feature that will show as both a timeline at the top and a list of instructions. Also, there is a DOM snapshot at each step. This is great to understand better how the page is structured, especially since we can pick and test Locators.

To start it up, simply run `npx playwright test --ui`.

UI mode is definitely the way to go if you don't use VS Code. Choosing this or the extension is a matter of preference, as both tools are excellent.

A Great Workflow to Write and Debug Tests

I love using Playwright Test for VS Code because of one reason: it lets you run and debug your tests but also generate their code.

Here is my workflow when writing Playwright test:

1. **Generate**

    I usually first create my test with Record new. If the file exists, I can use Record at cursor.

2. **Verify**

    Then I execute what I just generated, to verify that my configuration and latest additions to the test are working as intended. If not, I fix whatever is needed to fix.

3. **Refactor**

    Clean it up, refactor it, and rerun it to verify that it still works. I recommend using Turn on Continuous Run to have a watch mode: when the test file is saved, the test will re-run.

CHAPTER 2   WRITE TESTS EFFICIENTLY

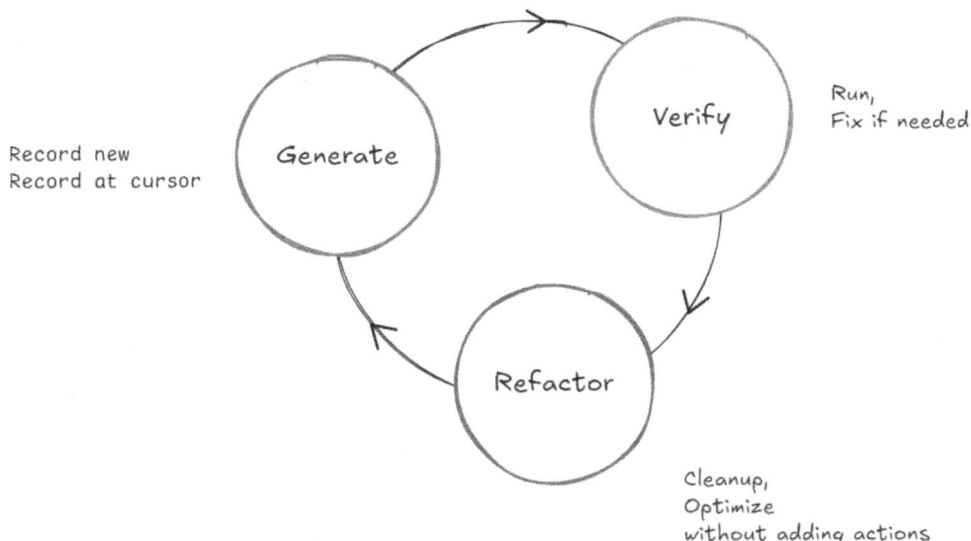

Figure 2-5. Generate with Codegen, verify, refactor

Here is the cool thing: when you `Record at cursor`, it will use whatever state from the browser under test. So it means you can continue test generation where you left it. This means that after step 3, you can use `Record at cursor` to add new things to your test; this is step 1 **Generate**.

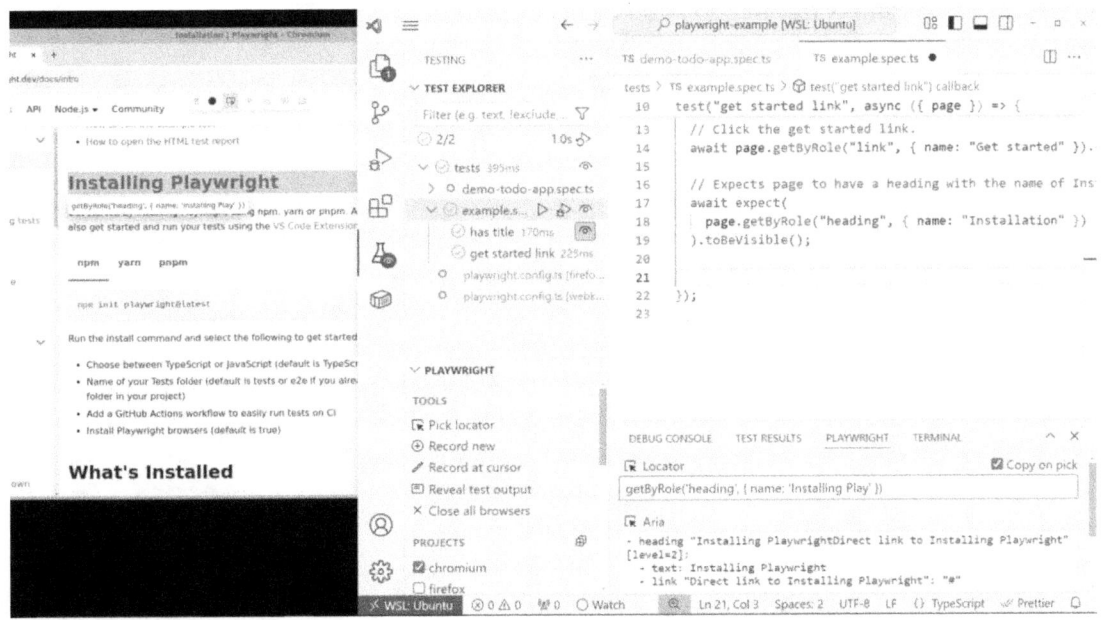

Figure 2-6. Writing a Locator with Playwright Test for VS Code and opened browser

For more complex Locator and Locator refactoring, I use `Pick Locator` and the Playwright tab. This tab allows trying out Locators directly, including more complex ones with filtering, for example.

Summary

This chapter was quite dense. Don't hesitate to practice and come back later with a new perspective on this part.

We covered

- **Actions** on links, forms, but also drag and drop or file upload
- A detailed review of **assertions**
- Keep in mind that **web-first assertions** verify things in the browser. This is **asynchronous**!
- Snapshots, visual regression testing, and the better **Aria snapshots**
- How and where to configure Playwright Test
- Tooling and my workflow to **Generate, Verify, and Refactor**

The next chapter is dedicated to a key notion of Playwright: Locators.

CHAPTER 3

Locators

This part is a deep-dive into one of the great features of Playwright. Locators are a crucial part of Playwright Test and Playwright Library as they are an API to access the Document Object Model of a web page. More precisely, they represent a way to find an Element. You can think of it as a pointer to an HTML element, that will be resolved when we use an action or an assertion.

Playwright offers many different Locators. We will see the most common ones in detail, and also how to combine them to get the perfect ones that will allow you to have more reliable tests. More importantly, by following best practices, you will make better apps thanks to testability and accessibility.

CSS and XPath

They are well-known selectors to get Elements, but are they usable and adapted for end-to-end testing?

CSS

Most, if not all, end-to-end testing frameworks offer CSS selector. It's probably the most used way to query the DOM of a page. Like in JQuery and now the native `querySelector()`, your favorite browser DevTools, and well… CSS.

The good thing is that as a frontend of full-stack developer, you probably know well CSS selectors. You can write CSS Locator with a selector string as argument of the `locator()` method; `css=` is usually not obligatory as Playwright will auto-detect CSS Selectors.

```
await page.locator('css=button').click();
```

Playwright Documentation recommends user-facing Locators instead of using CSS selectors, but they are not all bad. You can select an Element easily, or a class if it is carefully crafted and you don't use utility classes framework like Tailwind.

To avoid:

- + next sibling combinator
- ~ subsequent sibling combinator
- > child combinator

You should avoid selectors linked to parents and child, as they are tied to the DOM structure of your page. This is implementation detail. Your users don't care if a button is inside a div inside a span. It makes no sense for the user and has no impact. The thing is developers don't care either for these implementation details, so it can and will be refactored, rewritten, and changed.

Examples of better selectors:

```
header
.card
#login-btn
header button
```

Playwright adds pseudo-classes such as `:has-text()`, `:has()`, or `:visible()`. I would recommend filtering Locators instead as it is clearer and more obvious, making better code with a clear intent.

```
// :has-text pseudo-class
page.locator('article:has-text("Playwright")');
// filter
page.locator("article").filter({ hasText: "Playwright" });
```

Tip Pretty much all browsers' DevTools console provides dollar functions selectors.

$() lets you try a CSS selector, like `document.querySelector()`.

$$() will return all corresponding Elements, like `document.querySelectorAll()`.

$0 will return the latest selected Element; including your selection in DOM inspector!

XPath

XPath is a language to query XML documents. It is widely supported by browsers, automation libraries, and various programming languages. Xpath is very powerful; it can also be used to transform XML, similarly to XSLT.

I personally don't recommend XPath. First, it's overcomplicated for what we want to achieve with Playwright Test. It's also way too easy to write a selector that is tied to the implementation details. If you add the fact that Xpath Locator doesn't pierce the shadow DOM in Playwright, it makes a lot of downsides.

I believe there is a value in unlearning things. I developed on Blackberry, J2ME, and it turns out that these skills and knowledge are not very much in demand right now. Unlearning things declutter your memory for better, more useful things. And what is important and useful from these experiences will stick. So, really, there is no need to feel attached to a technology that becomes obsolete.

Legacy and Experimental Locators

There are experimental locators that are specifically tailored for Vue.js or React. They allow getting Locators by component and by property. They only work against not minified application builds. I don't find them very useful, and I never had to use them. However, it's a good inspiration of what can be done with custom Locators.

There are also `text` and `data-testid` Locators. They are valid, but they are considered legacy, and you should prefer their Testing Library inspired counterparts as seen in Listing 3-1.

Listing 3-1. text and data-testid

```
page.locator('text=Log in');
// should be
page.getByText('Log in');

page.locator('data-testid=submit');
// prefer
page.getByTestId('submit');
```

CHAPTER 3   LOCATORS

Testing Library Queries

CSS selectors, XPath, and alike were all what was available to get a Locator in Playwright. It's powerful but lacked in a few aspects. You got no auto-complete or checks on the selector syntax, so you could make a typo and won't find out before running the test. API discoverability was missing too: you couldn't count on your IDE to see what is available. Kent C. Dodds is the creator of the famous Testing Library. So, he discussed with the Playwright team to bring a better API to find DOM elements reliably.

> *The more your tests resemble the way your software is used, the more confidence they can give you.*
>
> —Kent C. Dodds

The Playwright team created a new set of methods to create Locators easily. Available on `Page`, `Locator,` and `FrameLocator,` it allows locating Elements in a similar fashion to how people use applications. Think about it: you don't interact with a web application by checking the style or divs. You look for text, buttons, links, label. Even more so if you use assistive technology, like a screen reader.

Warning   This is NOT Testing Library. The `getBy*` methods are the own implementation for Playwright. There are several details that differ, such as `getBy*` will match multiple Elements, waiting mechanism is totally different, there are no variant `queryBy*` or `findBy*`.

Sometimes these differences bite me when I use Testing Library.

Let's list them all:

- `getByAltText()` to locate an element, usually image, by its alt text
- `getByLabel()` to locate a form control by associated label's text
- `getByPlaceholder()` to locate an input by placeholder
- `getByRole()` to locate by explicit and implicit accessibility attributes
- `getByTestId()` to locate an element based on its `data-testid` attribute

- `getByText()` to locate by text content
- `getByTitle()` to locate an element by its title attribute

The Playwright Documentation on these Locators is extensive; I recommend reading it in addition to this chapter. The section **Locating elements** also has a great use: every Locator has examples with a simple live HTML sample. Like in Figure 3-1, you can try Locators against this page!

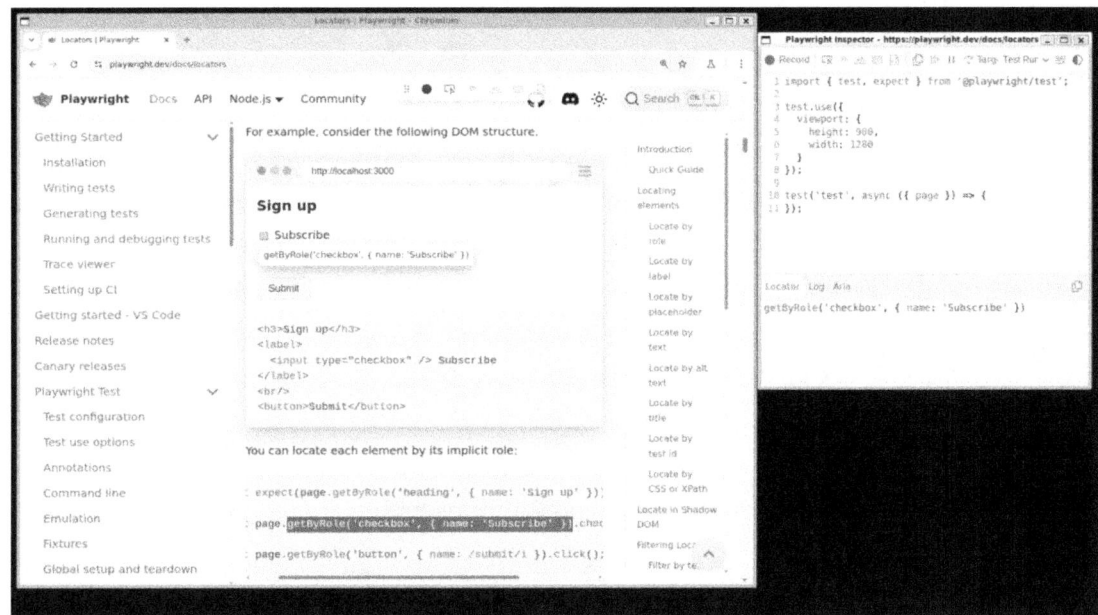

Figure 3-1. *Start Codegen and try Locators along with this chapter!*

Find it at https://playwright.dev/docs/locators#locating-elements.

For example, the Playwright documentation gives these examples for getByRole() (see Listing 3-2).

Listing 3-2. getByRole examples

```
await expect(page.getByRole('heading', { name: 'Sign up' })).toBeVisible();

await page.getByRole('checkbox', { name: 'Subscribe' }).check();

await page.getByRole('button', { name: /submit/i }).click();
```

CHAPTER 3   LOCATORS

Let's try it for ourselves:

1. Start Codegen from the CLI to open the documentation page.

   npx playwright codegen https://playwright.dev/docs/locators

2. Deactivate the test **Record**.

3. In the web page, scroll to the **Locate by role** section.

4. Try the Locator, without expect or page, in the **Locator** text area.

   getByRole('heading', { name: 'Sign up' })

getByText

```
getByText(
  text: string | RegExp,
  options?: {
    exact?: boolean;
  }
): Locator;
```

text and the exact option offer many possibilities on how to match an Element as shown in Listing 3-3.

- By default, text makes a substring match and ignores case.

- You can change this behavior with the exact option.

- Or you can set name to a regex. In this case, exact has no effect.

Listing 3-3. Examples for getByText

```
// substring match
getByText("llo Worl");
// ignore case
getByText("hello world");
// full string match
getByText("Hello World", { exact: true });

// substring match
```

```
getByText(/World/);
// full string match, ignore case
getByText(/^hello world$/i);
// matches "hello world", "hello Jane", and more
getByText(/Hello .+/i);
```

The next Locator offers the intuitiveness of getByText, plus some hints about accessibility and is more reliable.

getByRole

```
getByRole(
  role: string,
  options?: {
    checked?: boolean;
    disabled?: boolean;
    exact?: boolean;
    expanded?: boolean;
    includeHidden?: boolean;
    level?: number;
    name?: string | RegExp;
    pressed?: boolean;
    selected?: boolean;
  }
): Locator;
```

In my opinion, this is probably the single most important Locator. If there is one that you should remember, it's this one. getByRole allows locating Elements by their ARIA role. For example, button, listitem, or link. Thankfully, you usually don't have to manually add an ARIA role to your HTML since many Elements have implicit roles. For example, a <button> Element will have the button role implicitly. <a href=""> is link, <ul> is list, <li> is listitem, and so on...[1]

Because selecting every <button> of a page is probably not good enough, getByRole allows locating an Element by its role and its **accessible name**.

---
[1] Check the W3C spec for a full list: https://www.w3.org/TR/html-aria/#docconformance.

This is deduced by different information to get a name to present to assistive technologies. For button, the MDN web docs states

> *[for button role] The accessible name is either the content of the element or the value of an aria-label or element referenced by an aria-labelledby attribute, or description, if included.*

```
Styles    Computed    Layout    Accessibility
▶ Accessibility Tree
▼ ARIA Attributes
    aria-label: close
▼ Computed Properties
  ▼ Name: "close"
      aria-labelledby: Not specified
      aria-label: "close"
      From label: Not specified
      Contents: "x"
      title: Not specified
    Role: button
    Invalid user entry: false
    Focusable: true
▶ Source Order Viewer
```

Figure 3-2. *Chrome accessibility properties of a close button*

Figure 3-2 shows Chrome displaying accessibility properties and how the name is computed. Notice that you can use different means that lead to the same result. All the three ways in Listing 3-4 create a button that has the same accessible name.

Listing 3-4. Three buttons, same name

```
<!-- text -->
<button>close</button>

<!-- aria-label -->
<button aria-label="close">&times;</button>
```

```
<!-- image alt -->
<button><img src="path/to/button.svg" alt="close" /></button>
```

To locate such button, we'll use

```
getByRole('button', { name: 'close' })
```

name and exact options have similar matching mechanism to getByText().

In addition to the accessible name, other criteria based on the ARIA attributes can be used; They are basically based on the state of the element: `checked`, `disabled`, `expanded`, `pressed`, `selected`.

`level` is useful for headings. Here is how to locate a <h3> Element:

```
getByRole("heading", { name: "Sign up", level: 3 })
```

Warning Playwright Documentation reminds us that role selector **does not replace** accessibility audits and conformance tests, but rather gives early feedback about the ARIA guidelines.

I've met users of Playwright that are literally shocked by the usage of text-based Locators. The truth is a good Locator should fail when there is a change affecting the user. It's on purpose. Did you change the text for the login button? You may have to update a test, or a Page Object Model. This login changes from a button to a link? Yes, it should break.

> To make tests resilient, we recommend prioritizing user-facing attributes and explicit contracts.

—Playwright Documentation

A common concern is how to manage internationalization (i18n) with text Locators. It is quite easy to leverage regular expressions to locate an Element in different languages `page.getByRole('button', { name: /Message|Nachricht/ });`. As an alternative, it's possible to load the language files of your application in your tests if needed.

Alternative: getByAltText

```
getByAltText(
  text: string | RegExp,
  options?: {
    exact?: boolean;
  }
): Locator;
```

getByAltText allows locating Elements, usually images, that have an alternate text. Alt text describes an image for persons that use assistive technology.

Note that you can achieve the same result with getByRole() but getByAltText() is more expressive as it clearly shows the intent of matching on alt.

```
page.getByAltText('playwright logo');
// is the same as
page.getByRole('img', { name: 'playwright logo' });
```

getByLabel

```
getByLabel(
  text: string | RegExp,
  options?: {
    exact?: boolean;
  }
): Locator;
```

A `<label>` gives more information about another HTML Element. It is widely used with form Elements as it has many advantages:

- It provides a text explaining what the input is about. For example, how do you know what a checkbox does without a label?
- The label is linked with the input. It means that if you click on the label, the focus will be on the input. This helps a lot when you are on mobile.

The label can be set either by enclosing the input inside it or by using `for` and `id` keywords.

Listing 3-5. Label HTML example

```
<label>
  Do you like peas?
  <input type="checkbox" />
</label>

<label for="peas">Do you like peas?</label>
<input id="peas" type="checkbox" />
```

Either way the label and the input are linked, so locating the label means we can get the input.

```
getByLabel("peas");
```

Alternative: getByPlaceholder

```
getByPlaceholder(
  text: string | RegExp,
  options?: {
    exact?: boolean;
  }
): Locator;
```

Having a `<label>` is good for accessibility and a best practice when dealing with forms. However, when an input has no label, you may locate it with its placeholder.

```
<input type="email" placeholder="name@example.com" />
```

getByTestId

```
getByTestId(testId: string | RegExp): Locator;
```

When there are no better alternatives, or because sometimes we want to use an explicit contract, we can add an id for the sole usage of locating Elements in tests. It is possible in HTML to use the `data-*` attribute to make such contract between the DOM and tests. The most used custom data attribute for automation is `data-testid`.

```
<button data-testid="directions">Itinéraire</button>

getByTestId('directions');
```

CHAPTER 3 LOCATORS

By default, the Playwright test id is `data-testid`. You can change it in your test with use or in the Playwright configuration.

Listing 3-6. Configure test id with use

```
test.use({
  testIdAttribute: "data-test-id",
});
```

Listing 3-7. Configure test id with playwright.config.ts

```
import { defineConfig } from '@playwright/test';

export default defineConfig({
  use: {
    testIdAttribute: 'data-test-id'
  }
});
```

Playwright Test for VS Code will use the configuration from playwright.config.ts when generating test.

For Codegen, you need to change the test id via a CLI option.

```
npx playwright codegen --test-id-attribute=data-test-id
```

Tip What if the usage of test id is inconsistent in your web application (or across two applications under test)?

You can resort to CSS selectors in this case.

```
locator('[data-testid="first"]')
locator('[data-test-id="second"]')
```

Alternative: getByTitle

```
getByTitle(
  text: string | RegExp,
  options?: {
    exact?: boolean;
  }
): Locator;
```

Some Elements don't have accessible text, or alt; it doesn't necessarily mean that you must add a `data-testid`.

`title` is usually rendered as a tooltip. Frankly I seldom see it used, but I find it particularly useful in two cases: SVG and iframe.

Advanced Patterns

In some situations, even the best Locator doesn't make the cut. Let's see what can be done in such cases.

Working with iframes

Some of you may remember iframe from the glorious days of DHTML. They were used massively at the beginning of HTML, for example, for menus. Nowadays, iframes still have valid use cases such as displaying a preview or integrating a third party.

An iframe is technically another document, another page, than the main one. Because of that, Playwright won't locate Elements directly: you have to do it from within the iframe.

The easiest way to target an iframe is by using a regular Locator, then use `contentFrame` to get "inside" the iframe.

```
const frameLocator = page.locator("#embedded").contentFrame();

await frameLocator.getByRole('button').click();
// ...
```

You can also get the iframe from the browser programmatically, by name or even by URL!

```
// Get frame using the frame's name attribute
const frameLocator = page.frame('frame-login');

// Get frame using frame's URL
const frameLocator = page.frame({ url: /.*domain.*/ });

await frameLocator.getByRole('button').click();
// ...
```

Filtering Locators

Sometimes crafting the right locator is difficult, and we need a way to differentiate seemingly similar Elements. Think about it: web apps are often made of lists. Lists of movies in your favorite streaming service, list of menu items, list of products in an ecommerce website.

Consider the following example, in Listing 3-8. How do you select the list Element with "Product 1"?

Listing 3-8. A list of products

```
<ul>
  <li>
    <h3>Product 1</h3>
    <button>Add to cart</button>
  </li>
  <li>
    <h3>Product 2</h3>
    <button>Add to cart</button>
  </li>
</ul>
```

Using the first one would be hazardous as the order is not guaranteed in a product list. A data-testid could help, if it is on the <li> Element. In this case, getByRole won't work. Unlike a button Element, list item does not get its accessible name from its content.

The solution is filtering, which is very similar to `Array.filter()` in JavaScript. Here we can filter Elements that has a text. Or has a Locator.

```
// simply with a text
const product1 = page
  .getByRole("listitem")
  .filter({ hasText: "Product 1" });

// by Locator
const product2 = page
  .getByRole("listitem")
  .filter({ has: page.getByRole("heading", { name: "Product 2" }) });
```

Then you have the negative version.

```
// simply with a text
const product1 = page
  .getByRole("listitem")
  .filter({ hasNotText: "In promotion" });

// by Locator
const product2 = page
  .getByRole("listitem")
  .filter({ hasNot: promotionLocator });
```

Warning Don't confuse `hasText` and the accessible name used in `getByRole`. Accessible name means "the meaningful name of the Element for the user," whereas `hasText` means "contains a text, somehow, somewhere."

There is a third filter: `visible`. I personally use it with responsive content. Let's say that you have a menu for mobile and a menu for desktop, and CSS is changing the visibility. Then one way to be sure to target the right Element is to filter by visibility.

One last thing: you can combine filter options.

```
const product1 = page
  .getByRole("listitem")
  .filter({ hasText: "Product 1", visible: true });
```

Great, but what if I want to click on the button "Add to cart" of this list Element?

CHAPTER 3   LOCATORS

Chaining Locators

You can narrow down Locators by looking for them inside a Locator.

Figure 3-3. *Among the items, we select the one with "Doc Martins". We click its "See product details" button*

Listing 3-9. Chaining Locators

```
await page
  .getByRole('listitem')
  .filter({ hasText: 'Doc Martins' })
  .getByRole('button', { name: 'see product details' })
  .click();
```

In this example, we get an item by looking for the one that holds the text "Doc Martins" in lines 1–3 of Listing 3-9.

By simply chaining the call (i.e., call the `Locator.getByRole()`), we can get the button "See product details" within this item as shown in Figure 3-3.

The syntax is quite flexible; we could also extract the Doc Martins card Locator.

```
const card = page.getByRole("listitem").filter({ hasText: "Doc Martins" });
await card.getByRole("button", { name: "see product details" }).click();
```

Or we can use the `.locator()` function to chain it with another syntax.

```
const button = page.getByRole("button", { name: "see product details" });
await page
  .getByRole("listitem")
  .filter({ hasText: "Doc Martins" })
  .locator(button)
  .click();
```

Or both!

```
const card = page.getByRole("listitem").filter({ hasText: "Doc Martins" });
const button = page.getByRole("button", { name: "see product details" });
await card.locator(button).click();
```

Craft Better Apps with Semantic HTML

HTML is the language that describes web pages, being a document or a full-featured highly interactive application. For that purpose, you have different tags available. Basic elements that describe a page like heading, sections, or paragraph. But also, interaction elements such as buttons, inputs, forms. You have multimedia ones like video or canvas.

Semantic HTML is simply leveraging the possibilities of the HTML language to create markup that does not only "work" but also makes sense and expresses the meaning of the web page content.

Common tags include headings, paragraph, header, footer, link AKA anchor, button... `<div>` and `<span>` do not express any meaning; they are only used to group elements together. This is why you should only use them when you have no other options.

Semantic HTML has many benefits. First, it is what HTML is meant for: Hypertext Modeling Language is describing, well, (hyper) text. It means that this language is here to model and describe the content of a web page. With rich CSS features and modern JavaScript frameworks, it's sometimes easy to forget that fact.

As a developer, using semantic HTML helps to understand at first glance what the markup is about. Clear and descriptive code is way better than what is sometimes called "div soup".

Semantic HTML is really important to help machines to make sense of a webpage. Having a well-structured page makes it easier for browsers, search engine bot, automation tools (such as Playwright), and search engines. More importantly, good tags help assistive technologies like screen readers.

Semantic HTML is the first step to great and accessible web applications.

Writing good HTML means consciously using tags that convey meaning by themselves. A button, a paragraph, a link. Now, let's say that you've created an awesome component that acts like a button. In this case, you should rely on the `role` attribute.

```
<div role="button">
  {
    // The best button ever
    // ...
  }
</div>
```

Each semantic element has an implicit role. In this case, we'll set the `role` explicitly to notify whatever is reading the HTML that this is a `button`. The `role` sounds familiar? Yes, it is precisely what is used in the `getByRole()` Playwright Locator. Role is actually a specification of the Web Accessibility Initiative – Accessible Rich Internet Applications (WAI-ARIA). Every time you use `getByRole()` in Playwright, you rely on the accessibility. That's great. If you can locate your button with Playwright, it means that it's built-in with accessibility.

Because it encourages you to write semantic HTML, relies on user-facing and accessible name, `getByRole` is a great Locator that you should use as often as possible. Let's see other recommendations.

Locators Good Practices

Now that we know how semantic HTML is good for users and testability, let's have a recap of the different Locators and which one to favor. In addition, we'll list some more recommendations.

Locators Tier List

Playwright provides a great variety of different Locator strategies. As usual, Playwright turns out to be feature-rich and gives you great flexibility. This table helps by summarizing what, I believe, are the best Locators (and less suitable).

> *To make tests resilient, we recommend prioritizing user-facing attributes and explicit contracts.*
>
> —Playwright Documentation

Table 3-1. Locators tier list

Locator	Recommended	Notes
getByRole()	✓ Always	Best because it makes use of semantic HTML.
getByLabel()	✓ Always	Ideal for form input. getByRole("textbox") works too
getByPlaceholder()		To use when getByLabel() is not suitable
getByTestId()	✓ Good	
getByText()	⚠ Sparingly	Text alone is usually not good enough. Is this text displayed as a title? In a paragraph? Then you could use getByRole() and/or filtering
getByAltText()		For images only
getByTitle()		Can be useful for iframe, as you can set a title
CSS	⚠ Sparingly	Only with HTML element, well-known class or attribute
CSS utility class, XPath	✗ Never	

The great thing about Codegen is that it implements these rules when choosing a Locator. That's why it is such a useful tool, except on rare occasions it will get the right Locator for you effortlessly. The same goes for the VS Code extension.

Dos and Don'ts

I often encounter mistakes that are not necessarily basic, but at least easily avoidable. This section lists some common mistakes and good practices linked with Playwright Locators.

Do Lint Your Test

ESLint is a static code analyzer that will check your code and find syntax issues and potential bugs. This tool can be used in command line via an npm script, in Continuous Integration, and directly into your favorite IDE. Displaying issues directly in your editor ensures a short feedback loop: you have the error right in front of you, and is updated immediately once you fix it. I personally use the VS Code ESLint extension to do so, avoiding round-trips between my IDE and the CI.

Mainly two things are asynchronous in Playwright: actions (like `goto()`, `click()`...) and assertions (`expect().to...()`). To benefit from Playwright auto-waiting and retry mechanism, you need to await actions and assertions.

A very useful ESLint rule is `@typescript-eslint/no-floating-promises`; it will ensure that you don't forget to add await when needed.

```
// ❌ Incorrect
expect(page.locator('#promotional-banner')).toBeVisible();
```

```
// ✅ Correct
await expect(page.locator('#promotional-banner')).toBeVisible()
```

You should also give a try to ESLint Plugin Playwright,[2] a plugin that helps you to follow Playwright Test good practices and find gotchas.

---

[2] https://www.npmjs.com/package/eslint-plugin-playwright

Don't Wait

When an action or an assertion fails on a Locator, it is sometimes tempting to wait for some time just to be extra sure that this Locator is present. This can be done with `page.waitForTimeout()`, but should never ever be done.

Waiting explicitly for an arbitrary time makes the test unreliable. You are waiting for 1 second, why? Why not 2 seconds? What works on your machine may not in CI, or if the internet connection varies. A somehow better way is to use `waitFor`:

```
await orderSent.waitFor();
```

In this example, `orderSent` is a Locator for a confirmation banner that appears once the backend has finished processing an order. `waitFor` is helpful because it returns immediately if the element is already present or waits until it appears.

However, I advise using an assertion as it expresses clearly the intent to do a check.

```
await expect(orderSent).toBeVisible();
```

Do Refactor

As the number of your end-to-end tests grow, you may find ways to reuse code, improve things that are unclear, and remove unused code. Refactoring the tests code to keep it clean and easier to understand is necessary and never a waste of time.

Among useful refactoring, there you can extract a constant to have explicit naming.

```
// extracting a complex Locator to a const with clear name
const modalOK = getByRole().filter().locator(button);
```

Then if you can also create utility functions, maybe regroup them as a fixture. Some people find Page Object Model design pattern useful. Whatever helps you to make your tests easy may emerge from usage and refactoring.

Don't Add data-testid Everywhere

Using data attributes means that the application code and tests should be written by the same person, ideally at the same time. Otherwise, you will waste

- Time by asking others for missing data-testid
- Resources by guessing what to test first, at the risk of adding too much or too little

Sprinkle data-testid everywhere will not make your app easier to test

Having the ability to write the tests and code together is not always possible with end-to-end tests. Sprinkle data-testid everywhere will not make your app easier to test. The same goes with accessibility attributes. You should add `aria-role` only if the semantic HTML doesn't work for you.

Since you are using strict Locators, using the recommended ones with filtering or chaining, it should be fairly easy to find the cases where data-testid makes sense.

Summary

Semantic HTML makes for a better web, and for easier automation. We've seen the various Locators of Playwright and how they can be used for different use cases. With alternatives, tips, advanced filtering and chaining patterns, you can now craft reliable Locators.

Takeaways:

- Favor **semantic HTML**.
- getByRole and other **Testing Library-inspired Locators** are the best; they also encourage good practices.
- Use filtering and chaining to precisely find unique Elements, to keep Playwright **strictness**.

You now have everything needed to write tests, but they have the most value when running automatically. That is in Continuous Integration.

CHAPTER 4

Continuous Integration

In this chapter, you will set up a CI pipeline from scratch with explanations on how to get results, test reports, and traces. The example is with GitHub, but don't worry, I provide an alternative (GitLab CI), and the explanations and principles are the same whatever CI system used.

We will also use Docker to get a more consistent testing environment. The last part is about debugging after the tests are run. You'll find that Playwright shines in this situation.

Why Adding Playwright to Your CI?

Continuous Integration is an eXtreme Programming practice that is now a standard in modern development. It states that changes to the code of a project should be checked in and integrated in a continuous manner. For this, we generally use pipelines that will build the project and perform a series of tests automatically to check for any regressions. Many teams practice Continuous Integration by having a pipeline that performs the following steps in a few minutes: check code style, make a static analysis, check types, run unit tests and integration tests, build the application.

But somehow the end-to-end tests are forgotten, or may be relegated to nightly tests in the best cases. That hurts the feedback loop that we need as developers, by making it way too long. Imagine, everything seemed fine including unit tests, so we deployed the app after a change. Turned out, the end-to-end tests failed overnight. The thing is the developers who made the regression are already working on something else, so they have to pause it, switch context, and investigate what happened. You can make it take days if you add a QA service that has to go through some management to report an issue and actually have someone to fix it.

CHAPTER 4   CONTINUOUS INTEGRATION

We somehow accepted that end-to-end tests need many hours, but modern testing solutions are changing that. Playwright is fast, like blazing fast. Thanks to great performances with one worker, and the ability to scale horizontally and vertically, your end-to-end tests can run in minutes instead of several hours. Playwright Test is great if you want to put back end-to-end testing to Continuous Integration.

> **Warning**   Implementing Continuous Integration means adding your work to the code base on a regular basis. It can be achieved through Pull Requests with proofreading, but also through Peer Programming or Mob Programming. It also means building and packaging your application quickly (less than 10 minutes), collaborating with colleagues and other teams to avoid breaking everything. A pipeline is one of the tools of Continuous Integration, but it's not enough.

Our Pipeline with Playwright Test and GitHub

We will this how to build a pipeline to run Playwright test. In this chapter, I chose to build the pipeline with GitHub Actions, but I will give you all the keys to make it with your other CI solutions.

The steps of our pipeline will be as follows:

- Checkout our code
- Install dependencies
- Install Playwright Browsers
- Run the tests

Also, look at the end of this part to learn about **act**, a tool to try your pipelines locally.

Prerequisites

In this first step, we will scaffold our workflow file with the right prerequisites, then git checkout the code.

GitHub Workflows are saved under a .github/workflows folder; let's create our file playwright.yml. Remember Chapter 1? To run Playwright test, we need a Debian or Ubuntu Linux distribution, along with Node.js. We will use actions for this, i.e., reusable code.

Listing 4-1. *playwright.yml*

```
name: Playwright Tests
on:
  push
jobs:
  test:
    runs-on: ubuntu-latest
    steps:
    - uses: actions/checkout@v4
    - uses: actions/setup-node@v4
      with:
        node-version: lts/*
```

The action/checkout helps you by doing a git checkout of your repo.

Install Dependencies

The next step is to install the test project Node.js dependencies with the command npm ci. Note that in this context, "ci" stands for "clean install." Unlike install, it will totally remove the node_modules folder and will not resolve dependencies, but rather rely on the package-lock.json file.

It has several advantages for Continuous Integration:

- It's a clean install; you have no risks of using previous or outdated files.

- An installation with the lock file is faster since it will not perform package resolution.

- It's always the exact same versions, which is good for stable, reproducible builds.

Listing 4-2. playwright.yml

```
name: Playwright Tests
on:
  push
jobs:
  test:
    runs-on: ubuntu-latest
    steps:
    - uses: actions/checkout@v4
    - uses: actions/setup-node@v4
      with:
        node-version: lts/*
    - name: Install dependencies
      run: npm ci
```

Install Playwright Browsers

npx executes the installed playwright package or installs one for you when necessary. By using npx after installing our Node.js dependencies, we ensure that it will be the right playwright that installs the right browsers. In a CI, we want a fixed version of Playwright, with its browsers, and the system dependencies that fit the browsers.

Listing 4-3 is the updated file, where we install the browsers with their deps.

Listing 4-3. playwright.yml

```
name: Playwright Tests
on:
  push
jobs:
  test:
    runs-on: ubuntu-latest
    steps:
    - uses: actions/checkout@v4
    - uses: actions/setup-node@v4
      with:
        node-version: lts/*
```

```yaml
    - name: Install dependencies
      run: npm ci
    - name: Install Playwright Browsers
      run: npx playwright install --with-deps
```

You may be tempted to cache browsers, but it's usually less efficient due to the number and nature of the files needed for the browsers and the system dependencies. A Docker image is more fitting; we'll discuss more on that later in this chapter.

Run the Tests

This one is super-easy: we are ready to run our tests! Because we may have specific options passed to the Command Line Interface, I advise you to create an npm script dedicated to end-to-end. It's more flexible, and we can add more tests depending on our needs.

```json
{
  "scripts": {
    "test:e2e": "playwright test",
    "test:e2e:smoke": "playwright test --grep=smoke"
  }
}
```

We now have our final version of the workflow.

Listing 4-4. playwright.yml

```yaml
name: Playwright Tests
on:
  push
jobs:
  test:
    runs-on: ubuntu-latest
    steps:
    - uses: actions/checkout@v4
    - uses: actions/setup-node@v4
      with:
        node-version: lts/*
```

CHAPTER 4   CONTINUOUS INTEGRATION

```
  - name: Install dependencies
    run: npm ci
  - name: Install Playwright Browsers
    run: npx playwright install --with-deps
  - name: Run Playwright tests
    run: npm run test:e2e
```

Maybe you noticed that the resulting workflow file `playwright.yml` is almost identical to the one in Playwright Documentation, or the one generated by `npm init playwright`. It's intended! With all the key steps in mind, it's easy to write a pipeline for other technology than GitHub Actions.

Run GitHub Actions Locally with act

act is a handy utility that lets you run your GitHub Actions locally. It does so by using the power of Docker to run your workflows. It is available on a variety of Linux distributions, as well as macOS and Windows.

Running your pipeline locally has great benefit when writing actions file:

- The feedback loop is much shorter. You'll get your build, or an error message, in seconds instead of minutes.

- You don't use cloud power. Sometimes it is paid, so you can save money by using act.

- No need to git push stuff over and over.

- Don't mess with your runners; leave it to your co-workers to use.

You can find act install instruction on its website: `https://nektosact.com`.
Once installed, you can list workflows simply with `act --list`.

```
# list workflows
$ act --list
Stage  Job ID  Job name  Workflow name     Workflow file    Events
0      test    test      Playwright Tests  playwright.
yml    push,pull_request
```

CHAPTER 4   CONTINUOUS INTEGRATION

Then just use act command line with the event to run.

```
# to trigger event "on: push"
$ act push

⭐ Run Set up job
🚀  Start image=catthehacker/ubuntu:act-latest
🐳  docker pull image=catthehacker/ubuntu:act-latest
🐳  docker create image=catthehacker/ubuntu:act-latest
🐳  docker run image=catthehacker/ubuntu:act-latest
☑  Success - Set up job
☁  git clone 'https://github.com/actions/setup-node' # ref=v4
Non-terminating error while running 'git clone': some refs were not updated
☁  git clone 'https://github.com/actions/upload-artifact' # ref=v4
⭐ Run Main actions/checkout@v4
☑   Success - Main actions/checkout@v4 [3.241848ms]
⭐ Run Main actions/setup-node@v4
☑   Success - Main actions/setup-node@v4 [4.251531ms]
⭐ Run Main Install dependencies
☑   Success - Main Install dependencies [9.693623ms]
⭐ Run Main Install Playwright Browsers
☑   Success - Main Install Playwright Browsers [10.04631ms]
⭐ Run Main Run Playwright tests
☑   Success - Main Run Playwright tests [10.529734ms]
⭐ Run Main actions/upload-artifact@v4
☑   Success - Main actions/upload-artifact@v4 [3.150723ms]
⭐ Run Post actions/setup-node@v4
☑   Success - Post actions/setup-node@v4 [2.943379ms]
⭐ Run Complete job
Cleaning up container for job test
☑   Success - Complete job
🏁  Job succeeded
```

CHAPTER 4 CONTINUOUS INTEGRATION

Other CI Solutions

The official Playwright documentation has examples for the most popular solutions:

- Azure Pipelines
- CircleCI
- Jenkins
- Bitbucket Pipelines
- GitLab CI
- Google Cloud Build
- Drone

Our GitHub Workflow has to install everything needed to run the tests. GitLab CI, among others, have a different approach: the runner usually relies on Docker images. By using the official Docker images, it will make you save time and bandwidth by not downloading and installing browsers every time. As we said earlier, it is difficult to cache browsers with their dependencies. By using an official Docker image for Playwright, we can skip entirely the install Playwright step as seen in Listing 4-5.

Listing 4-5. .gitlab-ci.yml

```
stages:
  - test

tests:
  stage: test
  image: mcr.microsoft.com/playwright:v1.55.0-noble
  script:
    - npm ci
    - npm run test:e2e
```

Neat.

It's good practice to set an exact version for the job image. But what happens when you update your version of @playwright/test Node.js package? You get an error.

```
     Error: browserType.launch: Executable doesn't exist at /ms-playwright/
chromium_headless_shell-1161/chrome-linux/headless_shell

     Looks like Playwright Test or Playwright was just updated to 1.55.0.
     Please update docker image as well.
     - current: mcr.microsoft.com/playwright:v1.48.1-noble
     - required: mcr.microsoft.com/playwright:v1.55.0-noble

     <3 Playwright Team
```

This is great because

- It fails, as it should
- It gives you a clear message on what to do to fix your pipeline

Alternatively, GitHub Actions can also make use of containers. Let's see that in detail.

Docker and Playwright

Docker is a well-known container system that allows you to build, package, and run software in a controlled environment. A Docker container allows you to run things from a Docker image that will set up OS, library, files that are needed. This is perfect with Playwright Test in a Continuous Integration.

Docker

Docker containers are more lightweight than virtual machines because they rely on the host machine Operating System. Because it is lightweight, scalable, and relatively easy to use, it is widely popular. As a developer, you should probably know or learn how to build a Docker image (with a `Dockerfile` definition) and run it.

Docker is very useful in CI, and this will be our main usage with Playwright Test. It is useful because you won't need to set up an OS, install Node.js, or install Playwright browsers and their dependencies every time you run end-to-end tests on your CI pipelines. Moreover, caching is easy since you already have everything in the Docker image.

Sometimes, it is also handy to run Playwright Test from Docker locally. There are two cases where it is useful:

1. Your OS does not comply with the Playwright Test system requirements we've seen in the first chapter. Maybe your Windows or macOS version is too old, or maybe you are not using a Debian-like Linux distribution.

2. You are doing visual testing. We'll see later on that the rendering of a web application does not only depend on the browser, but also the fonts installed, and many small details linked with the Operating System.

Use Official Docker Image with GitHub Actions

Microsoft conveniently provides official Docker images for Playwright. There are different variants, based on the programming language you want to use, the version of Playwright (as it is preinstalled with the corresponding browsers), and the Ubuntu version code name.

```
# Node.js, 1.55.0, Noble Numbat (Ubuntu 24.04)
docker pull mcr.microsoft.com/playwright:v1.55.0-noble

# other languages variants
docker pull mcr.microsoft.com/playwright/python:v1.55.0-noble
docker pull mcr.microsoft.com/playwright/java:v1.55.0-noble
docker pull mcr.microsoft.com/playwright/dotnet:v1.55.0-noble
```

We can also use Docker with GitHub Actions. In Listing 4-6, I have adjusted the Workflow to use a container with a 1.55.0 image. I also removed the setup of Node.js and the installation of browsers, as they are included in the Playwright image.

In my experience, it is slightly faster (at least 30s) and has no downside.

Listing 4-6. playwright.yml

```
name: Playwright Tests
on:
  push
jobs:
  test:
```

```yaml
    runs-on: ubuntu-latest
    container:
      image: mcr.microsoft.com/playwright:v1.55.0-noble
    steps:
    - uses: actions/checkout@v4
    - name: Install dependencies
      run: npm ci
    - name: Run Playwright tests
      run: npm run test:e2e
```

Taylor Your Own Docker Image

You may want to build and use your own Docker image for Playwright Test for different reasons. Maybe you need the latest version of Node.js or you don't need all the default browsers (Chromium, Firefox, WebKit). On the contrary, you might need to run tests on Edge or Chrome, which Playwright can install for you. It's also possible to install any Chromium-based browser like Brave, Chrome, Vivaldi, … Then with some configuration, Playwright Test will be able to use them via CDP (Chrome DevTools Protocol).

To do this, we will make a simple Dockerfile that satisfies the prerequisites of Playwright: Node.js on a Debian distribution.

Listing 4-7. Dockerfile

```
FROM node:22-bookworm
# install different browsers
RUN npx playwright@1.55.0 install edge firefox webkit --with-deps

# more custom things
```

You can easily add extra things as needed, such as another browser that is not prepackaged in the Playwright Docker image. On top of the three default browsers, there is also Chrome, Edge, and variants. Run *npx playwright install --help* to get the full list.

Once we created the `Dockerfile`, we can build an image, tag it, and try it out.

```
# build
docker build . -t pw
# use
docker run --rm -it pw bash
```

Using your own Docker image, or the official one, is not only useful for Continuous Integration but guarantees a consistent development environment without hassle. This is crucial for visual testing.

Gotcha: Visual Regression Testing and CI

Visual regression testing is great until it's not. In addition to choosing the right thing to test, mask unwanted parts and animation, there is yet another difficulty with toHaveScreenshot(). Imagine, the tests all pass on your machine, but not on your colleague's. I've met developers who just didn't care about others because they use Windows or a Mac, or another Linux distro than theirs. This is not considerate to others, makes collaboration difficult, and is just anti-productive.

If your hardware and software setup differ from other contributors, chances are that it also differs from the Continuous Integration runners you are using. The toHaveScreenshot() results can vary depending on obvious things like different browser rendering engine, or the installed fonts. It turns out it can also vary on different hardware, like the type of CPU.

> *Browser rendering can vary based on the host OS, version, settings, hardware, power source (battery vs. power adapter), headless mode, and other factors. For consistent screenshots, run tests in the same environment where the baseline screenshots were generated.*
>
> —Playwright Documentation

To fill the gap, or at least most of it, we'll use the same Docker image on the CI and on our machine to generate image snapshots.

We want to update snapshots, inside a Docker container. We'll use a throwaway one.

Listing 4-8. Docker run

```
docker run --rm \
  -v $PWD:/app \
  -w /app \
  --network=host --ipc=host \
  mcr.microsoft.com/playwright:v1.55.0-noble \
  bash -c "npx playwright test snapshot -u"
```

Explanation of the docker run command line arguments used in Listing 4-8:

- `--rm` – Automatically removes the container when it exits
- `-v $PWD:/app` – Binds the current directory with /app in the container
- `-w /app` – Working directory
- `--network=host` – Use the host network
- `--ipc=host` – Playwright Documentation recommendation for Chromium
- `mcr.microsoft.com/playwright:v1.55.0-noble` – The Docker image to use; change it to your own if needed
- `bash -c "npx playwright test snapshot -u"` – bash executable, with a command

Another possibility that I didn't explain earlier is to tune the acceptable error rate to make `toHaveScreenshot()` a bit more lax. You can do it with

- `maxDiffPixels` – An option to set the acceptable number of different pixels
- `maxDiffPixelRatio` – To set an acceptable ratio of different pixels/total, as a number between 0 and 1

`toHaveScreenshot()` is based on `pixelmatch`, an image comparator that works at the pixel-level. There is also an experimental comparator `ssim-cie94`, based on structural similarity. It should give better results ignoring antialiasing differences.

```
await expect(page).toHaveScreenshot({
  _comparator: 'ssim-cie94',
});
```

There is a final way to manage visual tests that are difficult to maintain: delete them. No, really, delete them. You are wasting your time if they are not so stable. They might not be isolated enough, or maybe you should use something else.

CHAPTER 4   CONTINUOUS INTEGRATION

Advanced Pipeline

At this point, our Continuous Integration pipeline is done. That is, it is functional and ready for day-to-day duty. However, the remaining fine-tuning is more than just a "bonus." In this part, we will see how to get reports, and what to adjust in our test configuration.

Adjusting Parallelism and Timeout

When running Playwright Tests in continuous integration, some configuration may need to be adjusted. For example, you may need to adjust parallelism, be sure that nobody left a `test.only()` during debugging, or forbid headed browsers.

First thing first: `test.only()` is a syntax that allows you to debug easily the one test that you are working on. This should never go to the CI as it is meant for debugging only. Fortunately, the configuration created by `npm init playwright` already has this.

```
/* Fail the build on CI if you accidentally left test.only in the source
code. */
forbidOnly: !!process.env.CI,
```

Take a look at your runners. Do you have a big CPU? Many runners available? You'll need to set the number of workers accordingly.

```
workers: process.env.CI ? 1: undefined,
```

Setting it to 1 is often a good idea in Continuous Integration. We will optimize it further later on.

If some of your tests are regularly failing in CI, it may be because their execution takes too long time and reach the test timeout of 30000ms. First, it should be one of your goals to have fast, concise tests.

If many of your tests fail, you might want to tune the test timeout in the configuration file. While we are at it, we'll use `reportSlowTests` so that Playwright Test marks slow tests and doesn't tolerate too many of them.

```
export default defineConfig({
  timeout: 60_000,
  reportSlowTests: { max: 5, threshold: 30_000 },
  // ...
}
```

But that might be too broad to change the default timeout for all your tests. If only a few of them need some extra time, you can use test.slow().

```
test('slow', async ({ page }) => {
  test.slow();
  // ...
});
```

slow() is great because it will triple the default timeout (i.e., the timeout from playwright.config.ts), can take a condition, and have a description. This allows giving more context on why the test is slow, that will be shown as an annotation in the HTML report.

```
// Mark test as slow
test.slow();
// With a condition and a description
test.slow(browserName === 'webkit', 'This feature is slow in Safari');
// With a description (and a truthy condition)
test.slow(true, "The game takes up to a minute to load");
```

Retrieve Reports As Artifacts

Reporting is a must-have because it is the best source of information about a test run. Pipeline status and console log are not enough; we need something more readable and more complete.

First, don't forget to set up reporting in your Playwright Test configuration. Remember, we can use an environment variable to differentiate local and CI configuration.

Another must-have is adding Trace. Trace is your time machine to get logs, snapshot, and more on what happened when a test failed. It will be available from the HTML report automatically.

```
export default defineConfig({
  // ...
  reporter: process.env.CI ? [['html'], ['github']]: 'html',
  use: {
    trace: 'retain-on-failure',
  },
}
```

Then we need to make the report accessible. In most CI systems, this means uploading an artifact. Artifacts usually contain installer binaries, reports, intermediate builds, or documentation.

In our pipeline, we will add a GitHub action to upload artifacts as seen in Listing 4-9.

Listing 4-9. playwright.yml

```yaml
name: Playwright Tests
on:
  push
jobs:
  test:
    runs-on: ubuntu-latest
    steps:
    - uses: actions/checkout@v4
    - uses: actions/setup-node@v4
      with:
        node-version: lts/*
    - name: Install dependencies
      run: npm ci
    - name: Install Playwright Browsers
      run: npx playwright install --with-deps
    - name: Run Playwright tests
      run: npm run test:e2e
    - uses: actions/upload-artifact@v4
      if: ${{ always() }}
      with:
        name: playwright-report
        path: playwright-report/
        retention-days: 30
```

Reporting

Playwright Test offers several built-in reporters. Basically, you can separate them in two categories: reporters for humans and reporters for machines.

For humans:

- HTML reporter is by far the most useful. It will create a folder that can be served as a web page. It holds results for the tests and any attachments: trace, screenshot, video.

- List prints a line for each test being run.

- Line is more concise; it's meant for interactive terminal, as it will update a line with the latest finished test.

- Dot is even more concise: one dot per test.

For machines:

- JUnit will create an XML report with the format of the popular Java test framework. This format is understood by a variety of tooling. I used it to report test results in GitLab CI for example.

- JSON creates a report with a format specific to Playwright Test.

- Blob is mainly used for merging test results from several test runners (sharding, see Chapter 5).

- The GitHub reporter adds annotations when running in GitHub Actions.

As we've seen previously, you can set several reporters and configure them. Also, we can use the CI environment variable to have a differentiated behavior locally and in Continuous Integration.

```
reporter: process.env.CI
  ? [['list'], ['junit'], ['html', { open: 'never' }]]
  : 'html',
```

There are a number of third-party reporters available. Usually, the installation is straightforward: install the package, add the reporter by its name in the configuration. That's it!

Here is for Allure, a popular test reporting tool that will give you history, filtering, analytics…

Listing 4-10. Allure setup

```
npm install –save-dev allure-playwright
```

Listing 4-10a. Allure setup

```
// No specific import
import { defineConfig } from '@playwright/test';

export default defineConfig({
  reporter: 'allure-playwright',
});
```

You can also write your own reporter for Playwright Test. It is rather easy as we will see in Chapter 6.

Debugging Afterward with Logs, Reports, and Traces

A real difficult task is to make sense of a failed test on the CI. Also known as "it works on my machine." Or more probably because the pipeline is doing all the verifications that you may have forgotten. After all, that's the value of CI pipeline: being a safety net and giving you feedback. In this part, we will see the different options available for debugging, afterward.

Make Sense of Logs

The very first thing to check is the errors logged by the test script. Usually, it will give you clear clues on what happened.

It often goes down to two cases:

1. Locator was not found, hence an action failed. Usually, this means the action will fail after a timeout. Here you also need to pay attention to test setup, compilation errors, and which timeout failed exactly, i.e., an action will time out when there are no Locators, but a test can fail if it is too slow.

   ```
   1) [chromium] › tests/demo4.spec.ts:3:5 › test
   ```

   ```
   Test timeout of 30000ms exceeded.
   Error: locator.click: Test timeout of 30000ms exceeded.
   ```

CHAPTER 4 CONTINUOUS INTEGRATION

```
Call log:
  - waiting for locator('text=mxschmitt')
  14 |    await expect(page1).toHaveURL('https://github.com/
          microsoft/playwright');
  15 |    // Click text=mxschmitt
> 16 |    await page1.locator('text=mxschmitt').click();
     |                                          ^
  17 |    await expect(page1).toHaveURL('https://github.com/
          microsoft/playwright/commits?author=mxschmitt');
  18 |    await expect(page1.locator('text=woof')).toBeVisible();
  19 |
    at /builds/jfgreffier/playwright-demos/tests/demo4.spec.
    ts:16:41
attachment #1: trace (application/zip)
```

```
test-results/tests-demo4-test-chromium/trace.zip
Usage:
    npx playwright show-trace test-results/tests-demo4-test-
    chromium/trace.zip
```

2. An assertion failed. In this case, the assertion will give a clear message about what was expected and what was the actual value.

```
Error: expect(received).toBe(expected) // Object.is equality

Expected: 0
Received: 1

  150 |    const result = parseTestRunnerOutput(testProcess.
           output);
  151 |    expect.soft(result.passed).toBe(0);
> 152 |    expect.soft(result.failed).toBe(0);
      |                               ^
  153 |    expect.soft(result.didNotRun).toBe(2);
  154 |    expect.soft(result.output).not.toContain
           ('worker process exited unexpectedly');
  155 | });
```

99

CHAPTER 4   CONTINUOUS INTEGRATION

```
    at /Users/runner/work/playwright/playwright/tests/playwright-test/
    runner.spec.ts:152:30

Error: expect(received).toBe(expected) // Object.is equality
```

HTML Report

The HTML report is much more user-friendly than digging through Continuous Integration logs. Additionally, you'll have more context available.

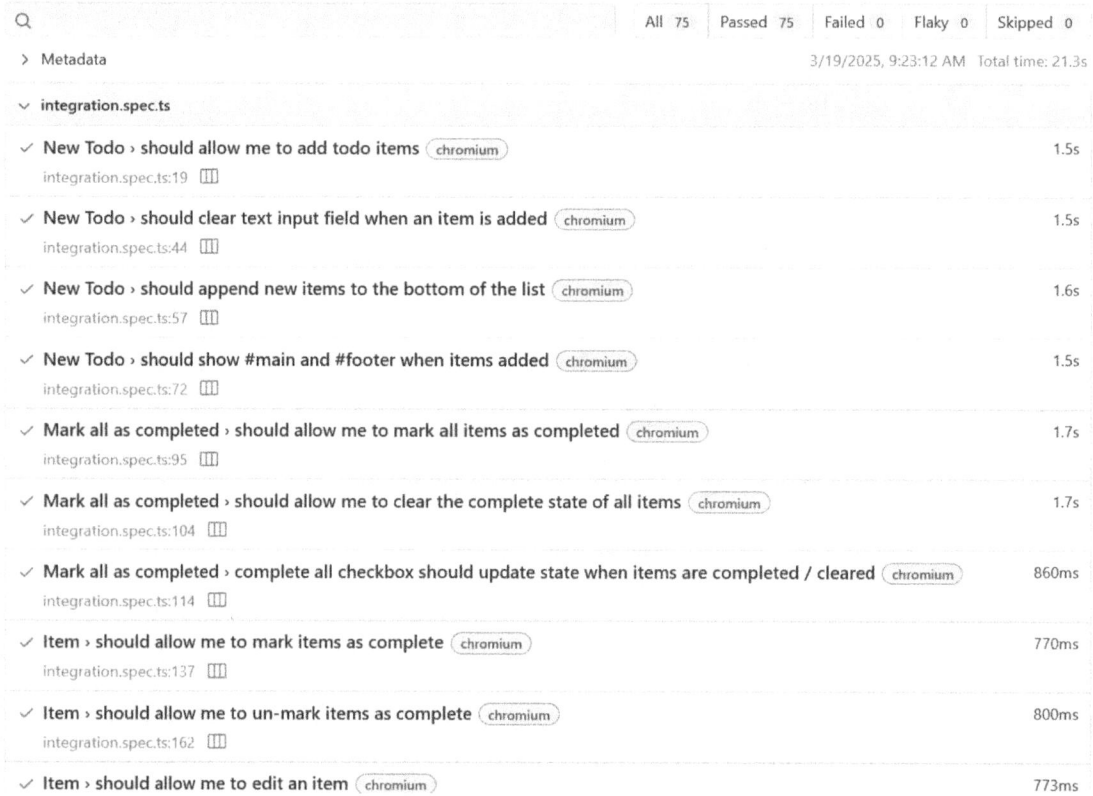

Figure 4-1. *HTML report*

To view the report, you'll need to either host it or download it and consult it on your machine with `npx playwright show-report`. You can check an example HTML report here: `https://demo.playwright.dev/reports/todomvc/`.

CHAPTER 4 CONTINUOUS INTEGRATION

You can easily navigate the results and filter them by result (Passed, Failed, Flaky, Skipped) and by tags. There are tags for the different configured projects, but also the tags you may add to your tests to organize test suites.

It's very interesting to use filtering and try to make sense of what happened when several tests failed. Maybe it's only one particular browser? Or are all of your tests failing? It may mean that it's a setup issue. Perhaps a particular subset of tests is failing?

On the test itself, you will get steps and Playwright API calls, as well as error logs and attachments.

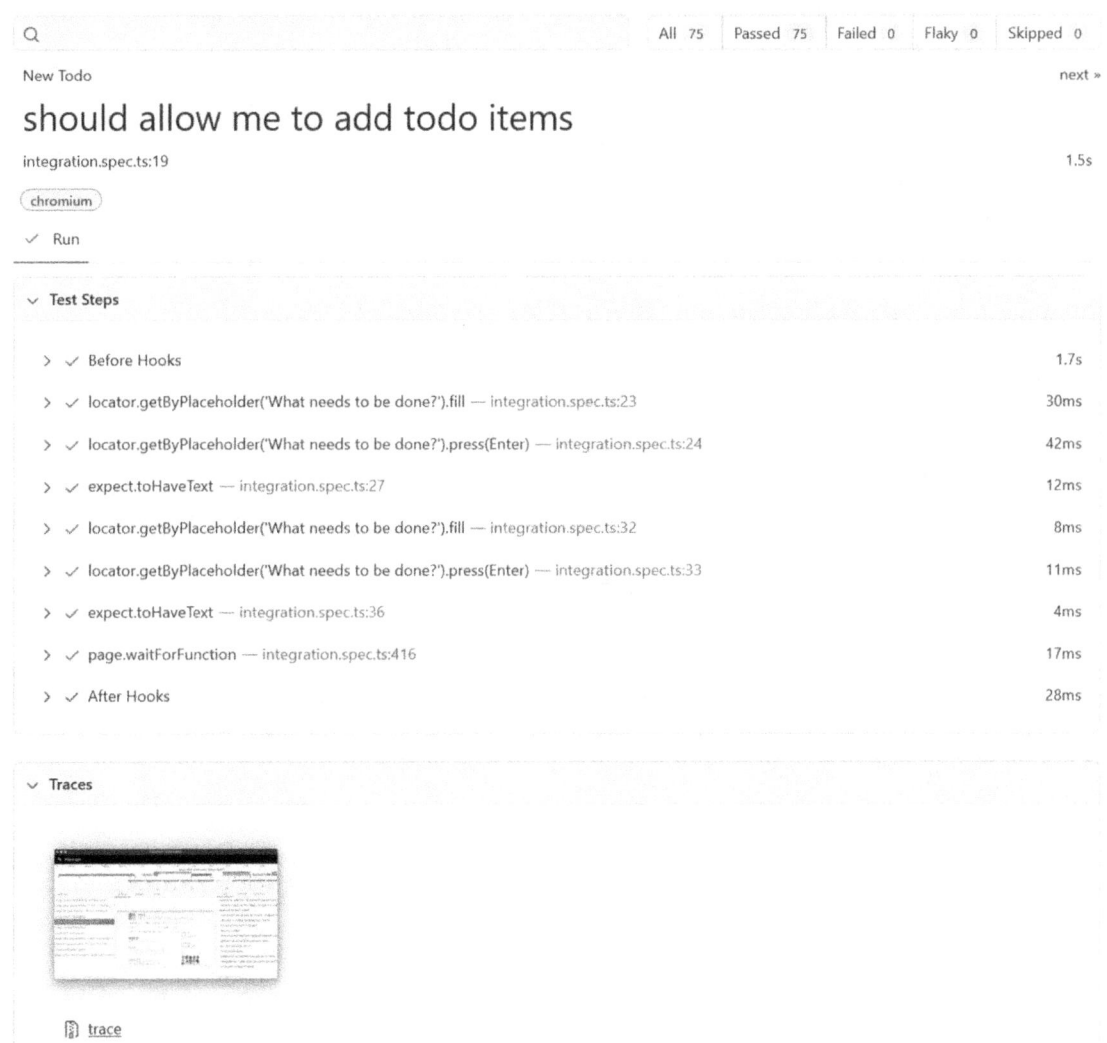

Figure 4-2. Test result details

101

There is also a new shiny `Copy prompt` button in case of failure. It's meant to copy a prompt for an AI agent. If you don't use AI, it's a great way to have a clear text explanation of a problem since it gives context information like the test itself, what failed, and an ARIA snapshot.

Time-Travel with Traces

Years ago, I was a developer in a team using end-to-end tests that were so long that they had to run overnight. Then you had to try and figure out what the hell happened, only from logs. Now we can make screenshots, or videos, to have a better grasp on what happened during the pipeline run. That's good, but usually not enough. For a long time, that and logs were the only options to understand what happened.

Playwright's Traces show command history, browser console, network, screenshot… and even DOM snapshots. When I discovered it, Playwright's Trace blew my mind. The Trace viewer is truly a killer-feature: no other tool offered such a comprehensive analysis and diagnosis possibilities. Plus, it is free and just works out of the box.

Here are the options to consult the traces of a test:

- Directly from the HTML report.

- Download it and launch the Trace viewer from CLI.

    `npx playwright show-trace trace.zip`

- Use the online trace viewer `https://trace.playwright.dev`.

    Either by uploading the trace file or by passing the URL with the path to a publicly accessible zip. `https://trace.playwright.dev/?trace=<trace.zip>`

CHAPTER 4   CONTINUOUS INTEGRATION

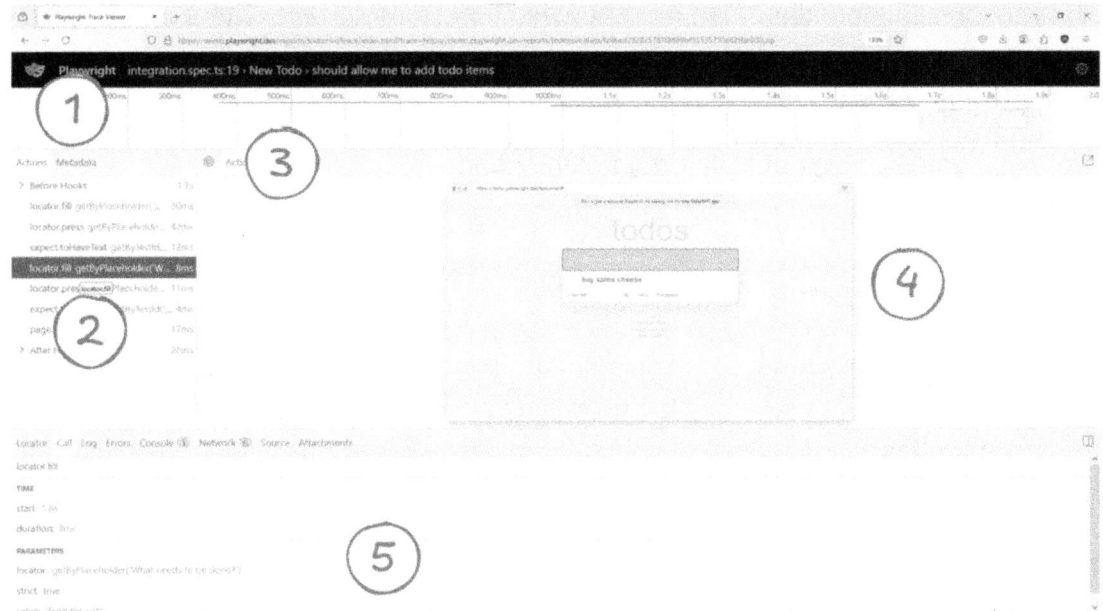

Figure 4-3. Trace viewer

Here is an overview of the Trace viewer as seen in Figure 4-3:

1. Timeline with DOM events and screenshots
2. Calls to Playwright, i.e., actions and assertions
3. Pick Locator
4. DOM snapshot
5. Test a Locator
6. Details on each call, e.g., `goto` with the parameters used
7. Console of the browser during the test
8. Check the source code of the test
9. Network calls

Warning Be careful on how and to whom you share your trace files. Traces hold many information, some of them might be sensitive. For example, network calls may give clues on API endpoints, network headers may leak API token, response

CHAPTER 4   CONTINUOUS INTEGRATION

JSON may hold more data than it is shown in the User Interface. There is the code source of your test as well. In some cases, in can be the source code of your app (think source maps).

Note that you can customize the recording options.

Select a Time Frame

The timeline not only allows to visualize events, but also to narrow down the trace information to a time. By selecting a time frame on the top, the trace Viewer will display the corresponding actions, logs, console calls, and network events that happened during that period.

Pick Locator

Not unlike Playwright Test for VS Code, you can pick a Locator or write a Locator interactively. It's perfect to debug and fix a Locator that broke, e.g., the page changed greatly, and it needs to readjust the test accordingly. It's very valuable because you can fix and write Locators back in time at the right point in time of the test.

DOM Snapshot

The center view shows a snapshot of the page at that time during the test. But it's not only a screenshot: it's a DOM snapshot, HTML, and CSS. It means that you can inspect the DOM with your browser DevTools, you can pick and try Locator. But you also have a full view of the web page, including layout and style. The CSS animations work too.

This is invaluable because you have a browser time machine!

Network

Similarly to the network panel of many browsers' Developer Tools, you can filter requests by their type such as Fetch (also called XHR in some tools), HTML, JS, CSS, Font, Image. The most interesting one for me is `Fetch`. These are the requests done programmatically by the application under tests. Note that it is called `Fetch` but it is technology-agnostic: it is exactly the same if you use the Fetch API, XMLHttpRequest, or any third-party like Axios.

Once you've clicked on a network call, you'll get more details: URL, method, request, and response headers... But more than that, you will get the response body! It's very handy to get the JSON response from the backend.

With the request, you can

- Copy as cURL – e.g., for debug purpose.
- Copy as Fetch – to execute as JavaScript.
- Copy as Playwright – it will use the request API, useful for API testing with Playwright Test.

And More

You also have detailed information on the Playwright call (action or assertion), logs, console message of the browser during the test. There is the source code of the test as well.

Run It on Your Machine

By this point, you must have a good understanding of what happened and what should be fixed. Or maybe you don't. Either way, we need to go back to developer mode.

There are several ways to debug a Playwright test; we'll see here what I personally find useful. In order, I'd recommend

- VS Code debugging
- UI mode in addition to adjust Locators easily
- Inspector if you don't use VS Code

Playwright Test for VS Code

My favorite way to debug Playwright tests is to use VS Code as it resembles my current workflow with developing and debugging frontend applications.

You can set your breakpoints directly in VS Code and execute tests step by step. You can also inspect Locators. When on a breakpoint, you can actually inspect Objects and execute code in a REPL in the debug console. We can also show the browser and open its console.

If you happen to also develop the app under testing, it's useful to see the application code and debug it alongside your tests!

UI Mode

I sometimes navigate between the VS Code extension and the UI mode. I love the trace mode; it's really a great developer experience to be able to inspect the DOM snapshot at that exact point in time. It's easy then to rewrite Locator.

Playwright Inspector

The Playwright Inspector allows step-by-step execution or inspecting Locators. It's perfectly usable, but I do prefer VS Code debugging.

`npx playwright test --debug`

The --debug option will make a number of changes in execution:

- Browser launches in headed mode
- Playwright Inspector appears
- Default timeout is unset
- Max failures is 1

Summary

In this chapter, we covered

- A GitHub pipeline, **built step by step.**
- Steps we covered remain basically the same whatever your CI solution.
- **Docker** is great to run tests in a controlled environment.
- How to retrieve **artifacts.**
- Reporting**.**
- And more important: **debugging**.

To make Continuous Integration, we should ensure that our test suite is run automatically, regularly, and quickly. In the next chapter, we'll list different good practices, tips, and tricks and find out how fast Playwright Test can be.

CHAPTER 5

Make It Fast

The first four chapters of this book covered the basics of end-to-end testing with Playwright Test. At this point, you have everything in your hands to write and maintain high-quality tests with Playwright. Now to have more value, they should run quickly in your Continuous Integration. This chapter is made of good practices, tips and tricks, and tooling to make your tests blazing fast.

Playwright Test has a reputation for being fast. It's not only a reputation as benchmarks[1] shown that it is in fact faster in most situations, even for large test suites. Without parallelization, that is. It means two things: it is good enough as it is, and it can be even faster with some optimization.

I try to follow two principles about Continuous Integration:

- Ten-minute build
- No premature optimizations

The Ten-minute build is a practice from eXtreme Programming. It states that the entire automatic build and tests of a system should not take longer than ten minutes. You will likely switch to another task if it's longer, or worse, you will forget that you added code to integrate. This is rather short for end-to-end testing, so don't take it as a hard limit, but more as the ideal to keep in mind. If it's longer than ten minutes, it means that it's time to optimize things.

It is said that premature optimization is the root of all evil. I agree, so please if your Playwright tests are fast enough, just skip this chapter. You'll come back here eventually when you need it.

---

[1] Cypress vs Selenium vs Playwright vs Puppeteer speed comparison by Giovani Rago: https://www.checklyhq.com/blog/cypress-vs-selenium-vs-playwright-vs-puppeteer-speed-comparison/.

CHAPTER 5   MAKE IT FAST

Make it work, make it right, make it fast.

—Kent Beck

Previously, we've seen how to set up Playwright Test and how to write tests efficiently. That's the easy part: make it work.

Only once you have working tests can you refactor your code and improve your tests as you unveil the intrinsic complexity of your application. It means that only once you've written some tests will you know what can be improved and you can ask yourself questions such as: Do I need custom fixtures? Should we use POM? How many tests do we really need? It takes some practice and knowledge to make your tests maintainable and to follow the best practices. In other words: make it right.

As the last step, we will see in this chapter how to lower the execution time of your tests. Faster tests mean that we can keep them in Continuous Integration, and easily improve the Developer eXperience by providing a short feedback loop. Make it fast, on CI and locally.

Parallelism

One way to have faster tests is to run them in parallel, by adding more workers on the same machine. Workers are the Operating System processes that are running the tests. The workers are created by Playwright Test according to its settings. Each worker starts a browser, so you can see it as a 1 worker = 1 browser instance.

This chapter encourages you to run your tests in parallel for faster results. Either with multiple workers on one machine, several machines, or cloud-based solutions. However, there is a downside to it: parallel tests can be less reliable. For example, two parallel tests running against a shared database can conflict. The best approach is to build your test suite with parallel execution from the beginning. You will thank yourself later.

How Many Workers Should You Use?

By default, Playwright Test will use up to 50% of your CPU logical cores. You can limit the number of workers via the command line.

```
npx playwright test --workers=1
```

Or in the configuration file as seen in Listing 5-1. In this case, the value `undefined` means the default setting.

Listing 5-1. playwright.config.ts

```
import { defineConfig } from '@playwright/test';
export default defineConfig({
  // Limit the number of workers on CI, use default locally
  workers: process.env.CI ? 1: undefined,
});
```

Instead of a number of workers, you can set a percentage of your CPU logical cores. This can be handy when you don't know the exact configuration of the machine that runs the tests.

```
npx playwright test --workers=50%
```

Note If you want to make full use of your CPU, you can set the value to 99%. Because the internal algorithm will calculate the number of workers and floor it, it effectively means 100% minus one (that we will use for the test coordinator process).

On my machine, it means 27 workers!

Depending on the machine you are running tests on and your test suite, the optimal configuration can be different. You should experiment to find the sweet spot that works.

OK, but how many workers, really?

Ivan Tanev gave the answer years ago in a blog post about Jest.[2] It consists of making benchmarks with **hyperfine**, a simple open source project that compares the execution time in the command line. You can parameterize runs with either a number that iterates (like a `for` loop) or a list of values. Just run the command and go grab a coffee and wait for the benchmark to complete.

---

[2] Make Your Jest Tests up to 20% Faster by Changing a Single Setting https://ivantanev.com/make-jest-faster

CHAPTER 5   MAKE IT FAST

```
hyperfine --parameter-scan w 1 10 --runs 1 'npx playwright test
--workers={w}'
```

Here is a sample result:

```
$ hyperfine --parameter-list w 1,25%,50%,75%,99% --runs 1 'npx playwright
test --repeat-each=5 --workers={w}'

Benchmark 1: npx playwright test --repeat-each=5 --workers=1
  Time (abs ≡):       219.712 s

Benchmark 2: npx playwright test --repeat-each=5 --workers=25%
  Time (abs ≡):        42.182 s

Benchmark 3: npx playwright test --repeat-each=5 --workers=50%
  Time (abs ≡):        31.495 s

Benchmark 4: npx playwright test --repeat-each=5 --workers=75%
  Time (abs ≡):        27.927 s

Benchmark 5: npx playwright test --repeat-each=5 --workers=99%
  Time (abs ≡):        27.391 s

Summary
  npx playwright test --repeat-each=5 --workers=99% ran
    1.02 times faster than npx playwright test --repeat-each=5
    --workers=75%
    1.15 times faster than npx playwright test --repeat-each=5
    --workers=50%
    1.54 times faster than npx playwright test --repeat-each=5
    --workers=25%
    8.02 times faster than npx playwright test --repeat-each=5 --workers=1
```

99% ran the fastest, but 75% is very close. We can also see that the default setting of 50% is very reasonable.

It's very instructive to figure out what gives much better performance, and where there are only marginal improvements. Test it for yourself and keep in mind that there are more parameters than raw calculation power: more workers mean more CPU usage, but also concurrent access to memory, storage, and network resources.

Your Machine vs. a CI Agent

You can fire dozens of workers on your local machine without problem. Continuous Integration agents, also called runners, are often a magnitude less powerful than a developer's computer.

CI runners are (virtual) machines that are used to perform automated tasks. They are usually small to remain cost-effective, and they don't have the same requirements as a personal computer – no UI, short-lived tasks, usually not too demanding tasks, non-critical.

Playwright team does not give clear system requirements in terms of CPU and memory usage, mainly because they vary greatly depending on the web application under test. From my experience, the minimal requirements should be close to the following:

- 2 CPU cores, to run the test runner and the browser
- 1 extra CPU core if you run your front-end application alongside the tests. For example, with the webServer setting
- 2GB of memory

The thing is, browsers are heavy applications that need more power than typical CI agent tasks. If you don't control your CI settings yourself, go talk to your team's or company's people that are in charge of your Continuous Integration infrastructure.

Table 5-1. *Standard GitHub-hosted runners for public repositories*

Virtual Machine	Processor (CPU)	Memory (RAM)	Storage (SSD)	Architecture
Linux	4	16 GB	14 GB	x64
Windows	4	16 GB	14 GB	x64
macOS	4	14 GB	14 GB	Intel
macOS	3 (M1)	7 GB	14 GB	arm64

The standard GitHub Linux runner has 4 CPUs and 16GB of RAM. If you run your tests and your app, you'll need 2+1 CPU cores. You can probably add a worker safely.

```
npx playwright test --workers=2
```

This example is trivial, but for other cases you can also use `hyperfine` to benchmark your settings against your CI agent to find the optimal setting.

Understand the Different Parallelism Options

As long as you have more than one worker, Playwright Test will run test files in parallel. There are no guarantees in which order the test files will run. We'll see later on that you can set dependencies between projects, but it's good practice that the tests remain independent.

Playwright documentation states that the tests inside a file are run in order. What does it mean, and what are the alternatives? Let's detail the three possible settings: `parallel`, `default`, and `serial`.

parallel

With this option, each test runs in parallel, without particular order. If a test fails, it will be retried independently. This is the most preferable situation, but it means that the tests should not have any relation whatsoever. Also, it means that a test cannot have side effects.

Listing 5-2. parallel.spec.ts

```
import test from '@playwright/test';

test.describe.configure({ mode: 'parallel' });

test('runs in parallel 1', async ({ page }) => {});
test('runs in parallel 2', async ({ page }) => {});
```

Also note that you can use `test.describe.configure()` whether you are using a `describe` block or not.

default

The tests run in order inside a file, one after another. If a test fails and is retried, it will be re-run independently.

Listing 5-3. default.spec.ts

```
import test from '@playwright/test';

test.describe.configure({ mode: 'default' });

test('runs first', async ({ page }) => {});
test('runs second', async ({ page }) => {});
```

serial

The tests are not only running one after another, but they are dependent on each other. It means that if a test fails, the following ones will be skipped. If there is a retry, Playwright will re-run the whole block, being a describe or a file.

Listing 5-4. serial.spec.ts

```
import test from '@playwright/test';

test.describe.configure({ mode: 'serial' });

test('runs first', async ({ page }) => {});
test('runs second', async ({ page }) => {});
```

Warning Using serial is a bad practice as it shows that your tests are not isolated. You should try to have smaller, focused tests. For something like a customer journey, use steps to separate the different phases of your test.

---

fullyParallel

This global setting (top-level or per project) is like setting parallel on every test file. It's great because it sets the bar higher by encouraging you to have parallelism and test isolation by default.

```
import { defineConfig } from '@playwright/test';

export default defineConfig({
  fullyParallel: false,
```

```
    projects: [
      {
        name: 'chromium',
        use: { ...devices['Desktop Chrome'] },
        fullyParallel: true,
      },
      // ...
});
```

This is not always easy to achieve. Let's say that you've opted in for fully parallel tests, but there is this one test that keeps breaking. In this case, you can opt out easily test by test, or per describe block.

```
test.describe('A, runs in parallel with B', () => {
  test('A1 runs in parallel with A2 and B', async ({ page }) => {});
  test('A2 runs in parallel with A1 and B', async ({ page }) => {});
});

test.describe('B, runs in parallel with A and its tests', () => {
  test.describe.configure({ mode: 'default' });
  test('in order B1', async ({ page }) => {});
  test('in order B2', async ({ page }) => {});
});
```

B2 will run after B1 in this example, but the rest of the file will run in parallel as it is the configuration file setting. I encourage you to always keep `fullyParallel` in `playwright.config.ts`, and keep in mind that you always have this escape hatch when you need it.

Sharding

We've seen scaling: multiplying the number of workers on a given machine. Sharding allows you to split the tests over several machines. Because Playwright's startup time is really short, splitting a test suite into three parts virtually means running the tests three times faster. This is well adapted to CI that often has many small runners available. Just keep in mind that each shard may need some preparation job: build and run the application, spinning up a database, etc.

CHAPTER 5   MAKE IT FAST

Scaling

Several workers

`npx playwright test --workers 2`

Sharding

Several CI jobs

```
npx playwright test --shard=1/3
npx playwright test --shard=2/3
npx playwright test --shard=3/3
```

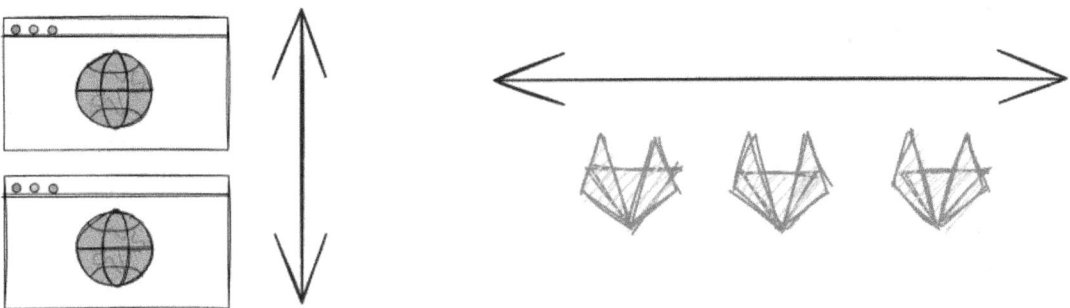

Figure 5-1. *Scaling and sharding*

The usage is simple: just tell Playwright which tests to run.

```
# Run the first third
npx playwright test --shard=1/3
```

By sending different test batches to different runners, we effectively split the tests between different machines.

For best efficiency, you should pay attention to the way your tests are organized. Because Playwright Test has no built-in centralized orchestration, it can't tell what the execution times are and how to split the tests efficiently. So, the tests should be of approximately the same size in order to "balance" the shards. The easiest way for that is to activate `fullyParallel` tests. It will allow Playwright Test to dispatch individual tests, instead of files.

If you don't have `fullyParallel` activated, Playwright Test will dispatch test files that have a much bigger granularity. In extreme cases, a shard will be bloated by long-running test suites in big files, while others have much less things to do.

CHAPTER 5   MAKE IT FAST

Set It Up with GitHub

Remember Nektos act? We will use it again to write and try out our GitHub pipeline locally.

For sharding, we need to make two changes:

- Applying a `matrix` strategy. This will create variations of our test job based on two variables.

- Use the `shardIndex` and `shardTotal` to build the shard parameter to pass to the test script.

This will create two jobs, one running with shard 1/2 and another with 2/2.

Listing 5-5.   playwright.yml

```yaml
name: Playwright Tests
on:
  push
jobs:
  test:
    runs-on: ubuntu-latest
    container:
      image: mcr.microsoft.com/playwright:v1.51.1-noble
    strategy:
      matrix:
        shardIndex: [1, 2]
        shardTotal: [2]
    steps:
    - uses: actions/checkout@v4
    - name: Install dependencies
      run: npm ci
    - name: Run Playwright tests
      run: npm run test:e2e -- --shard=${{ matrix.shardIndex }}/${{ matrix.shardTotal }}
```

You could also use the GitHub context variable `strategy.job-index` and `strategy.job-total`, but unfortunately they are not available in act.

It's even easier with GitLab CI with the use of `parallel`. The general pattern is the same. Parameterize jobs to define the different shards, then use the context variable or our parameter to build the Playwright Test command.

Listing 5-6. .gitlab-ci.yml

```yaml
tests:
  stage: test
  image: mcr.microsoft.com/playwright:v1.25.0-focal
  parallel: 7
  script:
    - npx playwright test --shard=$CI_NODE_INDEX/$CI_NODE_TOTAL
```

Reconstruct Reports

Because reports are typically written on the file system, we need to collect the data from the different runners and merge them. When using one of the built-in reporters, we should create a `blob` report first, then use a tool to merge and create our final report.

To create the blob report, we can either pass an option in the command line `npm run test:e2e -- --reporter=blob` or set it conditionally in the Playwright Test configuration file.

```
export default defineConfig({
  reporter: process.env.CI ? 'blob' : 'html',
  // ...
});
```

We add an upload artifact step; this shares the files under `blob-report` folder to the next job. Note that the artifact should have a unique name, either based on the matrix parameters or the context. Here too we could use `strategy.job-index`.

Listing 5-7. playwright.yml sharding with report upload

```yaml
name: Playwright Tests
on:
  push
jobs:
  test:
```

CHAPTER 5   MAKE IT FAST

```
    runs-on: ubuntu-latest
    container:
      image: mcr.microsoft.com/playwright:v1.52.0-noble
    strategy:
      matrix:
        shardIndex: [1, 2]
        shardTotal: [2]
    steps:
    - uses: actions/checkout@v4
    - name: Install dependencies
      run: npm ci
    - name: Run Playwright tests
      run: npm run test:e2e -- --shard=${{ matrix.shardIndex }}/${{ matrix.shardTotal }}
    - uses: actions/upload-artifact@v4
      with:
        name: blob-report-${{ matrix.shardIndex }}
        path: blob-report
```

This new `merge-report` job depends on the previous one with the need keyword. So once our tests ran, we first download the artifacts in the `all-blob-reports` folder. Then we use the `npx playwright merge-reports` script before uploading our final HTML report as an artifact.

Listing 5-8. playwright.yml merge reports

```
merge-reports:
  runs-on: ubuntu-latest
  needs: test
  container:
    image: mcr.microsoft.com/playwright:v1.52.0-noble
  steps:
  - name: Download blob reports from GitHub Actions Artifacts
    uses: actions/download-artifact@v4
    with:
      path: all-blob-reports
      pattern: blob-report-*
```

```
      merge-multiple: true
 - name: Merge into HTML report dependencies
   run: npx playwright merge-reports --reporter html ./all-blob-reports
 - name: Upload HTML report
   uses: actions/upload-artifact@v4
   with:
     name: html-report
     path: playwright-report
```

To run this with act, we'll need to set up a path to save the artifacts files. It should be a temporary folder. At the end of the pipeline, we can retrieve and show the final HTML report!

```
# Run the pipeline
act --artifact-server-path=/tmp/artifacts

# The go to the artifacts folder
cd /tmp/artifacts/1/html-report
unzip html-report.zip
npx playwright show-report .
```

Third-Party Reporters

The general idea remains the same regardless of the report used:

- Generate report on each shard and upload all of them as artifact.
- Run a merge job that will use a Command Line Interface tool.

When using a third-party reporter, you should refer to their documentation for the exact details on how to generate the reports and how to merge them. You can sometimes use blob reporter as an intermediate format. On the contrary, Monocart reporter doesn't need a specific format for the intermediate shard report (and doesn't support blob reports). But then, they provide a CLI tool to merge the reports via a npx command.

Again, using act or a similar way to run pipeline locally will save you precious time when writing a Continuous Integration pipeline.

CHAPTER 5   MAKE IT FAST

Save Time and Money in CI

Adjusting parallelism and using sharding is only one part of the solution: you should also ensure that your testing practices and your settings are not slowing you down.

Optimize Your Application and Environment

Before using Playwright's features to get faster tests, let's start with your web application itself. Improving the weight and performance of a web page is always a good idea. For the user experience first, but it will also benefit the tests. Indeed, because Playwright is fast, the performance bottleneck will often be your own application. Without going to the point of over-optimization, it is often easy to improve performance.

The first step is to measure your web application's performance. A tool like Lighthouse, which is integrated in Chrome, can help to have a first overview of what obvious changes[3] can be made. Having gzip compression, a good cache policy, checking if the images are adapted in size and file format probably are the first things to look for. Most JavaScript bundle tools offer some analysis option to figure out if some libs take too much space, and if tree-shaking is applied. With these few checks, you should be able to guarantee that your app performs well in terms of network usage and reactivity. We aim to apply the Pareto principle here: 20% of causes make for 80% of problems.

The other crucial thing to take into account is the connectivity between the test runner and the application you are testing, i.e., good network bandwidth and latency. It may be interesting to have your test runner in the same geographical region as the application under test. Ideally, you should have Playwright and the content you are testing on the same network.

Warning   If the application under test and Playwright are on the same network, performance and size optimizations will have less impact on test speed. But they still matter to your users.

Better, Playwright can start one or more servers locally via a command, and wait for the server to be ready before launching the tests. This is done via the `webServer` option

---

[3] Look for Speed Index, First Contentful Paint, unused JavaScript.

in the configuration file. Another alternative is to have a sidecar container, or a service, that runs the server for you next to Playwright Test. I personally prefer the webServer option as I can run it locally as well.

Authentication

There is one step that takes significant time and that you probably repeat for many of your tests: authentication. If you already have a dedicated test to verify your login page, there is no need to repeat it again and again. So, we will write setup code that will run first, then we will run our tests.

Instead of doing a sign-in step in every test that needs it, we can use a setup script that will run once. We can sign in by interacting with the page, as usual. Then we save the storage state of the browser in a file: cookies, local storage, and optionally indexedDB.

You should never commit this storage snapshot file as it holds sensitive information, and anyway the token will expire eventually (it should). So don't forget to add the .auth folder in your .gitignore!

Listing 5-9. auth.setup.ts

```
import { test as setup } from '@playwright/test';

const STORAGE_PATH = './.auth/user.json';

setup('signin', async ({ page, context }) => {
  await page.goto('/');

  // Login
  // ...

  // Ensure that we are signed in
  await expect(locator).isVisible();

  // Save the storage
  await context.storageState({ path: STORAGE_PATH });
});
```

We can then retrieve this storage snapshot file and apply it with use, either in the test file or in the Playwright configuration. We will do it once, thanks to project dependencies.

You can declare that a project depends on one or more projects. In our case, we will declare that we depend on a setup project so that it runs beforehand. If several projects depend on our setup, it will run only once.

Listing 5-10. playwright.config.ts with project dependency

```
export default defineConfig({
  // ...
  projects: [
    {
      name: 'setup',
      testMatch: /.*\.setup\.ts/,
      workers: 1,
    },
    {
      name: 'with auth',
      use: {
        // Use prepared auth state.
        storageState: './.auth/user.json',
      },
      dependencies: ['setup'],
    },
  ],
});
```

This pattern does not only apply to authentication, but really to any setup that is common to all your tests. Think populating a database with test data, starting up a Kubernetes environment, ...

Because the ordering of such setup script matters, we will do two things to guarantee execution order. First, we will disable parallelism altogether in the setup project by setting only one worker. Note that this setting is only for this project; others will benefit from parallelism as usual. Second, we will set the file order. For that, we name our setup files to benefit from the alphabetic ordering Playwright Test applies by default, e.g., 01-database.setup.ts, 02-auth.setup.ts, that is, if you want to split your setup into different files.

Leverage --only-changed Option

The fastest tests are the ones you don't run. We will select a subset of your test suite as an efficient way to reduce the test execution time.

The `--only-changed` option allows running test files that changed, or test which dependencies changed. It is based on git; so it actually means that it will check files that changed against a git ref. It has two usages.

Run tests that have been modified since the last commit.

```
npx playwright test --only-changed
```

Or tests that changed compared to a Git ref, i.e., a branch, a tag, a commit, HEAD.

```
# Changes with the remote main branch
npx playwright test --only-changed=origin/main
```

Because we are writing end-to-end tests, there is no hard link between the application tested and Playwright tests. It means Playwright can't guess that you broke the login feature and that tests should be re-run. `--only-changed` will only see your changed tests (and their deps). Not your code.

Tip To verify your pattern and rules without actually running the tests, you can simply use the `--list` option.

```
npx playwright test --list
```

The first use of this option is to simply run modified tests locally. When you are working on an end-to-end test, but maybe also its utilities functions, fixtures, POM, you can verify quickly that the modifications don't stop your tests from passing. Remember to give UI Mode or Playwright Test for VS Code a try, as they both offer a watch mode.

Better than that, you can run changed tests whenever you commit or push code. Git hooks are shell scripts that run on certain events: pre-commit, pre-push, on commit message… It's fairly easy to set up manually, but you may want to use a tool to manage your Git hooks. I suggest using `simple-git-hooks`. Thanks to this tool, you can, for example, run modified tests and find issues even before pushing it to the remote Git repo.

Other usages of `--only-changed` are in the Continuous Integration pipeline. First, you can run changed tests before running the whole test suite. In this way, it fails fast by verifying what has more probability to break (changed tests and dependencies). We'll see later that this technique can also help us to get more reliable tests by running them several times and ensure their reliability and reproducibility in this way.

The other CI option is more aggressive: just run changed tests on Pull Request, and run the whole test suite later. Being overnight or on a schedule, you will save money at the expense of a longer feedback loop. If something unexpectedly breaks, you will not know before the next day. I personally don't want a feedback loop that long, so I don't choose something as long as nightly tests.

Pushing the Envelope

Finally, I propose in this part tips and tricks that will probably make your test faster, with a risk of having less stable tests. For each one, I will tell you what the tradeoff is.

Fail Fast

The first tip is simply to fail fast. Because of the auto-waiting and the test timeout of 30 seconds by default, failing tests typically take longer time than passing ones. Sometimes it does not make sense to continue the execution of your whole test suite after a given number of failures. If dozens of tests fail, it probably means there is a configuration or operational issue: maybe the website under test is down, or a central API. Below a certain point, it just doesn't make sense to wait for the whole test suite to fail.

For that, you can set up a maximum number of failures like in Listing 5-11.

Listing 5-11. playwright.config.ts

```
export default defineConfig({
  maxFailures: 10,
});
```

✓ **no risk**

It needs some tuning to see what value works for you, but the tests will not change.

Don't Wait

I got this one from Stefan Judis, a fellow Playwright Ambassador. Stefan figured out that goto() is waiting for requests to finish.[4] This is not exactly what users are doing, as they can read the main content while other parts are still loading, and they will probably interact with the website or web app as soon as it is possible.

Let's take a look at method goto()

```
goto(url: string, options?: {
  referer?: string;
  timeout?: number;
  waitUntil?: "load"|"domcontentloaded"|"networkidle"|"commit";
}): Promise<null|Response>;
```

The timeout is set to 0 by default: no timeout. It might be tempting to adjust this setting to fail earlier if the loading takes too long. But in practice the action, expect, or ultimately test timeout will take care of that.

waitUntil is more interesting. It tells goto() what event it should wait until we continue.

- commit: We received the response from the server and the HTML parsing starts.
- domcontentloaded: HTML document is parsed and scripts are executed.
- load: The page is fully loaded. This is the default value.
- networkidle: There was no connection for at least 500ms. This is discouraged.

Playwright is rather conservative as it waits by default for load instead of an earlier state. This is usually not needed because you don't need everything to be loaded to interact with a page, and Playwright's auto-waiting mechanism is resilient enough to not rely on goto() waiting.

```
await page.goto('/', { waitUntil: 'commit' });
```

✓ **moderate risk**

---

[4] https://www.checklyhq.com/blog/why-page-goto-is-slowing-down-your-playwright-test

This technique might unveil hydration issues, which I'd argue is a good thing but takes effort to fix.

Block Content

Finally, it is possible to block specific resources, such as images or certain domains if they are not necessary for the tests. Keep in mind that your tests will no longer exactly reflect the end user's experience. So, be careful not to change the application too much at the risk of creating unreliable tests (usually false positives).

You can block a set of URLs or a domain with page.route()

```
await page.route('https://*.ads.com/**', (route) => route.abort());

// Start your tests AFTER you've set up route
await page.goto('/');
```

Or by type of resource.

```
await page.route('**/*', (route) => {
  return route.request().resourceType() === 'image'
    ? route.abort()
    : route.continue();
});
```

The resource type is a browser interpolation of the content type. Among the possible values, there are stylesheet, image, media, and font. We will see later on that page.route() has more usage for mocking and emulation.

Not loading images, media, or fonts may alter your tests. But in my opinion, there is one kind of content that should be able to be blocked without any issues: advertisements and privacy tracking. Some of your users already do it by using ad blockers. Ghostery is such tracker and ad blocker, and it can easily be added to Playwright.

```
npm install --save-dev @ghostery/adblocker-playwright
```

It only takes two lines to initialize the blocker as seen in Listing 5-12. After that, you are good to go!

Listing 5-12. ad-blocking.spec.ts

```
import { test, expect } from '@playwright/test';
import { PlaywrightBlocker } from '@ghostery/adblocker-playwright';

test.describe('blocking', () => {
  test('with ad blocker', async ({ page }) => {
    const blocker = await PlaywrightBlocker.fromPrebuiltAdsAndTracking();
    blocker.enableBlockingInPage(page);

    await page.goto('https://canyoublockit.com/testing/');
    await page.getByRole('link', { name: 'Finish' }).click();

    await expect(
      page.getByRole('heading', { name: 'results' }),
    ).toBeVisible();
  });
});
```

Ideally, advertisements should be light, non-intrusive, and respectful of privacy.

From a testing perspective, blocking ads will probably make you save some bandwidth and time. Better than that, it can make your tests simpler and more reliable: no need to have a Locator handler to close random popup, or specific code to wait for interstitial, … It is a good idea to run tests with an adblocker, as real users may, to ensure that the app behaves correctly.

⚠ **risky**

By blocking content, you WILL lose something. Either some stability or test realism. Please use with care.

Tests at Scale with Testing Services

We saw earlier that you can trade a longer feedback loop for less cost, by using a cheap Continuous Integration runner. It can be the other way around: hundreds of tests in under a minute, for a fee. No more end-to-end tests that only run at night!

CHAPTER 5   MAKE IT FAST

> *These go to eleven.*
>
> —Nigel Tufnel, *This Is Spinal Tap*

Recently, we've seen the emergence of test services that provide massive parallelization for Playwright test. I'm listing here what I think are the most promising ones: Microsoft Playwright Testing and Endform.

Microsoft Playwright Testing

The Playwright Testing service is a cloud-based solution that offers the possibility to run your tests on multiple remote browsers. Note that this solution is developed by a Microsoft Azure team that is independent from the Playwright team. It means that their offering is not mandatory, are separated, and Playwright Test will stay free and open source. The service does all of the heavy lifting, not your CI that will only run the test runner itself acting as an orchestrator. This allows to run your test suites much faster, with high parallelism.

Another benefit of using remote browsers is the consistency in visual regression testing. Because you can use the service both on a local machine and on CI, image comparison is more reliable as it is effectively always the same test environment.

You can use up to 50 workers via Microsoft Playwright Testing; but I found it difficult to find the ideal number of workers to use. As we've seen in the parallelism part of this chapter, more workers don't necessarily mean much faster test. I recommend starting with a relatively low number of workers (maybe 20?) and see how it goes.

Find more on their website: `https://azure.microsoft.com/products/playwright-testing`.

Endform

Endform is another testing service for Playwright Test. It's made by the people that already experimented with play-lambda: Playwright Test in AWS Lambda functions for massive parallelization.

At the time of writing, Endform is still in an early state, but it looks very promising. The technical approach is different from other testing services as it attempts to defer a maximum of things to remote execution instead of simply offering remote browsers.

I had a great experience with Endform. The performances were better than what I expected and are really impressive. I especially appreciated that you do not need to choose a number of workers or fine-tune anything. It just works. The pricing is per billable minute; each test suite run shows exactly how many minutes were used.

Go check it at `https://endform.dev`.

Summary

Remember that you may not need to optimize your tests now. Make them work, make them correct, and useful.

Then make your tests faster by

- Using **multiple workers locally**
- Adjusting parallelism options, and favoring **fully parallel** tests
- Distributing tests on several workers with **sharding**
- **Optimizing your test environment**

Now that we have fast and reliable tests in Continuous Integration, in the next few chapters, we will see how to customize Playwright to our needs, extending its behavior, use fixtures, then emulation.

CHAPTER 6

Extending Playwright Test

In this chapter, you'll learn how to customize Playwright to fit your needs. Not only configuration, but all the different customization points to create your own test reporter, assertions, and more… Such tooling and utils are often called test harness. Test harness is the code we write to put a piece of software under test. There are many kinds of test harnesses like stubs, fixtures, and custom utility code. Having tailor-made tooling and utils allows you to focus on your tests.

Custom expect

One thing you want to tune is assertions. Not only can it be personalized for better readability, but you can also create your own.

Custom expect Message

You can personalize an assertion error message. It will make your tests clearer by giving an exact explanation of what failed and more context when assertions are not obvious.

Listing 6-1. expect message

```
test("better assertions", () => {
  // Arrange
  test.step("log in", () => {});

  // Act
  // ...

  // Assert
  expect(2, "to be 3: Adel, Filip, Frank").toBe(3); // custom
                                                    expect message
});
```

In case the test has an error, the result gives the explanation of why the assertion failed.

Listing 6-1a. The error is much clearer

```
Running 1 test using 1 worker
  1) [chromium] › tests/assertions/better.spec.ts:3:1 › better assertions

    Error: to be 3: Adel, Filip, Frank

    expect(received).toBe(expected) // Object.is equality

    Expected: 3
    Received: 2
```

Extend expect

A great way to make your tests clearer and more concise is to make your own assertions. It may be handy if you have specific things to check over and over, or more simply something that is complex to check with the existing assertions.

Assertions are called **matchers**, this is the vocabulary that is common with Jest and other test frameworks. Playwright assertions system took inspiration from Jest's expect library. Playwright is largely compatible with this library, so some extensions originally meant for Jest works. Sure, nothing is guaranteed, so you should experiment for yourself to find what works or not.

Let's use some matchers from `jest-extended`! This library adds additional matchers for more convenience, mainly adding checks on JavaScript Primitives (Array, Boolean, Date, …).

Listing 6-2. jest-extended.spec.ts

```
import { toBeFinite, toBeValidDate } from 'jest-extended';
import { test, expect as baseExpect } from '@playwright/test';

const expect = baseExpect.extend({ toBeFinite, toBeValidDate });
```

```
test('valid date', async () => {
  expect(new Date()).toBeValidDate();
  expect(new Date('01/01/2018')).toBeValidDate();
  expect(new Date('01/90/2018')).not.toBeValidDate();
});

test('passes when value is a finite number', () => {
  expect(1).toBeFinite();
  expect(Infinity).not.toBeFinite();
  expect(NaN).not.toBeFinite();
});
```

In this example in Listing 6-2, we import and use two matchers (`toBeFinite`, `toBeValidDate`) to extend Playwright's expect. Once this is done, it is as if these new matchers were parts of the API. Now let's see how we can write our own matchers.

Make Your Own CSS Matcher

Let's say that you want to do something that has the reputation to not exist: testing CSS. More precisely, you want to test your layout and the relative positions of Elements. For example, this can be handy to verify that the menu is on the left of the main content on desktop, and has a different position on mobile.

I find it rather difficult to understand how to build a matcher, so let's get help from TypeScript.

- The function should return a `MatcherReturnType` or a `Promise<MatcherReturnType>` if async. You probably want to have an async function, as it will allow you to resolve Locators and either make an action or call methods to get data from them. That is why all the web-first assertions are asynchronous.

- The arguments of a matcher function are way more lax. There is a "receiver" and other arguments of type any. The receiver is the parameter of the `expect()` function, while the rest is whatever you want.

In our case, we want a matcher that takes a second Locator as a parameter. This assertion means that the receiver Locator is at the right of the reference one. We now know the signature of our function, in Listing 6-3. That's much easier.

Listing 6-3. toBeRightOf signature

```
async function toBeRightOf(
  locator: Locator,
  reference: Locator,
): Promise<MatcherReturnType>
```

The logic of our matcher in Listing 6-4 is as follows:

1. We get the bounding box of each Locator. Lines 7–8.

2. If any of the bounding boxes are missing, it's a fail. This should only happen when the Locator has an issue. Remember, Locators are resolved only when we need them. In this case, when we get the bounding boxes.

3. We do a little math on line 12 to check if the candidate Element is at the right of the other one.

4. Notice line 15 that we need to take not into account by effectively inverting the result.

Listing 6-4. layout-matchers.ts

```
export async function toBeRightOf(
  locator: Locator,
  reference: Locator,
): Promise<MatcherReturnType> {
  let pass: boolean;

  const candidateBox = await locator.boundingBox();
  const refBox = await reference.boundingBox();
  if (!candidateBox || !refBox) {
    pass = false;
  } else {
    pass = candidateBox.x >= refBox.x + refBox.width;
  }
```

```
  if (this.isNot) {
    pass = !pass;
  }
  const message = pass ? () => 'wouhou' : () => 'nope';
  return {
    message,
    pass,
  };
}
export async function toBeLeftOf(
  locator: Locator,
  reference: Locator,
): Promise<MatcherReturnType> {
// ...
```

Our layout matchers are ready, but what if we want to use them along Playwright's matchers and also jest-extended?

Compose Your Matchers Collection

It is rather easy to centralize all your custom matchers in one place. You just need to import matchers and extend the Playwright expect, before re-exporting the result as seen in Listing 6-4a.

Listing 6-4a. my-expect.ts

```
import { expect as baseExpect } from '@playwright/test';
import { toBeFinite, toBeValidDate } from 'jest-extended';
import * as layoutMatchers from './layout-matchers';

export const expect = baseExpect.extend({
  toBeFinite,
  toBeValidDate,
  ...layoutMatchers,
});
```

Then simply import your custom enriched expect instead of Playwright's one (Listing 6-5).

Listing 6-5. expect-collection.spec.ts

```
import { test } from '@playwright/test';
import { expect } from './my-expect';

test('valid date', async () => {
  expect(new Date()).toBeValidDate();
  expect(new Date('01/01/2018')).toBeValidDate();
  expect(new Date('01/90/2018')).not.toBeValidDate();
});

test('passes when value is a finite number', () => {
  expect(1).toBeFinite();
  expect(Infinity).not.toBeFinite();
  expect(NaN).not.toBeFinite();
});

test('layout', async ({ page }) => {
  await page.setContent(`
  <table>
    <tr><td id='7'>7</td><td id='8'>8</td><td id='9'>9</td></tr>
    <tr><td id='4'>4</td><td id='5'>Reference text</td><td id='6'>6</td></tr>
    <tr><td id='1'>1</td><td id='2'>2</td><td id='3'>3</td></tr>
  </table>`);

  await expect(page.getByText('6')).toBeRightOf(
    page.getByText('Reference text'),
  );
});
```

Reporters

Test reporters are vital because they give the most information about a test run. The difficulty is sometimes getting the right information, in the right format. Especially when your system needs to communicate with another software.

Test results are useful information, so they should be easily accessible via a static URL, in your Continuous Integration tool, or in a Pull Request web page. Reports provide a clear overview as well as valuable details, and they are often the first step to fixing failed tests.

Add Extra Information

Before adding new reporters, we can leverage the standard one and add more information to the test results.

Tags

We've seen earlier that tags can be used to filter tests to execute. Tags also convey information and ease the reading of reports. For example, you can filter results by tagging in the HTML reporter.

Keep in mind that tags must start with @. Also, you are not limited to one tag per test: the `tag` parameter accepts a tag or an array of tags.

Listing 6-6. Adding tags

```
import test from "@playwright/test";

test.describe("1", { tag: ["@TV", "@slow"] }, () => {
  test("one", () => {});
});
```

Annotate

Annotations allow adding one or more information to your reports with an arbitrary `type` and `description`. This is handy to display additional context for the test, or pass data along for a reporter to process.

CHAPTER 6   EXTENDING PLAYWRIGHT TEST

Listing 6-7. Single annotation

```
test(
  'annotation',
  {
    annotation: {
      type: 'issue',
      description: 'https://github.com/microsoft/playwright/issues/23180',
    },
  },
  async () => {
    // ...
  },
);
```

Playwright's HTML reporter displays annotations and changes URLs into links.

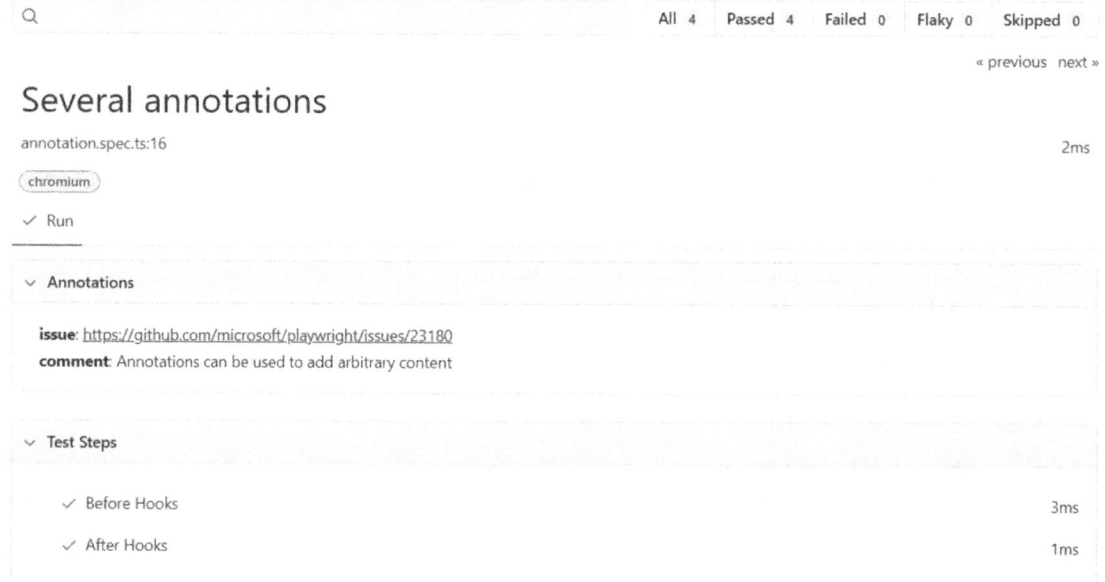

Figure 6-1. Several annotations in HTML report

To hide an annotation from display, `prefix` its type with an underscore. Notice how `_hidden` is defined in Listing 6-7a but not shown in Figure 6-1.

138

Listing 6-7a. Several annotations

```
test(
  'Several annotations',
  {
    annotation: [
      {
        type: 'issue',
        description:
          'https://github.com/microsoft/playwright/issues/23180',
      },
      {
        type: 'comment',
        description:
          ' Annotations can be used to add arbitrary content',
      },
      {
        type: '_hidden',
        description: 'https://en.wikipedia.org/wiki/The_Game_(mind_game)',
      },
    ],
  },
  async () => {
    // ...
  },
);
```

Attach

If you want to add data rather than just additional hints on a test, you can attach a file.

This can be either a file on the local system or it can be created in-memory (from a string or Buffer). In Listing 6-8, we will attach Axe scan results.

Axe allows performing automatic accessibility testing. It will help you catch accessibility issues early. For example, form elements without label, images without alternative text, poor color contrast that makes text hard to read... I suggest you adding Axe to your personal toolbox as it helps you to make better applications, and its integration with Playwright is trivial.

In Listing 6-8, we perform an Axe scan on lines 8–10. Note that it can be refactored to a custom fixture or a helper function. Then in line 12, we use testInfo.attach to simply add the Axe scan result as a JSON file.

Listing 6-8. Perform an Axe scan and attach its result

```
import { test } from '@playwright/test';
import AxeBuilder from '@axe-core/playwright';
import { AxeResults } from 'axe-core';

test('example with attachment', async ({ page }, testInfo) => {
  await page.goto('https://emma11y.github.io/tester-a11y/cas-pratique-5');

  const accessibilityScanResults: AxeResults = await new AxeBuilder({
    page,
  }).analyze();

  await testInfo.attach('accessibility-scan-results', {
    body: JSON.stringify(accessibilityScanResults, null, 2),
    contentType: 'application/json',
  });
});
```

Playwright Test attaches files in the same manner when adding a Trace file or image snapshots. The built-in HTML reporter will display attachments along with the test results.

HTML Report Title

Some reporter will take additional parameters when added with `playwright.config.ts`. In this case, it must be written as a **tuple**.

Listing 6-9. HTML reporter with a title

```
import { defineConfig } from '@playwright/test';

export default defineConfig({
  reporter: [['html', { title: 'Custom test run #1028' }]]
});
```

CHAPTER 6   EXTENDING PLAYWRIGHT TEST

If a title is defined, it will be displayed in the generated HTML report. Note that the text will be linkified.

> **Note**   A tuple is an Array of fixed structure and length. For example, [x, y, z].

Third-Party Reporters

All kinds of third-party reporters exist. There are reporters that will notify you on Slack, Teams, by email... If you are using a system holding your test results, there are reporters for Allure, ReportPortal, Xray, and more. There are also alternatives for human-readable reports that come as a replacement to the HTML reporter, like Monocart Reporter.

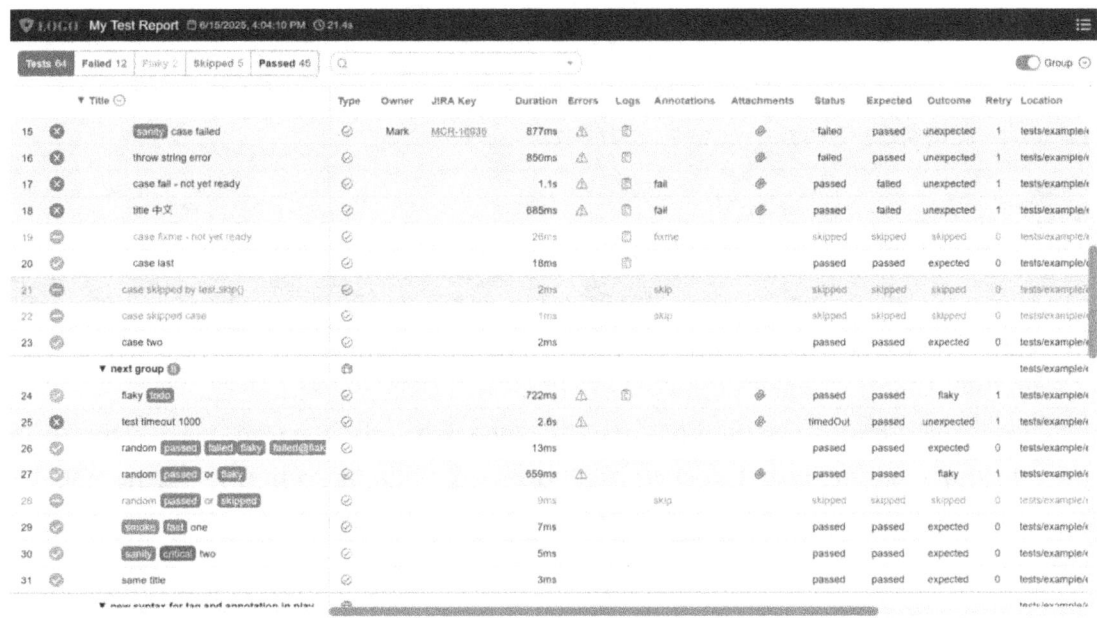

Figure 6-2. *Monocart Reporter*

Reporters often offer configuration points as **tuple**. You can see in Listing 6-10 the configuration of playwright-slack-report.

141

CHAPTER 6　EXTENDING PLAYWRIGHT TEST

Listing 6-10. playwright-slack-report configuration

```
import { defineConfig } from '@playwright/test';

export default defineConfig({
  reporter: [
    [
      "./node_modules/playwright-slack-report/dist/src/SlackReporter.js",
      {
        channels: ["pw-tests", "ci"], // provide one or more Slack channels
        sendResults: "always", // "always" , "on-failure", "off"
      },
    ],
  ],
});
```

Find more third-party reporters on Awesome Playwright: https://mxschmitt.github.io/awesome-playwright/#reporters.

Write Your Own

Writing your own reporter is not as difficult as it seems. It may be handy to report specific information to humans, or test results to a specific tool. In this part, we will write an Axe reporter that takes the attachments from earlier on and displays them as HTML.

For that, we simply have to implement the `Reporter` interface from Playwright. The test runner can then call our custom reporter on different events during the tests execution. All methods are optional, so it is up to us to choose which methods are useful for our reporter.

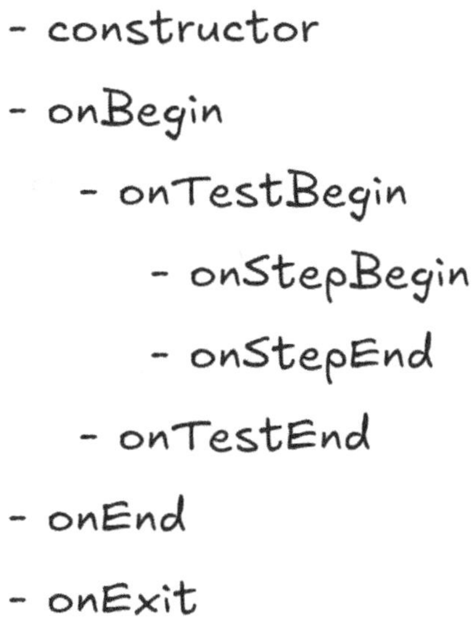

CHAPTER 6 EXTENDING PLAYWRIGHT TEST

- constructor
- onBegin
    - onTestBegin
        - onStepBegin
        - onStepEnd
    - onTestEnd
- onEnd
- onExit

Figure 6-3. *Tests lifecycle*

The calls lifecycle is as follows:

- **onBegin/onEnd** when the main test suite starts and ends
- **onTestBegin/onTestEnd** on each test
- **onStepBegin/onStepEnd** on each step, if any
- **onExit** before the test runner exits

Our Axe reporter will perform the following actions:

- Clean the report folder **onBegin**.
- Look for Axe scan result `attachment` **onTestEnd**, then create an HTML report thanks to the `axe-html-reporter` npm module.
- Display a message **onEnd**.

Listing 6-11. Our very own reporter

```
class MyReporter implements Reporter {
  path: string;

  constructor(options: { path?: string } = {}) {
    this.path = options.path ?? DEFAULT_PATH;
```

```
    console.log(`my-awesome-reporter path set to ${this.path}`);
  }

  onBegin(config: FullConfig, suite: Suite) {
    console.log(`Starting the run with ${suite.allTests().length} tests`);
    rm(this.path, { recursive: true }, () => {});
  }

  onTestEnd(test: TestCase, result: TestResult) {
    const attachment = result.attachments.find(
      (a) => a.name === 'accessibility-scan-results',
    );
    if (!attachment?.body) {
      return;
    }
    const scanResults: AxeResults = JSON.parse(attachment.body.toString());
    if (scanResults.violations.length === 0) {
      console.log(`${test.title} accessibility passed`);
      return;
    }

    console.log(`${test.title} accessibility failed`);
    createHtmlReport({
      results: scanResults,
      options: {
        reportFileName: `${test.id}.html`,
        outputDir: this.path,
      },
    });
  }

  async onEnd(result: FullResult) {
    console.log('To view the reports, run:');
    console.log(
      chalk.cyan(`
  npx serve ${this.path}
`),
```

        );
      }
    }
}
export default MyReporter;
```

Notice the constructor on line 4 of Listing 6-11. It takes a path option that can be set in `playwright.config.ts`.

```
export default defineConfig({
  reporter: [['./myreporter/my-awesome-reporter.ts', { path: 'reports' }]],
});
```

Test Data

Sometimes, we need to perform tests with various conditions, like different user or data. It means that we can have different test cases with the same testing logic. Only the input data changes. Let's see the various options we have to perform that easily.

Faker for Inclusive, Realistic Data

This library will help you create realistic but fake data for your tests such as name, postal address, email… In different languages. For that, you will be using different functions that will randomly generate the data for you. These functions are grouped by categories: person, airline, animal, phone number. This is perfect to fill a form with something else than "Jane Doe".

Using Faker with Playwright is straightforward; you just have to generate your data and write your tests as usual. Consider Listing 6-12 with different usages. Notice here that we chose to generate test data with the `fr` locale; this can be adjusted to your needs, or you may want a random locale.

Listing 6-12. Faker example with name, date, address, …

```
import { faker } from '@faker-js/faker/locale/fr';
import { expect, test } from '@playwright/test';

test('should create an account', async ({ page }) => {
  const dateBirth = faker.date.birthdate().toISOString().split('T')[0];
```
```

```
  await page.goto('https://practicesoftwaretesting.com/auth/register');

  await page.getByLabel('First name').fill(faker.person.firstName());
  await page.getByLabel('Last name').fill(faker.person.lastName());
  await page.getByLabel('Date of Birth').fill(dateBirth);
  await page.getByLabel('Street').fill(faker.location.streetAddress());
  await page.getByLabel('Postal Code').fill(faker.location.zipCode());
  await page.getByLabel('City').fill(faker.location.city());
  await page.getByLabel('Phone').fill(faker.phone.number());
  await page.getByLabel('Email').fill(faker.internet.email());
});
```

Faker will give you more realistic tests and may uncover problems that you would not detect otherwise. Here are some examples prone to bugs:

- Most family names are made of one character in China, like "Li" (李).

- Even when using Roman letters, one- or two-letter names are common. It means it's probably a bad idea to check for a minimal length.

- Many Indo-European languages have diacritics that may mess up with your encoding or rendering, like Jean-François.

- Here is a valid email address: lm1sds67@yahoo.co.jp. Does your home-made Regex take into account these kinds of domain names?

- German is very wordy, contrary to Chinese that is very compact (most words are two characters). This may break your styling.

i18n is hard because diversity is hard. Even if your app is meant for one specific demographic in one country, the reality is that people come from many different horizons. It means you sometimes have to think a little bit more than yourself and immediate surroundings, as they are probably not representative of the diversity of the real world. The least we could do is to not harm or exclude people with the software that we are writing.

It can be a problem that Faker creates new data on every call. You have three techniques for that (read along Listing 6-13).

1. If it doesn't cause any issue, leave it as is.

CHAPTER 6　EXTENDING PLAYWRIGHT TEST

2. Reuse the same value for the expected result if needed.

3. Set the seed. Pseudo-random generators generally use a seed value. If you set the same seed value, you'll get the same data. This is a bit like rolling a die and using its value every time.

Listing 6-13. Faker.js reproducible tests

```
test.describe('reproducible tests', () => {
  // 3. Re-seed the faker instance to guarantee test independance.
  test.afterEach(() => {
    faker.seed();
  });

  test('Reuse value for assertion', async ({ page }) => {
    const firstName = faker.person.firstName();
    const welcomeLocator = page.locator('.something');

    await page.goto('/');
    await page.getByLabel('First name').fill(firstName);

    // ...

    // 2. Reuse the generated value
    await expect(welcomeLocator).toContainText(firstName);
  });

  test('Seed', async ({ page }) => {
    // 3. Seed our faker instance with some static number.
    faker.seed(123);
    await page.goto('https://practicesoftwaretesting.com/auth/register');

    const dateBirth = faker.date.birthdate().toISOString().split('T')[0];

    await page.getByLabel('First name').fill(faker.person.firstName());
    await page.getByLabel('Last name').fill(faker.person.lastName());
    await page.getByLabel('Date of Birth').fill(dateBirth);
    await page.getByLabel('Street').fill(faker.location.streetAddress());
    await page.getByLabel('Postal Code').fill(faker.location.zipCode());
```

```
    await page.getByLabel('City').fill(faker.location.city());
    await page.getByLabel('Phone').fill(faker.phone.number());
    await page.getByLabel('Email').fill(faker.internet.email());
  });
});
```

Define Test Cases in JSON or CSV

Because Playwright Test is running in Node.js, you have the flexibility to leverage this and extend your tests with regular Node.js code. It means that you can feed your tests with all kinds of data sources and setups: read from a file, set up a database, call a server…

An easy and elegant solution is to set test data into a JSON file, as you will be able to import it directly, as seen in Listing 6-14.

Listing 6-14. Import test data from JSON

```
import { expect, test } from '@playwright/test';
import testData from './test-data.json' with { type: 'json' };

test('JSON', async ({}) => {
  expect(testData.username).toBe('test_user');
  expect(testData.role).toBe('admin');
});
```

In this second example (Listing 6-15), we read a CSV file thanks to the `csv-parse` library.

Listing 6-15. Import test data from CSV

```
import { expect, test } from '@playwright/test';
import { parse } from 'csv-parse/sync';
import { readFileSync } from 'fs';
import path from 'path';

test.describe('CSV', () => {
  const records = parse(readFileSync('./tests/input.csv'), {
    columns: true,
    delimiter: ';',
```

```
    cast: true,
  });

  const record = records[0];
  test(`foo`, () => {
    expect(record.some_value + record.another_value).toEqual(record.total);
  });
});
```

Parametrize Tests

Getting test data from a dedicated source is very flexible. You can generate data from a library like Faker or your own test data factory, you can import data or simply start by extracting constants.

We can go further: parametrize data, expected value, and test name. And do it for a list of tests.

We can enrich the example of Listing 6-15 and run different tests for the data described in `input.csv`. By calling the `test` method on each line of the CSV file, we effectively create different test cases.

Listing 6-16. Import test data from CSV

```
import { expect, test } from '@playwright/test';
import { parse } from 'csv-parse/sync';
import { readFileSync } from 'fs';
import path from 'path';

test.describe('CSV', () => {
  const records = parse(readFileSync('./tests/input.csv'), {
    columns: true,
    delimiter: ';',
    cast: true,
  });

  for (const record of records) {
    test(`foo: ${record.test_case}`, () => {
      expect(record.some_value + record.another_value).toEqual(
        record.total,
```

CHAPTER 6   EXTENDING PLAYWRIGHT TEST

```
      );
    });
  }
});
```

This is a great pattern because we can reuse the same code to test several different cases. Another usage could be testing a page with different devices, but it's more efficient to use projects for that.

Parametrize Projects with Test Options

Remember, we've said previously that projects are groups of tests with the same configuration. It means a group of tests can share the same testing data. Let's see how we can achieve that.

First, let's modify the test method to add our test data. Notice that we define the TestOptions type in line 3 of Listing 6-17. This helps us to be type-safe.

Listing 6-17. my-test.ts

```
import { test as base } from '@playwright/test';

export type TestOptions = {
  person: string;
};

export const test = base.extend<TestOptions>({
  person: 'John',
});
```

We successfully injected person by extending test. In our spec file, we just need to import our extended test instead of the Playwright base one.

Listing 6-17a. Using the modified test method

```
import { expect } from '@playwright/test';
import { test } from './my-test';

test('default value', async ({ person }) => {
  expect('John').toBe(person);
});
```

CHAPTER 6 EXTENDING PLAYWRIGHT TEST

Great, but it is hard-coded in our overridden test. By declaring our variable as an option, we can make it configurable in the Playwright configuration file (see Listing 6-18). We can then set the value in a project!

Listing 6-18. my-test.ts

```
import { test as base } from '@playwright/test';
export type TestOptions = {
  person: string;
};
export const test = base.extend<TestOptions>({
  person: ['John', { option: true }],
});
```

Listing 6-18a. playwright.config.ts project sets a person option

```
use: { ...devices['Desktop Chrome'], person: 'Alice' },
```

The usage in the spec file doesn't change. Notice that the value is now the one set up by the project, and not the default one defined in our modified test.

Listing 6-19. Test

```
import { expect } from '@playwright/test';
import { test } from './my-test';
test('default value', async ({ person }) => {
  expect('Alice').toBe(person);
});
```

We performed a Dependency Injection by extending test; that's actually one of the use cases of test fixtures. We will see in the next chapter that Playwright Test's fixtures are much more than that.

Summary

In this part, we've seen

- How to write our **own expect matchers**
- How to extend expect and get a **collection of matchers**
- **Third-party reporters** and test **attachments** to get a better grasp on our results
- **Parametrize tests** are an easy way to keep the code simple and have several test cases

Fixtures are the preferred way to extend tests and set the testing environment easily. They are a key part of Playwright; that's why, we will see fixtures in detail in the following chapter.

CHAPTER 7

Fixtures Deep Dive

In manufacturing, test fixtures are physical devices that create a controlled environment for testing. They allow standard conditions for repeatable and reliable tests. These pieces of equipment can make a test harness to contain the component under test, set up specific conditions that are always the same, add measurements...

Figure 7-1. *Fixture for testing textiles during a strength test*

In software, fixtures are usually pieces of code that set up state and data before each test, with optional cleanup after each. The traditional approach is to use test hooks like `beforeAll`, `afterAll`, `beforeEach`, and `afterEach`. We will see in this chapter that there are more than testing hooks.

We will use a **practical** example where Playwright Test fixtures improve test readability, make setup and teardown easier, and group your tests by their meaning instead of their technical setup. You are already using fixtures daily: page, context, or baseURL are fixtures. This chapter also details the popular Page Object Model design pattern, and how to integrate it as fixtures with Playwright.

Improve Your Tests with Fixtures

It is important to refactor existing code regularly to make it clearer and more maintainable. Every so often some code looks terrible, but remember that maybe it was written by someone else, or maybe it was yourself from the past. Anyway, they did the best they could, given their knowledge and resources at that time. Let's take a few existing tests and improve them, step by step.

> **Note** Go check the git repository that accompanies this book to explore the full example.
>
> https://github.com/Apress/Practical-Playwright-Test

The existing tests in our example are rather simple; they verify sign in to an application with different roles. They do not use custom fixtures, but they do use the built-in page fixture. We have two files that require your attention: home.spec.ts and settings.spec.ts.

Listing 7-1. home.spec.ts

```
import { expect, test } from '@playwright/test';
test.describe('normal user', () => {
  test.beforeEach(async ({ page }) => {
    await page.goto('/signin');
    await page.getByRole('textbox', { name: 'Username:' }).fill('user');
    await page.getByRole('textbox', { name: 'Password:' }).fill('user123');
    await page.getByRole('button', { name: 'Sign In' }).click();
    await expect(
      page.getByRole('heading', { name: 'Welcome to the App!' }),
```

```
      ).toBeVisible();
    });
    test.afterEach(async ({ page }) => {
      await page.getByRole('button', { name: 'Logout' }).click();
    });

    test('home should say hello', async ({ page }) => {
      await page.goto('/');
      await expect(page.getByRole('heading', { level: 2 })).toHaveText(
        'Hi user! 👋',
      );
    });
    // ...
});

test.describe('admin user', () => {
    test.beforeEach(async ({ page }) => {
      await page.goto('/signin');
      await page.getByRole('textbox', { name: 'Username:' }).fill('admin');
      await page
        .getByRole('textbox', { name: 'Password:' })
        .fill('admin123');
      await page.getByRole('button', { name: 'Sign In' }).click();
      await expect(
        page.getByRole('heading', { name: 'Welcome to the App!' }),
      ).toBeVisible();
    });
    test.afterEach(async ({ page }) => {
      await page.getByRole('button', { name: 'Logout' }).click();
    });

    test('home should say hello admin', async ({ page }) => {
      await page.goto('/');
      await expect(page.getByRole('heading', { level: 2 })).toHaveText(
        'Hello admin.',
```

```
      );
      await expect(
        page.getByRole('link', { name: 'Settings' }),
      ).toBeVisible();
    });

    test('settings page should display when admin', async ({ page }) => {
      await page.goto('/settings');
      await expect(page.getByRole('heading', { level: 1 })).toContainText(
        'Settings',
      );
    });
  });
});
```

Listing 7-2. settings.spec.ts

```
import { test, expect } from '@playwright/test';

test.describe('settings', () => {
  test.beforeEach(async ({ page }) => {
    await page.goto('/signin');
    await page.getByRole('textbox', { name: 'Username:' }).fill('admin');
    await page
      .getByRole('textbox', { name: 'Password:' })
      .fill('admin123');
    await page.getByRole('button', { name: 'Sign In' }).click();
    await expect(
      page.getByRole('heading', { name: 'Welcome to the App!' }),
    ).toBeVisible();
  });
  test.afterEach(async ({ page }) => {
    await page.getByRole('button', { name: 'Logout' }).click();
  });

  test('should display options', async ({ page }) => {
    await page.goto('/settings');
    await expect(
```

          page.getByRole('heading', { name: 'Application Settings' }),
).toBeVisible();
        await expect(
          page.getByRole('heading', { name: 'User Management' }),
).toBeVisible();
        await expect(
          page.getByRole('heading', { name: 'System Configuration' }),
).toBeVisible();
      });
    });

A few things are off:

- The tests are quite verbose, and the same admin login logic is repeated in the home and settings tests.

- Home tests are scattered in two describe blocks. It does not work well here, as our intent is to check the home in different cases.

- A test case for settings is in the home test file!?

Not great, not terrible. While some code repetition in tests is not a big deal, this is probably too much and will become a problem when we want to add new tests. Moreover, the tests are organized by the users logged in; I would personally prefer to organize them differently. This refactoring will lay out better bases for future tests. Time to level up and leverage fixtures to make the tests clearer.

Your First Fixture

Fixtures are alternatives to traditional testing hooks like `beforeEach()`, `afterEach()`. Let's write a simple fixture and see what the differences are.

To create our first fixture, we need to extend the `test` Object.

Listing 7-3. Override test to create myFixture

```
import { test as base } from '@playwright/test';
import { faker } from '@faker-js/faker/locale/fr';

export const test = base.extend<{ myFixture: string }>({
  myFixture: async ({}, use) => {
```

```
    console.log('Setup');
    await use(faker.person.firstName());
    console.log('Teardown');
  },
});
```

In Listing 7-3

- Line 4: We use the `test.extend()` function.
- Line 4: We define the fixture `myFixture`.
- Line 6: `use()` is when the test will actually run, and this is where we inject the first name.

Now, we need to import the overridden `test` Object in our tests and add our new fixture in the same manner as we do for built-in fixtures like page. Fixtures are on-demand; they will be active only when you add them to your test parameters.

Listing 7-4. Custom fixture usage

```
import { test } from './my-test';

test('example test', async ({ myFixture }) => {
  console.log(`Hello I'm ${myFixture}!`);
});
```

The test in Listing 7-4 retrieves what you passed in `use()` to display it.

Let's see the output when we run the test:

```
Setup
Hello I'm Suzon!
Teardown
```

Notice how the code before and after `use()` are setup and teardown, just like `beforeEach()` and `afterEach()`.

CHAPTER 7   FIXTURES DEEP DIVE

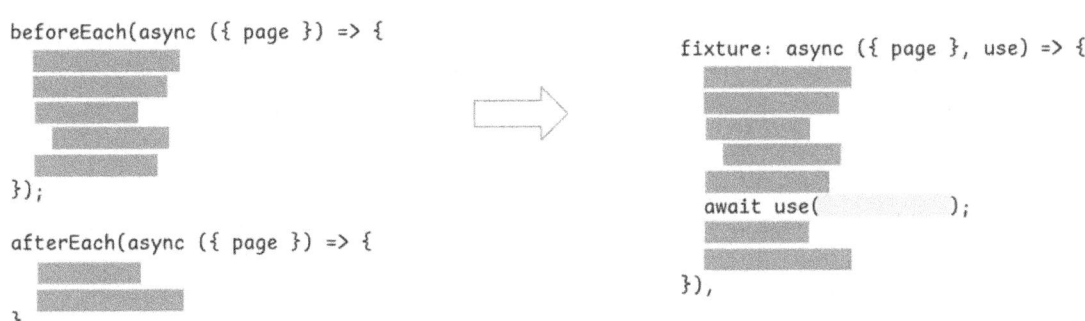

Figure 7-2.   From beforeEach/afterEach hook to fixture

Fixtures do the same preparation job as beforeEach and afterEach, except that they are not bound to a describe block! We can now improve our tests with this new knowledge.

Decoupling Setup and Test

OK, back to our tests. We could extract helper functions for login and logout, but even if it is an improvement, it is far from ideal. We will instead create fixtures to set up the test context for us.

Let's move the setup and teardown (i.e., beforeEach(), afterEach()) for user login into a fixture.

Listing 7-5.   my-test.ts

```
import { test as base, expect, Page } from '@playwright/test';
type MyFixtures = {
  loggedInPage: Page;
  loggedInAdminPage: Page;
};
export const test = base.extend<MyFixtures>({
  loggedInPage: async ({ page }, use) => {
    await page.goto('/signin');
    await page.getByRole('textbox', { name: 'Username:' }).fill('user');
    await page.getByRole('textbox', { name: 'Password:' }).fill('user123');
```

159

```
    await page.getByRole('button', { name: 'Sign In' }).click();
    await expect(
      page.getByRole('heading', { name: 'Welcome to the App!' }),
    ).toBeVisible();
    await use(page);
    await page.getByRole('button', { name: 'Logout' }).click();
  },
  loggedInAdminPage: async ({ page }, use) => {
    // ...
  },
});
```

```
export { expect } from '@playwright/test';
```

Notice in Listing 7-5 that we define the `MyFixtures` type to help TypeScript figure out what is added in the tests with our fixtures. Put in other words, it's the type of what is in `use()`.

We do the same with a `loggedInAdminPage` fixture. Then we can make a first rewrite of our home test by simply removing the `beforeEach()` and `afterEach()` for their fixture counterpart.

Listing 7-6. home.spec.ts, first rewrite

```
import { expect, test } from './my-test';

test.describe('normal user', () => {
  test('home should say hello', async ({ loggedInPage: page }) => {
    await page.goto('/');
    await expect(page.getByRole('heading', { level: 2 })).toHaveText(
      'Hi user! 👋',
    );
  });
  // ...
});

test.describe('admin user', () => {
  test('home should say hello admin', async ({
```

```
    loggedInAdminPage: page,
  }) => {
    await page.goto('/');
    await expect(page.getByRole('heading', { level: 2 })).toHaveText(
      'Hello admin.',
    );
    await expect(
      page.getByRole('link', { name: 'Settings' }),
    ).toBeVisible();
  });

  test('settings page should display when admin', async ({
    loggedInAdminPage: page,
  }) => {
    await page.goto('/settings');
    await expect(page.getByRole('heading', { level: 1 })).toContainText(
      'Settings',
    );
  });
});
```

The test is shorter while keeping its meaning. But we can go further and get rid of the "normal user" and "admin user" describe blocks. Because the setup and teardown are not linked to these blocks, we can now reorganize them as we wish. We'll also move back the "settings page should display" test. Listing 7-7 shows the final result of our refactoring.

Listing 7-7. home.spec.ts, refactored

```
import { expect, test } from './my-test';

test.describe('home', () => {
  test('should say hello', async ({ loggedInPage: page }) => {
    await page.goto('/');
    await expect(page.getByRole('heading', { level: 2 })).toHaveText(
      'Hi user! 👋',
```

```
    );
  });
  // ...

  test('should say hello when admin', async ({
    loggedInAdminPage: page,
  }) => {
    await page.goto('/');
    await expect(page.getByRole('heading', { level: 2 })).toHaveText(
      'Hello admin.',
    );
    await expect(
      page.getByRole('link', { name: 'Settings' }),
    ).toBeVisible();
  });
});
```

Listing 7-8. settings.spec.ts, refactored

```
import { expect, test } from './my-test';

test.describe('settings', () => {
  test('settings page should display when admin', async ({
    loggedInAdminPage: page,
  }) => {
    await page.goto('/settings');
    await expect(page.getByRole('heading', { level: 1 })).toContainText(
      'Settings',
    );
  });

  test('should display options', async ({ loggedInAdminPage: page }) => {
    await page.goto('/settings');
    await expect(
      page.getByRole('heading', { name: 'Application Settings' }),
    ).toBeVisible();
```

```
    await expect(
      page.getByRole('heading', { name: 'User Management' }),
    ).toBeVisible();
    await expect(
      page.getByRole('heading', { name: 'System Configuration' }),
    ).toBeVisible();
  });
});
```

If you prefer a user/admin dichotomy, this is fine too. The key point is that now you can organize your tests by their meaning, what makes sense to you, and not their common technical setup.

Composition

There is yet another characteristic of fixtures that is useful to improve tests. Maybe you noticed, our `loggedInPage` and `loggedInAdminPage` are using fixtures too! Moreover, a fixture can depend on another custom fixture.

Listing 7-9. Fixtures dependencies

```
import { test as base } from '@playwright/test';

type MyFixtures = {
  one: string;
  two: string;
};

export const test = base.extend<MyFixtures>({
  one: async ({}, use) => {
    await use('Hello');
  },
  two: async ({ one }, use) => {
    await use(`${one} world`);
  },
});
```

In Listing 7-9, the fixture two transparently relies on fixture one. It's the same thing for our previous fixture `loggedInPage` that uses page, a built-in fixture that itself is based on `context`. Even better, the test does not need to know about the fixture "one".

Listing 7-10. Fixtures dependencies usage

```
import { test as base } from '@playwright/test';

test('dependency', async ({ two }) => {
  console.log(two); // "Hello world"
});
```

Wrap-Up

Test fixtures are an alternative to test hooks, with some unique characteristics. We've seen the following key benefits:

- Encapsulation
- Decoupling
- On-demand
- Composition

Encapsulation allows having setup and teardown in the same function. This makes the reuse of fixtures much easier.

Fixtures and tests are decoupled. This means that you are not bound to `describe` block anymore to set up tests, and can organize tests logically rather than by common setup.

Because they are on-demand, fixtures will not clutter tests unnecessarily. There are no risks of slowing down tests because of the number of reusable fixtures you defined.

Fixtures can transparently rely on other fixtures by composition. No more hassle with complex before/after code that must be set in the right order.

Page Object Model

The Page Object Model is a design pattern that was popularized by Selenium WebDriver. It consists of using objects that represent areas of the web application under testing, be it a page or even something smaller. To be precise, the Page Object represents the services offered by a page as methods.

POM Class

With Playwright, POMs are usually written as a TypeScript class that takes page as a constructor parameter. Listing 7-11 may appear lengthy but is very simple.

Listing 7-11. POM class

```typescript
import { expect, type Page } from '@playwright/test';
export class CheckoutPage {
  readonly page: Page;

  constructor(page: Page) {
    this.page = page;
  }

  async fill() {
    await this.page
      .getByPlaceholder('email@example.com')
      .fill('user@example.com');
    await this.page.getByPlaceholder('Full name').fill('John Doe');
    await this.page
      .getByRole('button', { name: 'Enter address manually' })
      .click();
    await this.page.getByPlaceholder('Address line 1').fill('adress');
    await this.page.getByPlaceholder('Postal code').fill('10000');
    await this.page.getByPlaceholder('City').fill('City');
    await this.page
      .getByPlaceholder('1234 1234 1234')
      .fill('4242 4242 4242 4242');
    await this.page.getByPlaceholder('MM / YY').fill('01 / 28');
    await this.page.getByPlaceholder('CVC').fill('123');
  }

  async submit() {
    await this.page.getByTestId('hosted-payment-submit-button').click();
    await expect(
```

```
      this.page.getByTestId('submit-button-success'),
    ).toBeVisible();
  }
}
```

Our `CheckoutPage` class in Listing 7-11 exposes two methods: `fill` and `submit`. They represent services that the page offers, namely, filling out a valid payment form and submitting it. When using both methods, you've performed a payment. We can also add Locators as members of the class, just for convenience.

The advantages of the Page Object Model (POM) are as follows:

- Reduction of duplicated code…

- …which means there is only one place to fix if the tested application changes.

- Readability. Selenium selectors are often difficult to read (think XPath or CSS selectors) and may depend upon the implementation details. An extra abstraction is welcome in this case; this may be one strong point of using POM with Selenium WebDriver. I will argue that it's less the case with Playwright.

In its original form, the pattern supposed that a Page Object should return a Page Object. Being originally used in Java several years ago, it also encouraged class inheritance. With the years passing by, and our practices changing, it seems these recommendations are not used anymore.

Now that we defined the class, we can instantiate it and use the methods of our Page Object to interact with our application.

Listing 7-12. Page Object usage

```
import { test, expect } from '@playwright/test';
import { CheckoutPage } from './checkout-page';

test('checkout', async ({ page }) => {
  await page.goto('/checkout');

  const checkoutPage = new CheckoutPage(page);
  await checkoutPage.fill();
```

```
  await checkoutPage.submit();
  // ...
});
```

POM with Fixture

Just like we used fixtures to initialize and add test data, we can conveniently instantiate our Page Object and pass it to the test. This allows us to delegate the creation of the Page Object to the fixture, making the test code more concise.

Note in Listing 7-13 the addition of typing to ease the usage of fixtures. We add an instance of CheckoutPage, so that's the type of the fixture.

Listing 7-13. Fixture allows us to instantiate the POM class

```
import { test as base, expect } from '@playwright/test';
import { CheckoutPage } from './checkout-page';

// Declare the types of your fixtures.
type MyFixtures = {
  checkoutPage: CheckoutPage;
};

export const test = base.extend<MyFixtures>({
  checkoutPage: async ({ page }, use) => {
    const checkoutPage = new CheckoutPage(page);
    await use(checkoutPage);
    // Clean up if any
  },
});
export { expect } from '@playwright/test';
```

The result is a simple-to-use fixture. We don't even need to care how checkoutPage was created, and TypeScript will help your IDE auto-complete to discover the POM methods.

Listing 7-14. Fixture usage

```
import { test, expect } from './fixtures';

test('checkout', async ({ page, checkoutPage }) => {
```

```
    await page.goto('/checkout');

    await checkoutPage.fill();
    await checkoutPage.submit();
    // ...
    await expect(page.getByRole('heading')).toContainText('Thank you!');
});
```

Using fixtures has several advantages. The POM is instantiated on-demand when you use the checkoutPage. You can perform setup and teardown in the fixture as needed, giving you great control over the lifecycle of the POM Object. Lastly, you still can use page: in our example, the checkout happens on the very same page. This is a good example of fixture composition.

More Fixtures Usages

This part lists some more advanced scenarios that we haven't mentioned yet. In addition to this chapter, I advise you to consult the official documentation. It lists even more details like overriding built-in fixtures, worker fixtures, timeouts, and so on.

Injecting Test Data

It's easy to use a fixture to add testing data conveniently, on-demand.

Listing 7-15. userData fixture

```
import { test as base } from '@playwright/test';

type MyFixtures = {
  userData: { firstName: string; lastName: string };
};

export const test = base.extend<MyFixtures>({
  userData: async ({}, use) => {
    const person = {
      firstName: 'Jane',
      lastName: 'Doe',
```

CHAPTER 7   FIXTURES DEEP DIVE

```
    };
    await use(person);
  },
});
```

Our custom fixture is accessible the same way as usual. Notice in Listing 7-15 that we define the MyFixtures type to help TypeScript figure out what is added in the tests with our fixtures. Put in other words, it's the type of what is in use().

Listing 7-16. userData fixture

```
test('get started link', async ({ page, userData }) => {
  // ...
  await locator.fill(userData.firstName);
});
```

That's already usable and interesting, but let's go one step further and generate our test data with Faker! We saw in the previous chapter that Faker can help us to generate realistic data, such as a person's name or address. The test remains unchanged.

Listing 7-17. Populate userData fixture

```
import { faker } from '@faker-js/faker/locale/de';
import { test as base } from '@playwright/test';

type MyFixtures = {
  userData: { firstName: string; lastName: string };
};

export const test = base.extend<MyFixtures>({
  userData: async ({}, use) => {
    const person = {
      firstName: faker.person.firstName(),
      lastName: faker.person.lastName(),
    };

    await use(person);
  },
});
```

Remember the Arrange Act Assert pattern? Here is a refresher:

- **Arrange** prepares the environment and data for the test case.
- **Act** performs an action that will create a change.
- **Assert** checks that the state of the web app is as expected.

Creating the test data like we did in our userData is part of the Arrange step. By having the generation of test data in a fixture, you can focus on your test itself and not worry about setup code too much.

Automatic Fixtures

We can make a variant of a fixture that will be added to every test without explicitly adding it. For that, we just need to add the auto option. It means the fixture will be automatically added when using this test Object.

Listing 7-18. forEachTest automatic fixture

```
import { test as base, expect } from '@playwright/test';

export const test = base.extend<{ forEachTest: void }>({
  forEachTest: [
    async ({}, use) => {
      console.log('setup');
      await use();
      console.log('teardown');
    },
    { auto: true },
  ], // automatically starts for every test.
});
```

Note the funky tuple syntax. In the same way as reporters with options, we now set the fixture to an Array made of the function and an option Object.

As seen in Listing 7-19, the usage is simple: you have nothing to do as long as you are importing and using the extended test Object. Unlike other fixtures that are set up on demand, our new forEachTest is an automatic fixture.

Listing 7-19. Automatic fixture usage

```
import { test, expect } from './myTest';
test('basic', async ({}) => {
  console.log('test');
});
```

Automatic fixtures can be useful for use cases like test annotations, logging, ... Consider automatic fixtures like a beforeEach/afterEach executed for every single test.

For example, we can re-create the screenshot-on-fail feature. The automatic fixture in Listing 7-20 will check the test result after its run, i.e., after use(). Then it will make a screenshot if the test fails.

Listing 7-20. Screenshot on failure auto fixture

```
export const test = base.extend<{ forEachTest: void }>({
  forEachTest: [
    async ({ page }, use, testInfo) => {
      await use();

      if (testInfo.status !== testInfo.expectedStatus) {
        const screenshot = await page.screenshot();
        await testInfo.attach('screenshot', {
          body: screenshot,
          contentType: 'image/png',
        });
      }
    },
    { auto: true },
  ],
});
```

Test Options

In the previous chapter, we used options to parametrize tests in projects. In this way, we can define a value in a project and use it in tests. Options are a kind of fixture, so they can be used in fixtures.

CHAPTER 7　FIXTURES DEEP DIVE

Let's improve our screenshot on failure fixture. It's an automatic fixture, but it doesn't mean we want it to be active all the time. We will add the possibility to configure when we want to generate screenshots.

We will need two things:

- Define `screenshotOnFail`, a boolean option. In the same way as automatic fixture, we use a tuple to pass the default value, and the fixture options.

- Use `screenshotOnFail` in the `forEachTest`. We simply use it like a fixture.

Listing 7-21. Screenshot on failure auto fixture, with an option

```
import { test as base, expect } from '@playwright/test';

export const test = base.extend<{
  screenshotOnFail: boolean;
  forEachTest: void;
}>({
  screenshotOnFail: [false, { option: true }],
  forEachTest: [
    async ({ page, screenshotOnFail }, use, testInfo) => {
      await use();

      if (screenshotOnFail) {
        if (testInfo.status !== testInfo.expectedStatus) {
          const screenshot = await page.screenshot();
          await testInfo.attach('screenshot', {
            body: screenshot,
            contentType: 'image/png',
          });
        }
      }
    },
    { auto: true },
  ],
});
```

Listing 7-22. Auto fixture usage; nothing to see here!

```
export { expect } from '@playwright/test';

test.use({ screenshotOnFail: true });

test('homepage has wrong title', async ({ page }) => {
  await page.goto('https://playwright.dev/');
  await expect(page).toHaveTitle(/DefinitelyWrongTitle/);
});
```

It's a convenient way to configure fixtures similarly to other Playwright setups. This example can easily be extended to add a path option; maybe in the form of a config Object for `screenshotOnFail`.

Create Your Fixture Collection

Once you start to have more fixtures, you will need to organize them in a clear fashion. This part explains how to organize your fixtures, mix them with third-party ones, all while keeping it simple.

Keep One Custom Test

I personally suggest grouping fixtures into a unique file that exports your custom `test`. Having different test Objects is overcomplicated and can be confusing (you may ask yourself "what test am I using?").

Depending on the number and complexity of your fixtures, you may either define them in-place, extract their definition to a constant, or even to separate files as seen in Listing 7-23.

Listing 7-23. Mix and match

```
import { test as base, expect } from '@playwright/test';
import { CheckoutPage } from './checkout-page';
import { userData, type UserData } from './user-data-fixture';

// Declare the types of your fixtures.
type MyFixtures = {
```

```
  checkoutPage: CheckoutPage;
  userData: UserData;
};
const checkoutPage = async ({ page }, use) => {
  const checkoutPage = new CheckoutPage(page);
  await use(checkoutPage);
  // Clean up if any
};
export const test = base.extend<MyFixtures>({
  checkoutPage,
  userData,
});
export { expect } from '@playwright/test';
```

Don't worry about making your custom test file "too big" and impacting performance. Remember that fixtures are loaded as needed.

Mix It with Third-Party

Another way to centralize fixtures is to merge tests. I find this particularly fitting with third-party libraries that already ship their own fixtures by exporting a test Object.

Listing 7-24. Merge different test

```
import { mergeTests } from '@playwright/test';
import { test as dbTest } from 'database-test-utils';
import { test as a11yTest } from 'a11y-test-utils';

export const test = mergeTests(dbTest, a11yTest);
```

Organize Fixtures and Helpers

My first piece of advice for better organizing your code is to clearly separate fixtures and helper functions from the tests. Regroup them in a dedicated folder, e.g., a fixtures folder. If you use POM, each POM class should be in its own file.

Don't make things more complex than they need to be. Often simpler folder structures are easier to navigate and maintain.

Listing 7-25. Flat structure

```
/fixtures/test.ts
/fixtures/checkout-page.ts
/fixtures/login-page.ts
```

Listing 7-26. Utils, with folders

```
/utils/test.ts
/utils/expects.ts
/utils/test-data/list.json
/utils/POM/checkout-page.ts
/utils/POM/login-page.ts
```

It's simple to compose fixtures, mixing and matching them as needed in a single test. This is thanks to Playwright Test fixture declarative dependency mechanism. Just like a page uses the same `context` as the one you can add to your test, you don't need to worry about what to add, in what order.

DRY vs. WET

You may have heard of the programming principle known as "Don't Repeat Yourself" (DRY). Avoiding code duplication is a popular practice. It makes sense: less duplicate code means fewer places to fix and maintain.

However, I'd argue that DRY can sometimes be counterproductive if not used sparingly. First, there are very low benefits if a function is only used in a few different places. Let's say you have similar code in two components, that is not already part of another abstraction. In this case, making a new function, maybe in a new `utils` file, may be too much effort for the benefits. Second, there is a risk of premature abstraction. Like there are premature optimizations, I believe there are premature abstractions. You have a similar need at first, but then one of the components needs something slightly different. You start to add options, and if you don't pay attention you'll end up with a generic "does-everything" function that is harder to read and maintain. DRY can become an anti-pattern.

That's why I recommend "Write Everything Twice," also known as WET. If you write the code twice, that's fine. If you need it a third time, then consider extracting it. Or if after a while the code doesn't change and is stable (i.e., you didn't make a premature abstraction), then you can extract it.

Keep in mind that the code you write for tests is not the code of your application. It has very different requirements in terms of architecture, performance, and reusability. If some test code is duplicated, it is not necessarily a problem. Not everything needs to be a Page Object, or a fixture.

Summary

Fixtures are a core notion and an important part of how Playwright Test works internally. Think of built-in fixtures like `context` or `page`; they are used everywhere. If you are new to test fixtures (like I was), give yourself some time. It is a rather complex and large topic.

Common usages of test fixtures are

- Preparing and injecting test data
- Testing options
- Passing along utility functions and helpers
- Grouping tests by meaning, regardless of the setup
- Having global setup and teardown
- Page Object Model

Playwright Test fixtures have many benefits that make it worth investing some time learning and practicing. It makes your tests more concise, focused on what is important. It does not have the constraints of test hooks (beforeEach, afterEach, etc.) as it will not dictate your test structure and organization. Fixtures are composable and on-demand. They are only initialized when you actually need them. Finally, and I can't emphasize this enough, you can adopt fixtures progressively. You can add them to your tests gradually and when it makes sense.

The next chapter is about mocking and emulation; both give you more control over the testing environment.

CHAPTER 8

Mocking and Emulation

In this chapter, we will see how to use device definitions and make our own to mimic the characteristics of real-life phones, computers, or TVs. We will also change the testing environment with locale and timezone, and travel through space and time!

My favorite mocking features give the ability to read, modify, or replace network requests. They give full control of what is retrieved from APIs. Finally, we will use advanced techniques to get even more control on the application under test and the Chromium browser itself.

To me, mocking and emulation are the sides of the same coin. They are both tools that will ultimately give you more in control of your application and its environment during testing. Let's start with emulating devices.

Device Emulation

Nowadays, the web is not only used on desktop computers but also on mobile phones, tablets, connected TVs… Often the user interface of our applications will adapt to these different devices, sometimes with big changes in terms of usability. Emulation helps to represent these different machines in our tests.

What defines a mobile device is the inconsistency. It's usually a device with a touch screen, less power than a computer, with network. It may or may not have a physical keyboard. The screens come in all kinds of shapes and sizes. The network can be excellent 5G, Wi-Fi, or 3G with huge latency and frequent cuts (think mobile network in a train).

Listing 8-1. iPhone 15 Pro device definition

```
"iPhone 15 Pro": {
  "userAgent": "Mozilla/5.0 (iPhone; CPU iPhone OS 17_5 like Mac OS X)
  AppleWebKit/605.1.15 (KHTML, like Gecko) Version/26.0 Mobile/15E148
  Safari/604.1",
  "screen": {
    "width": 393,
    "height": 852
  },
  "viewport": {
    "width": 393,
    "height": 659
  },
  "deviceScaleFactor": 3,
  "isMobile": true,
  "hasTouch": true,
  "defaultBrowserType": "webkit"
}
```

Different characteristics of a phone, tablet, or laptop are in the notion of device in Playwright. Let's take a closer look.

userAgent

"userAgent": "Mozilla/5.0 (iPhone; CPU iPhone OS 17_5 like Mac OS X) AppleWebKit/605.1.15 (KHTML, like Gecko) Version/26.0 Mobile/15E148 Safari/604.1",

The user agent is typically used to get a clue on what the device is (OS, browser, manufacturer, type of device…). Depending on this, some backends may serve different content. The best way to forge a realistic user agent is actually to get one from a real device. This is the best way, as user agents vary greatly with the device hardware and software (browser and sometimes firmware version). Several websites list user agents of common devices; this is a good alternative.

Changing this value will affect what is sent to the backend in the HTTP header User-Agent, and the value accessible to the frontend via `navigator.userAgent`.

screen, viewport, deviceScaleFactor

```
"screen": {
  "width": 393,
  "height": 852
},
"viewport": {
  "width": 393,
  "height": 659
},
"deviceScaleFactor": 3,
```

viewport is the actual usable space in a page. You can optionally override screen, that will represent the total size. Imagine a browser on a computer window that is not full screen. viewport is the usable page size in the window; screen is the computer's total screen size. In other words, it's the document size (document.documentElement.clientHeight) and the screen size (screen.height).

I frankly have mixed feelings about the usage of screen in Playwright. While it gives some clue of the usable space vs. screen space, it cannot represent more complex cases: mobile browsers will show or hide the navigation bar, and the same goes for the mobile's status bar. Some devices have a notch or Apple's dynamic island: an area that is not usable to display content (it's usually where there is the front camera and other sensors). Devices may report safe areas in CSS, but this cannot be fully emulated with Playwright as of today.

Listing 8-2. Viewport safe area with fallback

```
env(safe-area-inset-top, 20px);
env(safe-area-inset-right, 1em);
env(safe-area-inset-bottom, 0.5vh);
env(safe-area-inset-left, 1.4rem);
```

deviceScaleFactor is similar to the device pixel ratio, the ratio between physical pixels[1] and CSS pixels. This notion appeared when mobile phones started to have denser screens, i.e., got more pixels on the same form factor. To keep it workable and

---

[1] Well, actually it's the screen size reported by the operating system, which might be doing some scaling too compared to the native size of the screen.

have a consistent experience, the CSS pixels remained the same but with more pixels underneath. This allows crisper fonts, vector graphics, and images (when adapted). You may know this as Apple's Retina screen.

Viewport size will impact the application real estate, while the application under test might display different images depending on the DPR. As far as I know, screen only affects `window.screen`.

Is This a Mobile?

```
"isMobile": true,
"hasTouch": true,
"defaultBrowserType": "webkit"
```

You may wonder why `isMobile` and `hasTouch` are different settings.

- `isMobile` specifies if the HTML `<meta>` tag viewport is taken into account. This meta allows some control over the viewport and scaling. To add insult to injury, some devices that are not mobile might take meta viewport into account.

- Believe it or not, there was a time when smartphones didn't have a touchscreen. This is past, but now you might have a laptop with a touchscreen. So while they overlap, having two different settings is welcomed.

The `defaultBrowserType` can be either `chromium`, `firefox`, or `webkit`. This is super useful because the emulation will be closer to the real behavior, like using WebKit to emulate an iPhone.

Usage

Playwright's device list is not exhaustive but gives you definitions of common devices. Device definitions can be used in projects or directly in test files with `test.use()`.

Listing 8-3. playwright.config.ts

```
import { defineConfig, devices } from '@playwright/test';

export default defineConfig({
```

```
  projects: [
    {
      testDir: './e2e/smoke',
      name: 'Smoke',
      use: { ...devices['Desktop Chrome'] },
    },
    // ...
  ],
});
```

Listing 8-3a. with test.use()

```
import { devices, test } from '@playwright/test';

test.use( ...devices['Desktop Chrome'] );

// ...
```

The spread syntax (...) expands an Object, and you still can also override it as in Listing 8-3a if you set values after the spread. If needed, you can also create your own definition file with your collection of devices. Myself, I just set the device emulation at the project level.

Listing 8-4. Spread syntax with overrides

```
import { defineConfig, devices } from '@playwright/test';

export default defineConfig({
  projects: [
    {
      name: 'TV',
      use: {
        ...devices['Desktop Chrome'],
        userAgent:
          'Mozilla/5.0 (WebOS; Linux/SmartTV) AppleWebKit/537.36
          (KHTML, like Gecko) ChrOme/94.0.4606.128 Safari/537.36 LG
          Browser/8.00.00(LGE; 50UR7300PSA; 03.31.82; 0x00000001;
          DTV_W23P); webOS.TV-2022; LG NetCast.TV-2013 Compatible (LGE,
          50UR7300PSA, wireless)',
```

            },
        },
        // ...
    ],
});
```

The built-in device definitions can also be used in the command line, with Codegen for example.

```
npx playwright codegen --device="iPhone 11"
```

Mobile Testing

I mentioned that not everything can be emulated in Playwright, and this is only the tip of the iceberg. Things like subtle rendering differences, behavior in battery-saving mode, screen notch, and multi-touch are hard to emulate. The harsh truth is: nothing beats testing on a real device. Even better, a set of various devices.

Playwright Test offers experimental support for Android devices, letting you test on Chrome and Android WebView. WebViews are typically used for hybrid application frameworks like Ionic. Android support is achieved via the Android Debug Bridge `adb`. I can't really recommend it as not everything works. Moreover, it does not seem to be under active development.

iOS is a no-go at the moment. There are no means to run Playwright automation or tests against Safari.

Usually device emulation is "good enough" for functional testing. If you need automated tests on actual hardware, I suggest you explore other solutions such as Selenium WebDriver.

Space and time

In this part, we'll change user preferences and their environment:

- **Locale**: What language does the user prefer
- **Timezone**: Where is the user and how does it impact local and international time
```

- **Clock**: What time is it
- **Geolocation**: Where exactly are they

Locale

`test.use({ locale: 'en-US' });`

The locale defines the language preferences of the user. This means not only the text translation, but also how to represent a date, how numbers are formatted, how to collate elements of a list, ... You get it; locale will have an effect on the internationalization (i18n) provided by the tested application and the APIs it uses.

You can set a locale to a language-country pair like `fr-CA` (Canadian French) or just a language, `fr` (French). In this case, it will default to one variation of the language, i.e., `fr` will use France's French. `en` will use American English.

The locale matching mechanism is forgiving and can create issues. When preparing examples, I opened a browser with `npx playwright open --lang="en-UK"` and the date was '7/31/2025'. Wait, the 7th of the 31st month!

Can you guess why?

`en-UK` does not exist; it should be `en-GB`.[2] But the browser will recognize `en`; ignore the rest and fall back to American English with no errors.

The locale has several impacts:

- `navigator.language`, used for frontend language detection
- `Accept-Language`, an HTTP header automatically sent by the browser, which affects language detection in the backend
- Date formatting
- Number formatting, for example, with `.toLocaleString()` or `Intl.NumberFormat()`

Timezone

`test.use({ timezoneId: 'Europe/Paris' });`

---

[2] For "United Kingdom of Great Britain and Northern Ireland" and not Great Britain. Go figure!

CHAPTER 8   MOCKING AND EMULATION

At the same moment it's 9PM in Paris and 4AM in Shanghai. Timezones are very complex as they are based on the position on Earth (longitude) but also politics and history. China has one gigantic timezone, Nepal has an offset of UTC+5:45, some countries use daylight saving, some do not, some are geographically close but will not apply DST at the same dates…

If your tests rely on local time, they may break when running in a different timezone. This typically happens when your CI runners are not in the same location as your local PC.

In Playwright, you can emulate the timezone by setting an ICU identifier (International Components for Unicode) for the `timezoneId` setting. This means you can use values like `America/New_York` or `Asia/Shanghai`, but not an offset like `+09:00`.

The timezone will impact local time and date in the browsers. This option is useful to validate behavior for international users, Date manipulations, i18n, or scheduling. We didn't time travel here, but the Clock API can.

Clock API

We can control two things with this API: the current time, and timers. Great Scott!

`setFixedTime` makes `new Date()` and `Date.now()` return the fake time that you set. Playwright's documentation states that the timers are still running; this means that you can ask for the time every second in a `setTimeout` or `setInterval`, the current time is always the same. This mock is useful to write predictable tests when Date.now() is used.

For more complex use cases, the API becomes way more complex as well.

Now, let's say that you need to make a countdown. This can be to close a user session automatically after inactivity, to stop a game when the play time is reached, for a cooking timer… Our example app in Figure 8-1 will display a 5-minute countdown (1), a message when 1 minute remains (2), and finally a message when the countdown is over (3).

Countdown Timer

① 00:00

Only 1 minute remaining! ②

③ Time is up!

Figure 8-1. Countdown

For the sake of demonstration, we have two implementations: one that checks time regularly and another that actually counts down the remaining seconds. Bear with me, it will matter later.

Listing 8-5. Countdown

```
// This checks time every second
const endTime = Date.now() + 5 * 60_000;
const renderTime = () => {
  const diffInSeconds = Math.round((endTime - Date.now()) / 1000);
  // ...

  if (diffInSeconds <= 0) {
    document.getElementById("timesup").textContent = "Time is up!";
  } else {
    setTimeout(renderTime, 1000);
  }
};
renderTime();
```

CHAPTER 8   MOCKING AND EMULATION

```
// This counts every second
let totalSeconds = 5 * 60;
setInterval(() => {
  totalSeconds--;
  if (totalSeconds <= 60) {
    document.getElementById("warn").textContent = "Only 1 minute
    remaining!";
  }
}, 1000);
```

In this book, we've paid attention following best practices to write fast tests, so we can't reasonably wait for 5 minutes to test our countdown. So we will manipulate time. We need to install our fake clock first. This should be done before any time-related API call. Then we can just fast-forward 5 minutes with `clock.fastForward()`.

"Time is up!" is shown when running Listing 8-6, but not "Only 1 minute remaining!". This is because fast-forward is more like a jump in time, so it did not run through all the time intervals. In other words, the time changed, but the time didn't actually elapse.

Listing 8-6. Fast-forward

```
import { test, expect } from '@playwright/test';

test('countdown fast forward', async ({ page }) => {
  await page.clock.install();
  await page.goto('/countdown-timer.html');

  await page.clock.fastForward('05:00');

  await expect.soft(page.getByText('Only 1 minute remaining!')).
  toBeVisible();
  await expect(page.getByText('Time is up!')).toBeVisible();
});
```

On the contrary, `clock.runFor()` means that it will run all the timers for 5 minutes. If you run the test headful, you'll see the countdown run all the way to 0 (but faster).

Listing 8-7. Run

```
test('countdown run', async ({ page }) => {
  await page.clock.install();
  await page.goto('/countdown-timer.html');

  await page.clock.runFor('05:00');

  await expect(page.getByText('Only 1 minute remaining!')).toBeVisible();
  await expect(page.getByText('Time is up!')).toBeVisible();
});
```

Note Think of the difference between `fastForward` and `runFor` like watching Blu-ray, a DVD, or online video with chapters. If you skip to a chapter (`fastForward`), you jump in time but didn't watch what happened during that time. If you x2 the playback speed, you'll see everything (like `runFor`).

The fake clock has an impact on several APIs: Date, Timeout, Interval, AnimationFrame, IdleCallback, Performance.

Permissions

```
test.use({ permissions: ['notifications'], });
```

When a website needs sensitive information or features, the browser will ask the user if they wish to grant or deny access. It's usually things linked to privacy such as geolocation, microphone, notifications... Playwright will set the permissions listed by this setting programmatically instead of asking for a manual approval.

The Playwright documentation gives a list of permissions that "**may** be supported by **some** browsers." This is where differences between browsers make it difficult because they have wildly different behavior (aka fragmentation). According to MDN, only a handful of permissions are supported across Chrome, Firefox, and Safari: `camera`, `geolocation`, `microphone`, `notifications`, `push`. For others, you may have to verify browser compatibility and experiment by yourself.

Permissions are granted (or denied) for a `context`. This makes sense if you think of `context` as a browser session.

CHAPTER 8 MOCKING AND EMULATION

Remember, we can roughly consider that

- `browser` is Chromium, Firefox, WebKit…
- `context` is an incognito session
- `page` is a tab in this session

Geolocation

```
test.use({
  geolocation: { longitude: 48.1173, latitude: -1.6778 },
  permissions: ['geolocation'],
});
```

For geolocation, you'll need two things: grant the permission and set a location. This can be done with `test.use()` as seen in Listing 8-8, or in the Playwright Test configuration file.

Listing 8-8. Geolocation example

```
import { test } from '@playwright/test';

test.use({
  geolocation: { longitude: 48.1173, latitude: -1.6778 },
  permissions: ['geolocation'],
});

test('Geoloc', async ({ page }) => {
  await page.goto('https://www.bing.com/maps');
  await page.getByRole('link', { name: 'Accept' }).click();
  await page.getByRole('button', { name: '3D Flyover' }).click();
});
```

You can also set and modify the location afterward with `context.setGeolocation()`.

> **Warning** This setting only impacts the geolocation declared by the browser via the Geolocation API. Some websites may use other means to estimate your position, such as your IP address. For example, to restrict access based on your region (geofencing).

Network

Inspecting and mocking network requests needs more heavy lifting, but it's totally worth it. The route feature is one of my favorites as it makes it possible to reproduce conditions that may be difficult otherwise: variations of the backend responses, or partner APIs that may be unreliable, or avoiding real paid subscriptions on live environments.

Route

The page.route(), or context.route(), needs two parameters: a glob pattern to match[3] and a handler function. This mechanism will match network requests and let you handle them yourself.

I always found glob patterns a bit confusing. I often wondered what to do to capture subfolders in a file system or match an URL. The most common patterns are as follows:

* * matches any character but stops at the next /

* ** matches everything

* ? is a wildcard for one character

* {png,jpeg} matches exactly one of the strings

Table 8-1 shows glob pattern examples for common use cases of route matching.

---

[3] You can also use a regex or a predicate function, but globs are nice once you get it.

CHAPTER 8   MOCKING AND EMULATION

Table 8-1. *URLs glob pattern examples*

Glob pattern	Explanation
`https://www.example.com/**`	Any URL of a given origin
`**/users`	A path, regardless of the origin
`**/users*`	Same as above, ignoring query params
`**/*.{png,jpeg}`	Some images

The handle function is responsible for taking care of the request. You can either abort, continue, or fulfill it with modifications to the response. We already used a route handler to abort image requests in Chapter 5! In Listing 8-9, we abort or go on with the request, depending on a criterion.

Listing 8-9. Abort image route

```
await page.route('**/*', (route) => {
  return route.request().resourceType() === 'image'
    ? route.abort()
    : route.continue();
});
```

My personal favorite is to trick the frontend with a forged or modified API answer. In Listing 8-10, we just create our own JSON response.

Listing 8-10. Simple fulfill

```
await page.route('*/**/api/v1/fruits', async route => {
  const json = [{ name: 'Strawberry', id: 21 }];
  await route.fulfill({ json });
});
```

Even better, we can make a real API request and modify its answer before it goes to the frontend. In Listing 8-11, line 2, we use `route.fetch()` to request the backend and get the response. We then use this data and modify it before fulfilling the request on line 8. The frontend will have a mix of the real backend response with our modifications. We can change the JSON response, but we can also tamper with headers, response status, …

Listing 8-11. Fullfill with modified response

```
await page.route('**/api/v1/public/account/features*', async (route) => {
  const response = await route.fetch();
  const json = await response.json();

  const features: Feature[] = json.features;
  const proPlan = features.find((feature) => feature.name === 'Pro Plan');
  proPlan.status = FeatureStatus.ACTIVE;
  return route.fulfill({ json: { features } });
});
```

Writing routes can be a bit tricky: you have to make the right glob to capture the correct route, have knowledge of the API, and know exactly what to modify. To start, I usually write a simple function, make the request to the backend, and debug that in VS Code. It's much easier once you make sure that the route is captured and when you can inspect the returned data.

Listing 8-12. Use debugger to ease the writing of a route

```
await page.route('**/api/v1/fruits', async (route) => {
  const response = await route.fetch();
  const json = await response.json();
  // debug here the response and check it live in VS Code debug console
  debugger;
  await route.fulfill({ json });
});
```

Emulating a Slow Network

It may seem counterintuitive wanting to slow down the network when in Chapter 5 we tried to make our tests faster. It is not, because we will slow down the network on purpose to test that our web app works as intended. This time, network speed is consciously in our control instead of being a variable.

When we think of network speed, there are actually two notions: bandwidth and latency. The first one is how fast you can download data. It has more impact on large content like images. The second is the response time. Consider a request from an API: the time for the backend to build the answer, access a database, the round-trip time over the network, the time to initiate a request. All that waiting time adds up. Bandwidth and latency are different notions, but in our case it doesn't make much difference: either way, the network requests are fulfilled later.

So, let's introduce latency to our network calls with the Playwright Test "route" API. Follow along with Listing 8-13.

1. Catch every API call.

2. Wait for a while. Because the handler function is async, we'll do it with a Promise.

3. Continue.

Listing 8-13. Wait before proceeding with the request

```
import { setTimeout } from 'node:timers/promises';
import { test, expect } from '@playwright/test';

test('slow network', async ({ page }) => {
  // 1
  await page.route('**/api/v1/*', async (route) => {
    // 2
    await setTimeout(1_000);
    // 3
    await route.continue();
  });

  await page.goto(
    'https://todobackend.com/client/index.html?https://csharp-todo-backend.azurewebsites.net/api/v1/todo',
  );
  await page
    .getByRole('textbox', { name: 'What needs to be done?' })
    .fill('tomatoes');
  await page
    .getByRole('textbox', { name: 'What needs to be done?' })
```

```
    .press('Enter');
  await page.reload();
  await expect(page.getByText('tomatoes')).toBeVisible();
});
```

If you want to go further, you could use a random delay or even randomly fail. Moreover, I found that slowing down API calls only yields more interesting results. This is a technique inspired by chaos engineering that will create bad conditions on purpose to test your app resilience. In the next chapter on test reliability, we will use this to stress-test our tests as well.

Record and Replay HAR

Another way to mock network requests is to create a route from a HAR file. HTTP ARchive (HAR) is a format based on JSON that holds the network requests, usually between a browser and a backend, with request, response, headers… It's like a snapshot of the network view of your browser's DevTools. This format is widely adopted in various analysis tools and in browsers, in which you can easily record and save requests to HAR.

The syntax and mechanism of page.routeFromHAR() differ from page.route(). Here we are not handling a route with a function but more simply with a HAR file previously recorded and saved to Git. The first parameter is the path of the HAR file and the glob pattern to match is passed as a url option.

Listing 8-14. routeFromHAR

```
await page.routeFromHAR('./hars/fruit.har', {
  url: '*/**/api/v1/fruits',
  update: false,
});
```

To record an HAR file from Playwright, the easiest way is probably to add update: true in the page.routeFromHAR() options seen in Listing 8-14. With this, Playwright will perform the real network requests to the backend, then save them to the HAR file. You can then commit this file for future tests. You can also analyze HAR files with tools such as Google's HAR Analyzer or the VS Code extension HAR Viewer. Being JSON, HAR files can be modified fairly easily.

CHAPTER 8   MOCKING AND EMULATION

Warning Network requests recorded in HAR will contain sensitive information. Cookies, tokens, client data… anything that went through the network can be recorded.

Recording and replaying network calls in this way is very powerful and handy. However, I personally prefer `page.route()` as it is more fine-grained and gives me a lot of control over what is mocked, modified or left as is.

Injecting JavaScript

I was initially reluctant to write about JavaScript injection as I found that it is complex and overkill most of the time. But there is a hidden gem in Playwright's documentation for init scripts.

Let's start with `page.evaluate()` before going any further. This method will simply evaluate code in the browser land and return the value in your test script. You can use a string in a similar fashion to `eval()`. More conveniently, you can pass a function as in Listing 8-15.

Listing 8-15. Evaluate

```
const res = await page.evaluate('1 + 2');
console.log(res); // Prints "3"

const res2 = await page.evaluate(() => 1 + 2);
console.log(res2); // Prints "3"
```

The function will be serialized by Playwright first, then executed in the browser land. Keep in mind that the function you pass to `page.evaluate()` runs in the browser, not Playwright. That is why you can't use variables from your test directly. However, you can use arguments to `page.evaluate()` that will be passed along to the function. See Listing 8-16 for an example of do and don't.

Listing 8-16. Evaluate with parameters

```
const name = 'Jane';
// Displays "Hello "
```

```
await page.evaluate(() => document.writeln(`Hello ${name}<br>`));

// Displays "Hello Jane"
await page.evaluate((n) => document.writeln(`Hello ${n}<br>`), name);
```

There are several ways to execute and expose functions in the browser land from Playwright, but I find addInitScript particularly interesting because it can create mocks. Init scripts are executed before the page loads; this is somehow reminiscent of Chrome's extension content scripts. So, let's see the interesting bit from the documentation I was talking about.

Listing 8-17. Math random, mocked

```
import { test, expect } from '@playwright/test';

// Add script for every test in the beforeEach hook.
test.beforeEach(async ({ page }) => {
  const value = 42;
  await page.addInitScript(value => {
    Math.random = () => value;
  }, value);
});
```

In this example, the init script is used to modify Math.random() behavior. JavaScript is very flexible by nature, so with trickery you can redefine pretty much anything. This can be seen as a last resort when other methods don't apply, i.e., don't do this to mock geolocation or network as Playwright Test offers easier, better solutions out of the box.

Chrome DevTools Protocol

As a developer, you probably use Chromium's DevTools often, if not daily. It is actually a client-server application: the browser is the server and DevTools acts as the client. It means that with this client you can connect to another debug server such as a remote browser on a smartphone or a Node.js application, as it also implements the DevTools Protocol.

CDP allows for automation, and this is precisely what Puppeteer was created for: automating Chrome via its debug protocol. Sound familiar? That's the same approach used by Playwright. That's no coincidence, since part of the Playwright team is behind CDP and Puppeteer.

Using Chrome DevTools Protocol is leveraging low-level features of Playwright and Chrome. We will use its possibilities to do something that is not available in higher-level APIs of Playwright.

Using CDP to Slow Down the CPU

Now is the time for some kind of sorcery. We will ask a Chromium browser to slow down the CPU for us to emulate a slower machine. Nowadays, personal computers and high-end smartphones are extremely powerful machines. As developers, we often have access to machines with 20+ cores, 32 GB of RAM, SSD. These do not reflect everyone's configuration, and it's a good idea to check that an app works on low-end devices.

We will use the Chrome DevTools Protocol to tell the browser to slow down. See in Listing 8-18 how we filter out browsers that are not based on Chromium. Then we create a new CDP session from the `context`. Finally, we can set the CPU slowdown by sending a `setCPUThrottlingRate` command.

Listing 8-18. page with and without CPU throttling

```
import { test, expect } from '@playwright/test';

test('CPU throttling', async ({ context, browserName }) => {
  if (browserName !== 'chromium') {
    test.skip();
  }

  const page1 = await context.newPage();
  await page1.goto('https://dacris.github.io/jsmark/benchModern.html');

  const page2 = await context.newPage();
  const client = await page2.context().newCDPSession(page2);
  await client.send('Emulation.setCPUThrottlingRate', { rate: 4 });
  await page2.goto('https://dacris.github.io/jsmark/benchModern.html');
});
```

The documentation for this CDP command is as follows:

`Emulation.setCPUThrottlingRate`

Enables CPU throttling to emulate slower CPUs.
Parameters

- **rate** (number): Throttling rate as a slowdown factor (1 is no throttle, 2 is 2x slowdown, etc.)

Using Chrome DevTools Protocol directly is pretty straightforward. Here are two great resources to begin with:

- A getting started guide with several examples.

  `https://github.com/aslushnikov/getting-started-with-cdp`

- The Chrome DevTools Protocol itself. The website allows navigating and searching the complete protocol documentation. Note that the Git repository contains the protocol definition itself, in JSON.

  `https://chromedevtools.github.io/devtools-protocol/`

Summary

Real hardware and manual testing are useful for exploratory testing. But for automated tests, emulation and mocks give you great control on your test environment.

Main takeaways from this part:

- Using Playwright's or your own **device definitions** makes tests more realistic.
- You can easily change **space and time**. At least in a browser.
- Route and HAR mocking let you **change network response**.
- You can also **simulate a slow network**.
- We even saw how to have **fine control on the browser with JavaScript injection and CDP**.

Let's continue with advanced topics and see how to handle flaky tests and make our tests more reliable.

CHAPTER 9

Gain Confidence Thanks to Reliable Tests

The working title for this book was *Confidence with Playwright Test*. Because my goal is that you, the reader, become confident in your usage of this tool but also that you can have confidence from your tests. Confidence that your system works, that you didn't break anything with a new development and that you can refactor your code safely. I believe that good tests give more freedom, build trust in your code, and increase confidence in your team.

This is why automated tests should be reliable. You can't trust them if they sometimes fail for no reason, or even worse, pass when they shouldn't. Flaky tests are a common problem for end-to-end testing. In this chapter, we will see common Playwright Test mechanisms that help: auto-waiting and retry. We will also learn how to detect flaky tests and how to fix them for good.

Built-In Reliability: Auto-Waiting, Retries, and Timeouts

I sometimes came across beginners who misunderstood Playwright's capabilities. They claim that Playwright is unreliable, but forget to use `await` for asynchronous functions. Or some may say that Playwright's auto-waiting is just a marketing claim.

While it's incorrect to say that a test framework is inherently flaky or reliable, it can encourage good practices. Consider this part a refresher: we will review good practices and concepts for actions, assertions, and retries. We will also go deeper into the different mechanisms of Playwright Test that make for reliable tests.

Understanding Actions Auto-Waiting

When I write a Locator that does not find an Element and use the action `click()`, it will fail after 30000 ms. So, Playwright just waited over and over? What is automatic about it?

```
await page.locator('fail').click();
```

We actually hit the timeout for a test, because actions don't have timeout by default, i.e., actions won't time out but the test eventually will. You can set a timeout for action either in the configuration file, as in Listing 9-1, or for a single action as in Listing 9-2.

Listing 9-1. playwright.config.ts

```
import { defineConfig } from '@playwright/test';

export default defineConfig({
  use: {
    actionTimeout: 5_000,
  },
});
```

Listing 9-2. Action with timeout

```
test('fail fast', async ({ page }) => {
  await page.locator('fail').click({ timeout: 5_000 });
});
```

Some may be puzzled by why this is called auto-waiting, since it seems that Playwright Test apparently just waits. It will automatically wait for actionability. Depending on the action, the checks are different:

- `click()` will wait for the Element to be visible, enabled but also receives events.
- `fill()` will check that the Element is editable (among others).

It is called **auto**-waiting because it automatically waits for the right state of Element. In the case of a Locator that never resolves, Playwright Test waits for a state on an Element that will not be there.

If we disable this auto-waiting mechanism, the test framework will click immediately. It may seem unnecessary to wait for readiness, so let's see what happens when we use the force option. Consider Listing 9-3 where a button is in the page, but disabled, before it is ready. This can happen because we are still fetching content, or the click listener is not registered yet, which is oftentimes called hydration.

Listing 9-3. Readiness problem

```
import test, { expect } from '@playwright/test';

test('clicks blindly (force)', async ({ page }) => {
  await page.setContent(`
    <button id="btn" disabled="true">Click me</button>
    <div id="message" style="display:none">Success</div>

    <script>
      setTimeout(() => {
        document.getElementById('btn').disabled = false;
      }, 1000);
      document.getElementById('btn').addEventListener('click', () => {
        document.getElementById('message').style.display = 'block';
      });
    </script>
  `);

  await page
    .getByRole('button', { name: 'Click me' })
    .click({ force: true });
  await expect(page.getByText('Success')).toBeVisible();
});
```

If Playwright clicks immediately, the action will never be triggered. Hence the test fails. To avoid that, we can add an assertion before clicking. However, to be complete, we would need to check for visibility and more.

Listing 9-4. Use expect to check readiness

```
import test, { expect } from '@playwright/test';

test('clicks blindly (force)', async ({ page }) => {
  // ...
  await expect(
    page.getByRole('button', { name: 'Click me' })
  ).toBeEnabled();
  await page
    .getByRole('button', { name: 'Click me' })
    .click({ force: true });
  await expect(page.getByText('Success')).toBeVisible();
});
```

Clicking immediately with force seems to be a performance optimization, but it is not: if the auto-waiting checks pass, Playwright will perform the action immediately.

What can fail: If you forget to wait for an action, or don't use auto-waiting, usually the next action or assertion will fail.

Web-First Assertions

We've seen in Chapter 2 that web-assertions are good because they are adapted for testing the DOM. I also mentioned that they are called auto-retrying assertions. Let's see what it means in practice.

Locator.textContent() returns, obviously, the text content of an Element. It returns immediately. Well, almost, because Playwright needs to resolve the Locator and get the text in the browser land. It means that this method should be awaited.

If we make a non-retrying assertion, it will look like Listing 9-5. Note how the expect().toBe() does not need to be awaited.

Listing 9-5. Non-retrying assertion

```
expect(await locator.textContent()).toBe('Hello');
```

This assertion will fail if the Element is not visible at this exact point in time. To improve that, we can retry the assertion until it is true with poll().

Listing 9-6. Retry non-retrying assertion

```
await expect.poll(async () => await locator.textContent()).toBe('Hello');
```

That looks like auto-retrying assertions with extra steps. You should use web-first assertions whenever possible.

Warning Don't forget to await your web-first assertions.

What can fail: Assertions fail randomly.

Fine-Tune Your Timeouts

You can set timeouts individually with the options of actions, assertions, tests... and also set these timeouts in the Playwright configuration file.

Listing 9-7. Every timeouts with their default values

```
import { defineConfig } from '@playwright/test';

export default defineConfig({
  timeout: 30_000,
  globalTimeout: 0,
  expect: {
    timeout: 5_000,
  },
  use: {
    actionTimeout: 0,
    navigationTimeout: 0,
  },
});
```

There are many fine-grained settings. This can feel overwhelming, but as usual, Playwright Test has reasonable defaults and gives you the possibility to adjust the settings.

My advice is to keep Playwright's defaults as they are rather low but reasonable. Then if a test needs more time, use `test.slow()` and tag it as `@slow`. Only if many of your tests are slow and you have already optimized them, you may consider changing the test timeout in the configuration file.

You can also set some individuals' expect timeout to 0 (no timeout), so Playwright will wait until hitting the test timeout. The error message will not be as clear, so this should be an exception.

Listing 9-8 demonstrates all these syntaxes in action.

Listing 9-8. A slow test with custom exception timeout

```
import { test, expect } from '@playwright/test';
test('extended timeouts', { tag: '@slow' }, async ({ page }) => {
  // Hello world appears after a long delay
  // ...
  test.slow();
  const locator = page.getByRole('heading');
  await expect(locator).toHaveText('Hello world', { timeout: 0 });
});
```

What can fail: Test fails with a test timeout (30000 ms), at different steps of the test.

Test Retry

In addition to auto-retrying assertions (such as toBeVisible) and retrying blocks (with toPass), there is a third level of test retry.

Playwright can retry a test when it fails: the framework will retry until the test passes, for a maximum number of attempts. This is very useful when a test is failing intermittently. Thanks to retry, a single unstable test will not throw away a whole Continuous Integration pipeline.

As usual, there is a setting for test retry in the Playwright configuration file as well as a CLI flag. Note how the settings created by npm init playwright set different values in CI in Listing 9-9.

Listing 9-9. playwright.config.ts

```
export default defineConfig({
  /* Retry on CI only */
  retries: process.env.CI ? 2 : 0,
  // ...
});
```

In Chapter 5, we've seen that the different parallelism options influence how tests are retried.

- parallel or fullyParallel: If a test fails, it will be retried independently.
- default: If a test fails, it will be retried independently.
- serial: Playwright will re-run the whole block, being a describe or a file.

When a test fails at first and eventually passes after one or more retries, Playwright Test will mark such a test as flaky. This is visible in the HTML report as in Figure 9-1. Even more than a resilient CI, to me the benefit of test retry is to detect such unstable tests.

CHAPTER 9   GAIN CONFIDENCE THANKS TO RELIABLE TESTS

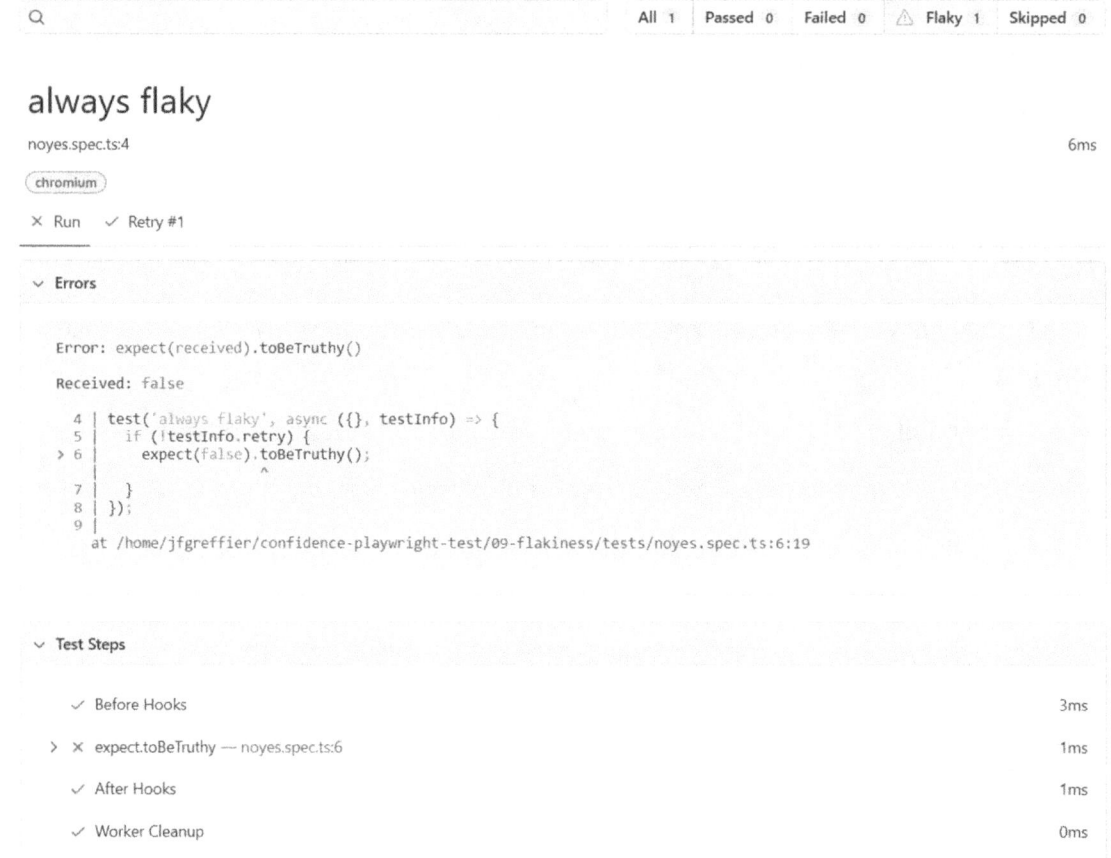

Figure 9-1.   Test marked as flaky

What can fail: Congratulations! Playwright Test detected a test as flaky.

Flakiness

Some tests are said to be "flaky." They are tests that are non-deterministic: not only are they fragile, but they act unexpectedly. It's like flaky tests are plotting against you. They may pass, or fail, in unexpected ways.

You may find different root causes such as a poorly written test, network conditions, test environment, or race conditions. It is difficult to untangle most of the time. Not only do these tests fail in a seemingly random way, but they also pass by chance. It works by accident.

Because failure is not 100% correlated with your tested application not working as intended, you just can't trust flaky tests. It's very problematic because the very purpose of tests is to give you more confidence in the current state of your web application. Having flaky tests will make developers suspicious of test results and may create alert fatigue. Because of the signal vs. noise ratio, nobody will pay attention to failed test results anymore. Then when the web app is really broken, nobody will notice.

In this part, we will see what causes flakiness, how to find flaky tests, how to avoid them, and finally how to **fix them for good**.

How to Detect Flaky Tests

Two things will help us find flaky tests: statistics and making the odds more favorable. More runs increase the chances of finding faulty cases. We can also artificially make the conditions worse for the tests, to make them randomly fail more often. But first, we should be able to find flaky tests in our daily workflows.

Find Flaky Tests Daily in CI

Your first line of defense should consist in a simple practice: pay attention to your CI tests results. Observe regularly your tests results and look for flaky tests. We saw earlier that test retries will help by not failing a whole test suite every time Playwright stumbles on an unstable test. Moreover, Playwright Test will mark these tests as "flaky."

Treat flaky tests as technical debt, i.e., it is not blocking right now but it will slow you down in the future. If you don't fix flaky tests, they will make your test suite slower, will add noise in the logs and reports, and make introducing new tests and features more difficult. If you let them, flaky tests will follow Murphy's law and fail at the worst possible moment, when you need to release a new version or apply a hotfix. Some teams have a zero-bug policy; it means that as soon as a bug appears they try to fix it. It's demanding but in the case of flaky tests, it's a good idea to not delay the correction of the tests and sometimes the application under test.

Test Burn-In

You just wrote a great end-to-end test, but how do you ensure that it is always reliable? It is important to build confidence in our tests by only adding trusted ones to the Continuous Integration. We will simply use statistics and run tests many times to find seemingly random failures.

Murat Ozcan calls this process test burn-in. I quite like this name because, like fixtures, it comes from real-life testing practice. In electronics, burn-in testing consists of running the components for a given time to detect any flaw early on. The component under test can also be subject to higher temperature, voltage, and many power-on cycles.

This is exactly what we will do to ensure that our test is reliable: make it battle-tested by running it a hundred times with the command line option --repeat-each. On top of that, I suggest deactivating retries. Indeed, here we already use repetition to detect flaky tests and the failed attempt will appear as a failure which is clearer in our context.

Listing 9-10. repeat each

```
npx playwright test --retries=0 --repeat-each=100
```

Great, but we may encounter another problem as we run all of our suites a hundred times. Playwright is fast but running a whole test suite a hundred times may lead to thousands or dozens of thousands of runs! That can take a tremendous amount of time.

The first approach is to test only what is needed, i.e., new tests, tests that changed, or tests affected by fixtures changes. This is exactly what --only-changed does. As seen in Chapter 5, this option can run tests that changed compared to a Git ref. Here we can use it to detect changes against the remote main branch.

Listing 9-11. Repeat each changed tests

```
npx playwright test --only-changed=origin/main --retries=0 --repeat-each=100
```

Test burn-in is also a nice use case for testing services at scale. Microsoft Playwright Testing and Endform are designed to run hundreds of tests, if not thousands, in a few minutes. See Chapter 5 for more details.

Finally, let's put this command in an npm script, as it is rather long and complex.

Listing 9-12. package.json

```
{
  "scripts": {
    "lint": "eslint .",
    "test": "playwright test",
    "test:burn-in": "playwright test --only-changed=origin/main --retries=0 --repeat-each=100"
```

```
  },
  // ...
}
```

When you run your new tests a hundred times, you have pretty good confidence that it will work without issues later on. If you already have end-to-end tests and never practiced test burn-in, now is a good time to try it on your test suite and go grab a coffee.

Chaos

Playwright makes reliable tests easy to write, so sometimes we need to create artificially bad conditions for the test faults to emerge. This is the same as Netflix's chaos engineering: making things bad on purpose to test resilience.

One popular solution is to clog your machine by starting many parallel workers. Ideally, it should be enough to make your CPU hurt. There is a great command for that: `--workers`. You can pass a number of workers but also a percentage of your logical CPU cores. The trick is to set it **higher than 100%**.

Listing 9-13. Real numbers from my personal machine

```
$ npx playwright test --workers=150%

Running 45 tests using 42 workers
```

We can also emulate a slow CPU. In fact, Chapter 8 describes how we can use Chrome DevTools Protocol to ask the browser to apply CPU throttling. Let's throw in a slower network as well. We achieved that in Chapter 8 with `page.route()`. Finally, we'll make this as a fixture that will be great not only to detect flaky tests but also to investigate and fix them.

Listing 9-14. Fixture to detect flaky tests

```
import { setTimeout } from 'node:timers/promises';
import { test as base, Page } from '@playwright/test';

export type MyFixtures = {
  chaos: () => Promise<void>;
};

export const test = base.extend<MyFixtures>({
```

```
  chaos: async ({ browserName, page }, use) => {
    await use(async () => {
      // 1
      if (browserName !== 'chromium') {
        test.skip();
      }

      // 2 CPU throttling
      const client = await page.context().newCDPSession(page);
      await client.send('Emulation.setCPUThrottlingRate', { rate: 4 });

      // 3 Slow XHR
      await page.route('**', async (route) => {
        if (route.request().resourceType() === 'xhr') {
          await setTimeout(1_000);
        }
        await route.continue();
      });
    });
  },
});

export { expect } from '@playwright/test';
```

Let's break down Listing 9-14:

- Line 11: Because we use CDP, this fixture is only for Chromium.

- Line 16: We tell the browser to apply a slowdown of 4. It means the browser will be 4 times slower than your machine. This may still be very good compared to a low-end smartphone, so don't hesitate to adjust this value.

- Line 20: We apply a wait to every XHR request. In my experience, slowing down API calls (usually XHR or fetch) yields better results than slowing down every network request. We could also add a random delay to introduce more chaos.

The fixture exposes a function but we could override page or add an option. I just find that a function that you must call is more explicit.

CHAPTER 9   GAIN CONFIDENCE THANKS TO RELIABLE TESTS

Case Study: TODO App

While preparing the example for route to slow down network, for Chapter 8, I actually ran into an issue. While the slowdown is fine, the test of Listing 8-13 does not always succeed.

This sample uses a simple TODO application with a client and backend. The test is as follows:

1. Add an item in the TODO list.

2. Reload the page.

3. Assert that the item is retrieved from the backend.

Without network delay, it would often fail in headed mode but not so much in headless. With our chaos fixture, it fails consistently at the assertion line 16 of Listing 9-15.

Can you guess why?

Listing 9-15. Flaky TODO

```
import { test, expect } from './fixtures';

test('flaky TODO', async ({ page, chaos }) => {
  await chaos();

  const backendURL = getBackendURL();
  await page.goto(`/`);

  const inputLocator = page.getByRole('textbox', {
    name: 'What needs to be done?',
  });
  await inputLocator.fill('tomatoes');
  await inputLocator.press('Enter');
  await page.reload();

  await expect(page.getByText('tomatoes')).toBeVisible();
});
```

Adding a new item will trigger an HTTP POST request for the backend to create a new entry. But then, we reload the page right after submitting the item. Let's take a look at what happened in the browser.

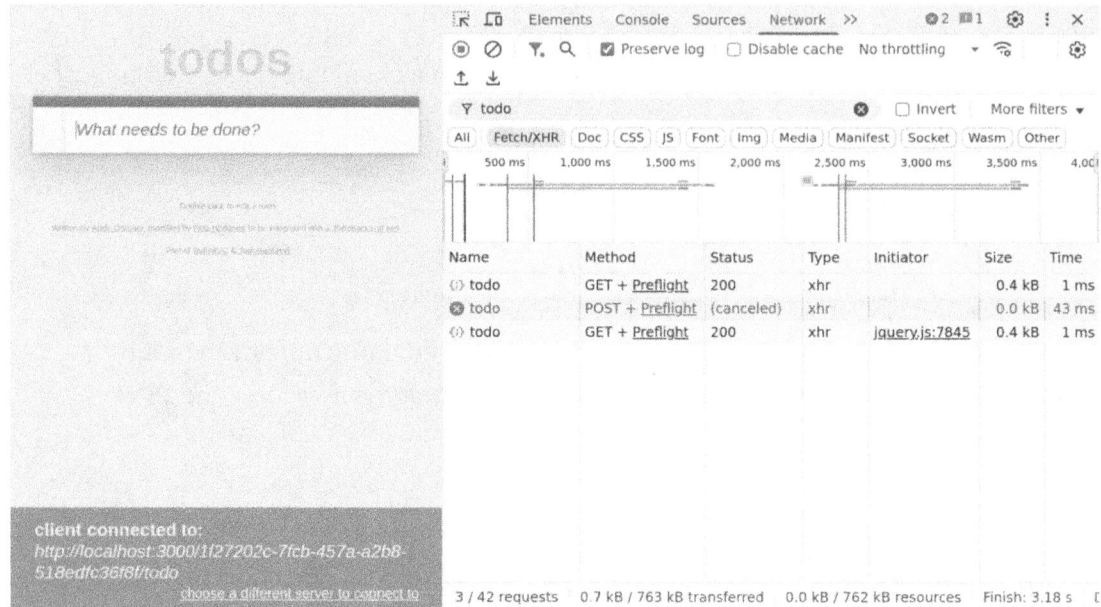

Figure 9-2. *The todo call was cancelled*

We reloaded the page before the POST had a chance to go through. If the POST request takes more than a few dozen milliseconds, the test fails.

Strategies to Fix Flaky Tests

Now that we have the means to detect flaky tests, we have to fix them. Whether we found flaky tests early with burn-in or noticed them later in Continuous Integration, if we can't fix them right away, we will have to mark them and put them in quarantine. In this part, we will also see how to fix flaky tests, for good.

Enforce Good Practices

The best way to avoid simple mistakes is to make them impossible, or difficult. Poka-yoke is a Japanese term for error prevention mechanism that made it in industry, design, and process. It's in the microwave that stops when you open the door, or the computer ports with different shapes.

CHAPTER 9   GAIN CONFIDENCE THANKS TO RELIABLE TESTS

The first way to avoid simple mistakes early is to use TypeScript. Using it rather than just JavaScript will help you catch issues when you write tests, thanks to type safety. Remember, you can write your Playwright tests in TypeScript even if the application under test doesn't use it. The app can be written with anything like JavaScript or even Blazor.

My favorite way to avoid simple mistakes is using a linter, also known as a static code analyzer. ESLint is probably the most popular; I personally use it both in CI and with the VS Code ESLint extension. It allows for a short feedback loop, as errors and warnings are visible right in the editor as seen in Figure 9-3. Not only will you avoid mistakes as you write tests, but you will be able to analyze a test at a glance and oftentimes fix issues quickly.

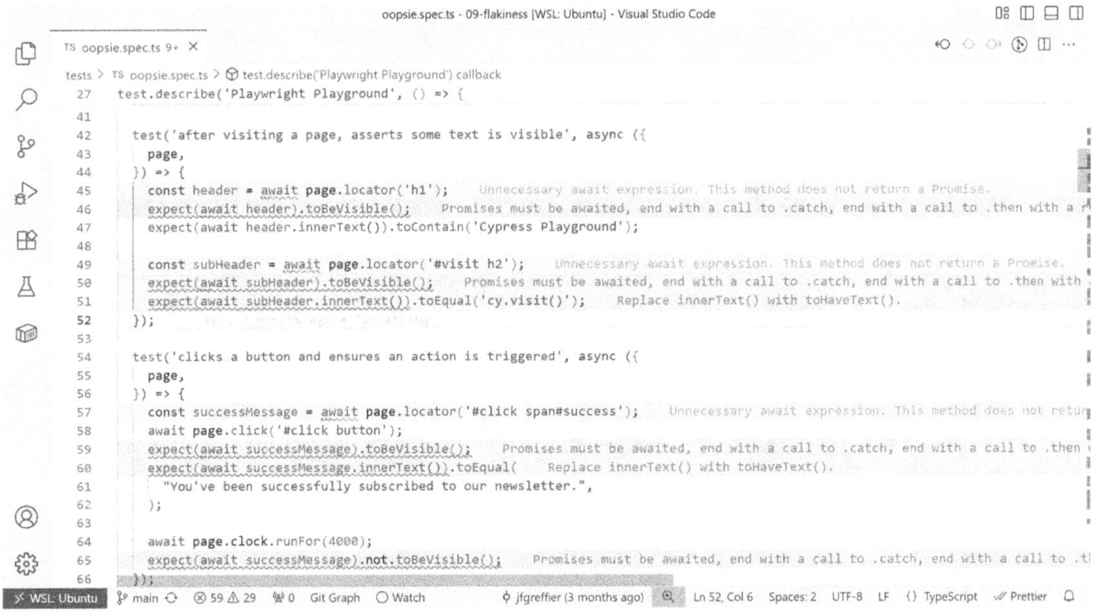

Figure 9-3. VS Code ESLint extension and Error Lens

The following are ESLint rules that I find useful. They are from typescript-eslint and ESLint Plugin Playwright.

`playwright/missing-playwright-await` is great to catch missing `await`. Indeed, to benefit from auto-waiting and auto-retrying assertions, we have to wait for them!

`@typescript-eslint/no-floating-promises` is more generic and not specific to Playwright; it will catch some edge cases that the previous rule doesn't.

213

CHAPTER 9   GAIN CONFIDENCE THANKS TO RELIABLE TESTS

Listing 9-16. Missing Playwright await

```
// ❌ Incorrect
page.getByRole('button').click();
expect(page.locator('#promotional-banner')).toBeVisible();

// ✅ Correct
await page.getByRole('button').click();
await expect(page.locator('#promotional-banner')).toBeVisible();
```

playwright/no-useless-await will look for await that are not necessary, such as with generic assertions. It's a nice addition because useless await harm the code readability and may confuse readers.

Listing 9-17. No useless await

```
// ❌ Incorrect
await page.getByRole('heading');
await expect(1).toBe(1);
await expect(true).toBeTruthy();

// ✅ Correct
page.getByRole('heading');
expect(1).toBe(1);
expect(true).toBeTruthy();
```

playwright/prefer-web-first-assertions will look for assertions that could be changed in favor of web-first assertions. As seen earlier in this chapter, these auto-retrying assertions make more reliable tests.

Listing 9-18. Prefer web-first assertions

```
// ❌ Incorrect
expect(await page.locator('.post').isVisible()).toBe(true);
expect(await page.locator('.post').isEnabled()).toBe(true);
expect(await page.locator('.post').innerText()).toBe('bar');

// ✅ Correct
await expect(page.locator('.post')).toBeVisible();
await expect(page.locator('.post')).toBeEnabled();
await expect(page.locator('.post')).toHaveText('bar');
```

> **Warning** Many of these rules need to configure TypeScript in order to work. A basic configuration can be done in only two steps: install TypeScript as a dev dependency, and init a simple `tsconfig.json` file.
>
> ```
> npm install --save-dev typescript
> npx tsc --init
> ```

These rules are auto fixable. It means that you can fix all of them safely with a single command.

```
npm run lint -- --fix
```

Using TypeScript and ESLint not only helps you follow good practices but will also catch potential issues, automatically. This allows you to focus on better, more interesting, problems.

Unfortunately, none of this helps for our TODO App. Time to put this test aside.

Quarantine

If we can't fix flaky tests right away, we are exposed to the risk of seeing them pile up. When this happens, the value of the whole test suite can decrease as you can't trust tests anymore.

Playwright already marks flaky tests in reports, but it's not quite enough. To avoid noise and avoid contaminating the healthy tests, we will use tags to put these tests in quarantine.

Listing 9-19. Tag and annotation

```
test(
  'flaky test',
  {
    tag: '@flaky',
    annotation: {
      type: 'issue',
      description: https://github.com/acme/app/issues/42',
    },
  },
```

```
  async () => {
    // ...
  },
);
```

Thanks to tags not only we can clearly identify unstable tests, but we can also exclude them from the CI. With grepInvert, in CLI or projects as in Listing 9-20 and Listing 9-20a, you can make different runs for the healthy tests and the unstable ones.

Listing 9-20. Grep invert as CLI option

```
npx playwright test --grep-invert @flaky
```

Listing 9-20a. . Grep invert in playwright.config.ts

```
import { defineConfig, devices } from "@playwright/test";

export default defineConfig({
  testDir: "./e2e",

  projects: [
    {
      // ...
      grepInvert: /@flaky/,
    },
  ],
});
```

Putting tests in quarantine doesn't mean that you shouldn't run them but rather have a differentiated pipeline or reporting. In this way, you can focus on what is important.

Isolate helps, but you still have to fix it. It's probably a good idea to file a bug and add its reference as a test annotation, as in Listing 9-19. Then, depending on your team working style you may want to fix this flaky test at a dedicated time, or right when they appear, or if a maximum is reached. Anyhow, flaky tests must be fixed.

Fix Flaky Tests for Good

We usually don't need to wait for an Element to be ready or to change, as action's auto-waiting is an implicit check. However, there are some cases where we need to perform an explicit check. It can happen when we navigate to a new page with `page.goto()` or if we make an interaction that won't use auto-waiting, e.g., moving the mouse, scrolling, using the keyboard.

To explicitly wait for a Locator, `waitFor()` is fine. But I think that using an assertion is better because it shows that we want to perform a check, before going on with the rest of the test. Also, a failing assertion is clear and easy to debug.

Listing 9-21. Check explicitly

```
// ✘ Never
await page.waitForTimeout();
// Fine
await orderSent.waitFor();
```

```
// ☑ Best
await expect(orderSent).toBeVisible();
```

Sometimes, auto-waiting fails. All checks for an action pass but nothing happens. This may be caused by an hydration issue. For example, a button is in the DOM, is available, and clickable but actually the application is not quite ready yet to process the click action. It may not be obvious, but usually our `chaos` fixture will find such case.

This can happen in frameworks that use hydration, partial rehydration, Incremental Static Regeneration… or more simply in any case where HTML is built and made available before interactions (e.g., JavaScript is still loading). Such hydration issues must be fixed in the application:

- Display a button; set it as disabled until it is ready.
- Show a loading wheel while submitting data to the backend.
- Display placeholders.

It is not always possible to fix the application under test. `expect.poll()` adds retrying to a generic assertion. `expect.toPass()` can be seen as a variant that allows retrying blocks of code. It is very useful in these tricky hydration situations: we will retry an action and make an assertion until it passes.

Listing 9-22. toPass()

```
await expect(async () => {
  await page.getByRole('button', { name: 'Click me' }).click();
  await expect(page.getByText('Success')).toBeVisible();
}).toPass();
```

Another form of race condition appears when running different tests in parallel and is due to lack of test isolation. I encouraged you to use parallelization at different levels: sharding in CI, files parallelization on local machine, test parallelization with `fullyParallel`, massive parallelization with hundreds of tests thanks to Microsoft Playwright Testing or Endform. But having fully isolated stable parallel test is not so easy.

Tests should be isolated, i.e., they should not have side effects. It is easy with unit tests, where you don't change the state of the application, but it's more difficult with end-to-end tests. For example, you might add new items, change user settings, delete a record.

There are usually two strategies to perform test isolation:

- Make a new state from scratch. For example, reset the database at the beginning of a test suite run. Unfortunately, it is too costly to make before every single test.

- Cleanup. The most common. We set up and tear down with `beforeEach`, `afterEach`, or fixture. But cleanup alone doesn't prevent collisions. Moreover, in case of a test failure, it's likely that cleanup also fails and infects other tests by leaving a bad state.

To have better test isolation, you can use scoped data, i.e., create a new user if needed, and make your changes in this new context. Also, you can leverage mocks when applicable.

Start with limited parallelism to avoid issues. It is probable that your CI is not using parallelism yet anyway. Having one worker on one CI agent is a common setup, and is often good enough. Ramp up parallelism gradually; use it first on your local machine to benefit from multicore CPU. Then try introducing sharding in CI. A great advantage of Microsoft Playwright Testing or Endform is that you can use them locally before scaling up in Continuous Integration.

CHAPTER 9   GAIN CONFIDENCE THANKS TO RELIABLE TESTS

Finally, there is one technique that fixes a flaky test for good: delete it. That seems radical, but if you cannot figure it out after adding explicit wait, careful setup, and debugging with traces, then just delete it. Delete it and then rewrite the test from scratch. Sometimes it's better to restart rather than trying to patch up an existing fragile code.

By that time, you probably have a good idea of what you want to verify with this test and maybe you have better knowledge of Playwright, and the application under test, than when the test was written. An alternative might be to resort to manual testing: maybe the functionality is not clear or needs a complicated setup that may benefit from some rework before automating the corresponding tests. Manual testing is sometimes a good opportunity to fine-tune a test before automating it.

Case Study Solution

We've identified earlier that our TODO App test was faulty because we reloaded the page right after creating a new entry. This effectively aborts the POST request to the backend if it is still in progress. Unfortunately, we can't wait for the new item in the list: it's added regardless of the POST request. Worse, the new item will be shown in the list even if the network is cut.

The best solution is to fix the TODO application so that it reflects the real state of the application. For example, it can add the item to the list only once the backend request is done, or it could show some kind of sync status.

To fix the test without changing the app, we will need to wait for another event. Since we know that a POST will happen, we can use `waitForResponse()` to wait for it.

Listing 9-23. Flaky TODO, fixed

```
import { test, expect } from './fixtures';

test('flaky TODO fixed', async ({ page, chaos }) => {
  await chaos();

  const backendURL = getBackendURL();
  await page.goto(`/`);

  const inputLocator = page.getByRole('textbox', {
    name: 'What needs to be done?',
  });
  await inputLocator.fill('tomatoes');
```

```
// 1 no await
const responsePromise = page.waitForResponse(
  (response) =>
    response.url() === backendURL &&
    response.request().method() === 'POST',
);
await inputLocator.press('Enter');
// 2 wait for POST
await responsePromise;
await page.reload();

await expect(page.getByText('tomatoes')).toBeVisible();
});
```

Notice how we create the response Promise before adding the TODO item (1 in Listing 9-23), but wait for the Promise after (2). In this way, we start listening to changes before acting on the application.

Another way to write this is to use `Promise.all()` to wait for every Promise to complete. Some find it much more readable because there's no additional variable.

Listing 9-23a. Flaky TODO, fixed with Promise.all()

```
import { test, expect } from './fixtures';

test('flaky TODO fixed', async ({ page, chaos }) => {
  await chaos();

  const backendURL = getBackendURL();
  await page.goto(`/`);

  const inputLocator = page.getByRole('textbox', {
    name: 'What needs to be done?',
  });
  await inputLocator.fill('tomatoes');
  await Promise.all([
    inputLocator.press('Enter'),
    page.waitForResponse(
      (response) =>
```

```
      response.url() === backendURL &&
      response.request().method() === 'POST'
  ),
 ]);
 await page.reload();

 await expect(page.getByText('tomatoes')).toBeVisible();
});
```

This is far from ideal because it relies on implementation details (the way the app saves an item). The TODO App has an underlying issue that should ultimately be solved.

Summary

I believe we write tests for the sole objective of gaining confidence in what we create. However, this only works if our tests themselves are reliable in all circumstances. That is why fixing flaky tests is not only useful but crucial.

In this part, we've seen

- An in-depth explanation of the various **auto-waiting** and **retry** mechanisms of Playwright Test
- A definition of **flakiness**
- Different ways to detect uncertainty like **test burn-in** or **chaos engineering**
- How to **fix flaky tests for good**

Up until now, we focused on using Playwright for end-to-end testing. But what else can we do with Playwright? We will explore automation, monitoring, and more types of testing in the next chapter.

CHAPTER 10

Automation and More with Playwright

So far, we have exclusively focused on end-to-end testing with Playwright Test. Not only the basics but the intricates of flaky tests, fixtures, performance optimization, and so on. For the last part of this book, we will focus on other usages, both in terms of automation and testing, and how to integrate Playwright Test to your testing strategy.

I remember a few years back when I gave my first public talk. It was on Playwright and my attempt at a definition for this new promising tool was: Playwright is a browser automation solution for end-to-end testing that rocks! While Playwright shines at testing, it is a very capable automation solution. In this chapter, we will explore other uses of Playwright. Automation with the Playwright Library, and the differences with the test runner. We will see examples of usage like scraping and content generation. Finally, I'll introduce Checkly, a synthetic monitoring tool based on our favorite end-to-end testing library.

Playwright Library

At the heart of Playwright Test, there is the automation part named Playwright Library. While Playwright Test provides tooling and architecture for end-to-end testing, Playwright Library is solely dedicated to browser automation without the whole testing framework.

Changing from one another feels a bit like switching from an urban bicycle to a unicycle. It works well, you can do nice tricks with it, but it's not practical to go to work daily and it's more difficult to begin with. Playwright Library and Test are just meant for different usages.

Playwright without any bells and whistles means you can't use assertions, or fixtures, and it is basically plain old Node.js. This also means that you can run directly with node ./getstarted.js which is nice.

Listing 10-1. Get started

```
const { chromium } = require('playwright');
(async () => {
  const browser = await chromium.launch({ headless: false });
  const context = await browser.newContext();
  const page = await context.newPage();
  await page.goto('https://playwright.dev/');
  await page.getByRole('link', { name: 'Get started' }).click();

  await context.close();
  await browser.close();
})();
```

Listing 10-1 is a simple example; it shows some specificities of the automation library. Instead of importing @playwright/test, you require playwright. Note that we use an IIFE (Immediately Invoked Function Expression) to be able to run an async function.

Note I am using CommonJS syntax, with require, in this chapter, as it works everywhere and this is what codegen will give you. You can switch to ES Module by renaming your .js files to .mjs or add "type": "module" to the package.json. With ESM, you can import modules and use top-level await.

You can use Chromium, Firefox, and WebKit. Also, the technical requirements are the same as Playwright Test (see Chapter 1). You'll need to write more code to create a browser instance, a context, then a page, and don't forget to close them. All that heavy lifting to get an isolated page is usually done automatically by Playwright Test. Fortunately, you can use Codegen to create your automation script easily with the necessary setup and teardown. For that, just select Library under Node.js as seen in Figure 10-1.

CHAPTER 10 AUTOMATION AND MORE WITH PLAYWRIGHT

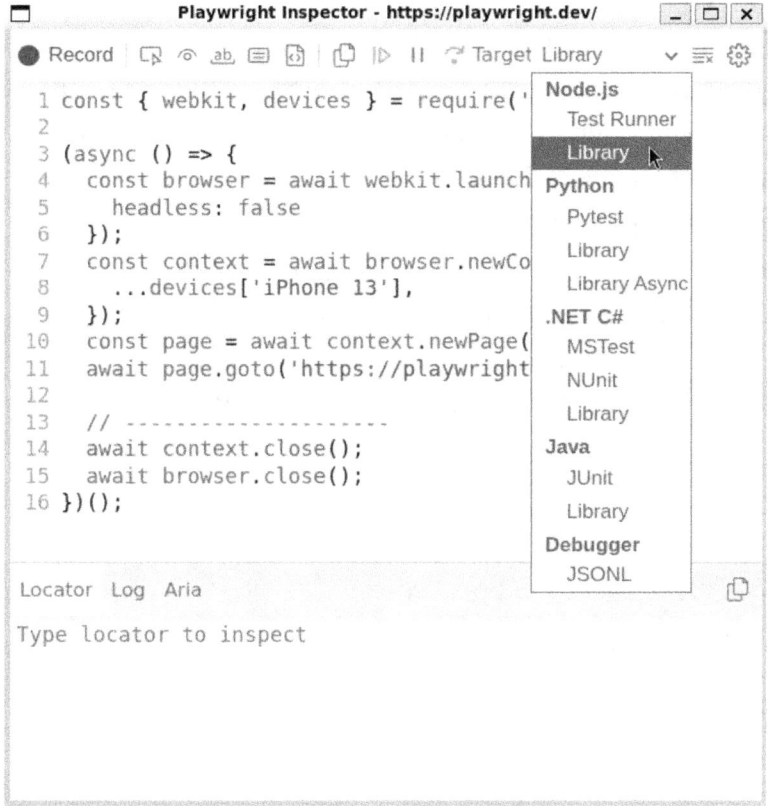

Figure 10-1. Codegen can generate Library code

Codegen is ideal for a record and playback workflow as it will record your actions: navigation, filing input, clicking, ...

Web Scraping

Sometimes public API are not available, incomplete, or not obvious to use. This is frustrating when you just need one piece of information from a web page. Think of checking whether a bicycle is in stock, or if the result of a survey has been published. It is rather easy to use a short Playwright Library script to look for a change on a page and get notified on update.

If we go further from these simple use cases, we extract structured data from a website. This is web scraping.

225

CHAPTER 10   AUTOMATION AND MORE WITH PLAYWRIGHT

> **Warning**   Always look for the terms of service and `robots.txt` file to understand what usage is allowed or not. For example, `https://playwright.dev/robots.txt` discourages crawling the "next" version of the documentation. Be gentle and don't flood a website by aggressively crawling it. Finally, don't steal art and other copyrighted material.

A nice practical usage of scraping is a price watcher. Back in 2022,[1] Sakis from Greece built a solution to track prices from different local supermarkets, allowing consumers to compare prices between shops and have a price history. Playwright Library is ideal for this usage, because it can render dynamic pages with JavaScript in a real browser and extract the information needed effortlessly.

The general workflow for scraping is as follows:

1. Launch the browser and open a page.
2. Go to the target URL.
3. Wait for a Locator to appear.
4. Extract text and/or images.

Listing 10-2. Web scraping example

```
const { chromium } = require('playwright');
(async () => {
  // 1. Launch browser
  const browser = await chromium.launch();
  const context = await browser.newContext();
  const page = await context.newPage();

  // 2. Go to the target site
  await page.goto('https://playwright.dev');

  // 3. Wait for a Locator
  await page.getByRole('link', { name: 'Get started' }).waitFor();
```

---

[1] See his blog for the full story: `https://www.sakisv.net/2024/08/tracking-supermarket-prices-playwright/`.

```
// 4. Extract text
const heading = await page.getByRole('h1');
console.log(`Heading is: ${heading}`);

  await context.close();
  await browser.close();
})();
```

You can see that the best practices for automation and testing are quite different. Methods that we have avoided so far such as `waitFor()` or `Locator.innerText()` are common here.

Playwright provides useful methods for data extraction:

- `innerText()` or `innerHTML()` to get text content
- `screenshot()` more details on that in the next part
- `Locator.allInnerTexts()` returns an array of text from all matching Elements

Unlike Playwright Test, where we want strict Locators that points to a unique Element, in scraping we often target a list of elements. For that, you can use `Locator.all()` to iterate on them.

Listing 10-3. Looping on Elements

```
for (const row of await page.getByRole('listitem').all()) {
  console.log(await row.textContent());
}
```

Once we get these data, we can add them to a database, or write them to a file. Using Node.js is very useful here to be able to manage the data we just got.

Note that you will have the responsibility to implement a solution for parallelization or rate-limit by yourself. Especially the last one, to avoid overloading servers and possibly being blocked. You can start with something as simple as no parallelization and the `slowMo` context option.

Generating Artifacts: Screenshots, PDFs, Videos

Playwright not only can test or interact with websites, it can also create content from them, be it screenshots, videos, or even PDFs.

Screenshots for Your Documentation

Capturing screenshots of a website or a web application can be useful, for example, to create up-to-date documentation. Just like with Playwright Test, we can use device emulation too as seen in Listing 10-4. That's perfect to generate a mobile screenshot, for example.

The screenshot options are the same as toHaveScreenshot(): you can specify an area with clip, make a screenshot of the viewport or the full page, apply a CSS style... Similarly, you can make a screenshot of the page or of a Locator. Because we want to save a file, and not a reference image like with testing, we usually want to specify the path.

Listing 10-4. Screenshot

```
const { chromium, devices } = require('playwright');
(async () => {
  const browser = await chromium.launch();
  const context = await browser.newContext({
    ...devices['Pixel 5'],
  });
  const page = await context.newPage();

  await page.goto('https://playwright.dev');

  // Full-page screenshot
  await page.screenshot({ path: 'home.png', fullPage: true });

  // Element screenshot
  const chart = page.locator('header');
  await chart.screenshot({ path: 'header.png' });

  await context.close();
  await browser.close();
})();
```

Recording Videos

I created a video to demo Playwright Library at my first talk. For that, I used the best way to make a video of a browser automation: recording it with Playwright.

You simply can add a `recordVideo` option when creating the context, with a path to the directory to save the videos. The only downside is that I had to explain why I used `slowMo` and `waitForTimeout` to my audience, while it was only to make a video easier to follow.

Listing 10-5. Video

```
const { chromium, devices } = require('playwright');
(async () => {
  const browser = await chromium.launch({
    slowMo: 1000,
  });
  const context = await browser.newContext({
    recordVideo: { dir: 'videos/' },
    ...devices['Pixel 5'],
  });
  const page = await context.newPage();

  await page.goto('http://playwright.dev');
  await page.click('text=Get started');
  await page.waitForTimeout(3000);

  await context.close();
  await browser.close();
})();
```

The video files are saved upon browser context closure. If you have issues with video recording, make sure you have awaited `context.close()` and it did not stop unexpectedly.

CHAPTER 10   AUTOMATION AND MORE WITH PLAYWRIGHT

```
1  const { chromium, devices } = require('playwright');
2
3  (async () => {
4    const browser = await chromium.launch({
5      slowMo: 1000
6    });
7    const context = await browser.newContext({
8      recordVideo: { dir: 'videos/' },
9      ...devices['Pixel 5']
10   });
11   const page = await context.newPage();
12
13   await page.goto('http://playwright.dev');
14   await page.click('text=Get started');
15   await page.waitForTimeout(3000);
16
17   await context.close();
18   await browser.close();
19 })();
20
```

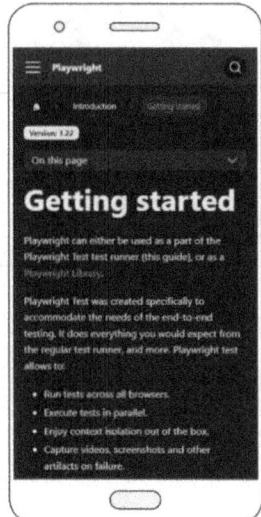

Figure 10-2. Code and result side by side

PDF Generation

A few years ago, I was working on a project where we needed to generate reports in PDF to be sent by email or downloaded by users. The backend was in Java, and after some research, we found that backend solutions we evaluated to generate PDF were not satisfactory. This makes sense: it's hard to render a document that looks great with different fonts, and includes charts and images. But we could get great results rather easily in the frontend. In the end, the team used browser automation to create a microservice that generates multi-page PDFs from a dedicated frontend-page effortlessly.

It's easy and efficient to generate PDF files with Playwright Library, either with the command line or in Node.js as you can see in the following examples.

Listing 10-6. Generate PDF in command line

```
npx playwright pdf https://example.com example.pdf
```

The option `--wait-for-selector` is very handy if you use the CLI. It allows you to wait for a specific selector. By selector, it means CSS selectors and legacy Locators as seen in Chapter 3, e.g., `"text=Log in"`, `"css=.class"`, or `"data-testid=submit"`. For something more complex, you'll have to write a Node.js script.

Listing 10-6. Generate PDF with Node.js

```
const { chromium } = require('playwright');
(async () => {
  const browser = await chromium.launch();
  const context = await browser.newContext();
  const page = await context.newPage();

  await page.goto('http://www.example.com/');
  await page.pdf({
    path: './example.pdf',
    format: 'A4',
  });
  // --------------------
  await context.close();
  await browser.close();
})();
```

Here are some points of attention:

- The browser can be changed and will have an impact on the final render.

- The paper format defaults to Letter, a paper size that is commonly used in North America. You may want to change it to A4, which is used in other countries.[2]

- You can set page range, margin, header and footer, scale…

Generating a PDF file with Playwright is very much like printing a document. This is perfect because you get the flexibility of automation (with CSS injection if needed) and benefits of the rendering fidelity of modern browsers.

---

[2] Insert random joke about system of units.

CHAPTER 10   AUTOMATION AND MORE WITH PLAYWRIGHT

Monitoring with Playwright and Checkly

Many efficient development practices aim to reduce the feedback loop between your changes and their results. TDD and pair programming give you feedback in seconds, CI in a few minutes, stand-up meeting with colleagues in a day, … What if, just like we do Continuous Integration, we could do Continuous Testing?

Even with thorough testing during development cycles, production can break: a component deployment unexpectedly affects another functionality, a third-party service is down or just too slow, you face a DNS problem in some region of the world… On the other hand, monitoring your production is not always enough, maybe the APIs are doing well and no errors are logged in the clients but a change in CSS prevents clicking a button. Testing your production end-to-end allows getting feedback very early on when something breaks. In this way, you can even detect issues before they affect your customers.

This is what Checkly is about. Checkly performs Playwright tests, in production, on a cadence.

Peace of Mind

Surely, you can slap together a CI pipeline and a Slack bot to get some form of alerting from your Playwright tests. But Checkly makes it easier and offers features related to monitoring instead of testing only.

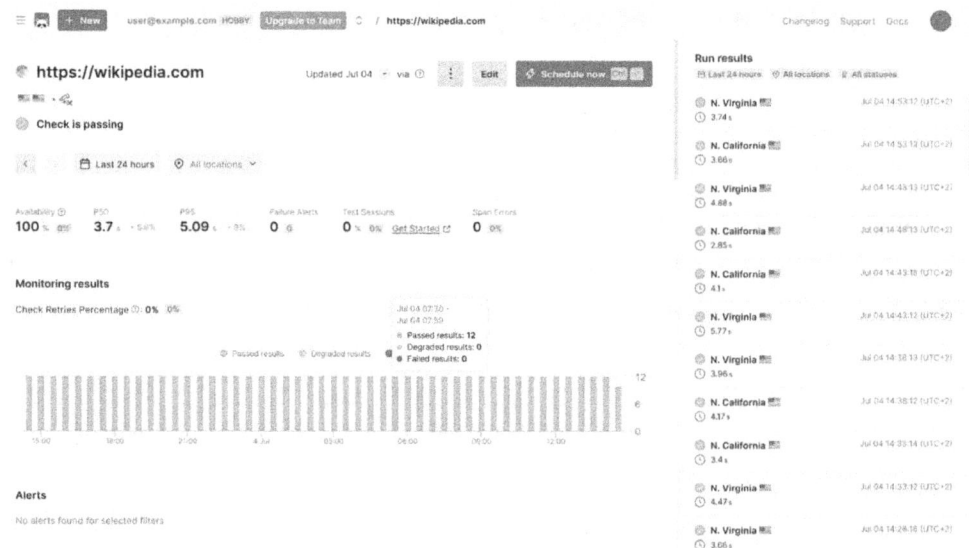

Figure 10-3. Checkly results

First, Checkly offers a monitoring dashboard with checks, their results with different server locations, your application availability, performance hints… In case a test has failed, you will have access to the Playwright Traces to investigate what happened.

Alerts can be sent via phone call, SMS, Slack, email, or pretty much anything since Checkly works with webhooks. With Continuous Testing and alerting, you can find out about issues before your users. Discover problems early and get Playwright Traces to diagnose help to get a shorter Mean Time Between Failure, i.e., short visible outages. Because Checkly is designed for monitoring, it offers fine-grained alerting levels and frequency of tests to have alerting for things that matter. This helps with alert fatigue, when teams are desensitized to notifications because of too many unimportant alerts.

Finally, Checkly provides a status page to make availability and incident status visible to your users.

Use with Playwright

Like Playwright, Checkly offers a command-line wizard. You can run `npm init` to get started (or `npm create` as the docs states, it's the same).

```
npm init checkly
```

Listing 10-7. Checkly CLI wizard

```
? Which template would you like to use for your new project?
    An advanced TypeScript project with multiple examples and best
    practices (recommended)
    An advanced JavaScript project with multiple examples and best
    practices
>   A boilerplate TypeScript project with basic config
    A boilerplate JavaScript project with basic config
```

For your first steps with Checkly, I advise you to select the "A boilerplate TypeScript project with basic config" option from the wizard. It will create a small, familiar project structure as seen in Table 10-1.

Take a look at __checks__/homepage.spec.ts; it's a plain old Playwright test.

Table 10-1. Files added by Checkly initialization script

File	
__checks__/homepage.spec.ts	A Playwright test!
__checks__	This folder holds more checks examples, that are not based on Playwright
checkly.config.ts	Checkly's configuration file
package.json	
.gitignore	

Checkly is an online service, so you will need to log in from the CLI before you can run tests locally, or deploy your configuration and tests to https://www.checklyhq.com.

```
# init
npm create checkly@latest
# login
npx checkly login
# local run
npx checkly test
# deploy your project to your Checkly account
npx checkly deploy
```

Benefits

Testing your application continuously is great because it gives you more confidence and peace of mind. Like end-to-end tests prove that your app works, Continuous Testing proves that users can actually interact with the app. Regardless of DNS, location, or time.

I find Checkly neat because you can leverage your existing Playwright tests and transform them into checks. I advise you to run smoke tests or a "happy path" rather than trying to run all your tests. Select something that is worth worrying about. For example, if users can't access their profile, it's bad but not as bad as if they can't log in. If you don't have tests that would make good checks, it's good that we learned how to write good, reliable end-to-end tests.

All the Checkly configuration can be saved and versioned in Git, as well as the checks. At the times of infrastructure as code, documentation as code, and pretty much everything as code, it's only logical to offer monitoring as code.

Summary

While **Practical Playwright Test** focuses on end-to-end testing, I wanted to give you an overview of what more is possible with Playwright. It allows you to automate tasks, extract content, generate artifacts (like PDFs), or monitor your application. Browser automation has surprising usages, and I believe that more will emerge.

I believe that Playwright Library is here to stay. It has a prominent role in browser automation as it is becoming the favorite building brick for many software applications. Look carefully and you will realize it's under the hood of many automation and testing solutions.

CHAPTER 11

Beyond End-to-End Testing

In this chapter, we'll continue to explore the possibilities of Playwright. Here we will focus on usages that are not the traditional end-to-end testing.

First, we will see how Behavior-Driven Development can be applied and still keep the advantages of Playwright Test. Then API testing, not only in complement to end-to-end testing, but mixed into a unified context. Finally, we'll try different ways to perform in-browser component testing. This allows us not only to test in isolation but also to actually experience and inspect components while we develop them.

Behavior-Driven Development

BDD is a testing practice that uses specifications written in natural language as executable tests. Its goal is to encourage collaboration between different parties: QA, developers, product owners, and business analysts.

The most common syntax to describe features in BDD is Gherkin with the Given, When, Then keywords as demonstrated in Listing 11-1.

Listing 11-1. Gherkin feature example

```
Given the Maker has started a game with the word "silky"
When the Breaker joins the Maker's game
Then the Breaker must guess a word with 5 characters
```

The Gherkin formalism comes from Cucumber, a tool that will help you use your feature specifications as executable tests. Cucumber is a highly popular test runner that is available for Java, JavaScript, and more.

CHAPTER 11   BEYOND END-TO-END TESTING

You can use Cucumber directly with Playwright, but then it means using Cucumber as the test runner. It is fine, but I personally feel it's a loss, as we won't have the benefits of Playwright Test like fixtures, project configuration, and so on. As developers, we already have a lot to learn, so it's best if we can use the same tooling across classic end-to-end and BDD tests.

Playwright-BDD

Playwright-BDD is a tool that will generate Playwright tests from your Behavior-Driven Development scenarios. In order to do that, you'll need to write your tests in Gherkin and implement "steps." In this context, steps are what will transform a sentence into actual code.

The setup is rather easy: install the package and tune the Playwright configuration file. Check the Playwright-BDD website for the exact details and latest instructions. https://vitalets.github.io/playwright-bdd

See Listing 11-2; this is the test itself written in natural language following the Gherkin formalism. Listing 11-3 are steps definition, that can be used across several tests. The steps form the "glue" between Gherkin and Playwright instructions.

Listing 11-2. Test in Gherkin

```
Feature: Playwright site

    Scenario: Check get started link
        Given I am on home page
        When I click link "Get started"
        Then I see a heading "Installation"
```

Listing 11-3. Steps

```
import { expect } from '@playwright/test';
import { createBdd } from 'playwright-bdd';

const { Given, When, Then } = createBdd();

Given('I am on home page', async ({ page }) => {
  await page.goto('https://playwright.dev');
});
```

```
When('I click link {string}', async ({ page }, name) => {
  await page.getByRole('link', { name }).click();
});

Then('I see a heading {string}', async ({ page }, keyword) => {
  await expect(page.getByRole('heading', { name: keyword })).toBeVisible();
});
```

Once you have your test and steps, you use Playwright-BDD to transform them into actual Playwright tests. Please note that it is advised to not commit the resulting tests as they are considered as intermediate artifacts only, i.e., the Gherkin test should be your unique source of truth. Finally, you run the Playwright tests as usual.

```
npx bddgen && npx playwright test
```

One thing that I appreciate is that the Given, When, Then structure is translated into Playwright steps! This makes the test report easier to read.

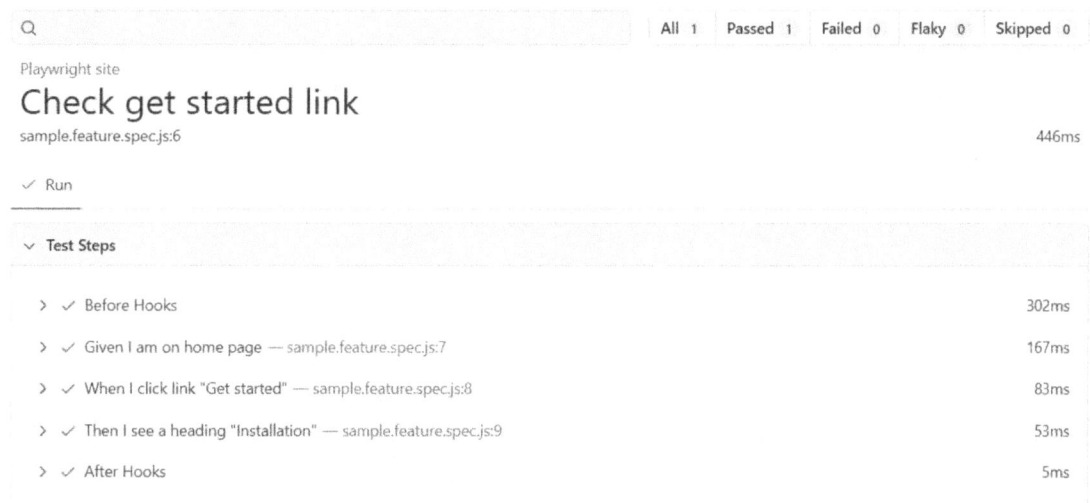

Figure 11-1. HTML test report

Alternative: Approval Testing

In my experience, product owners and the like will usually not write executable tests (even with the convenience of BDD). But they will be more than happy to review and discuss test results that are clear and human-readable. I believe that more than executable requirements, we need means for collaboration.

CHAPTER 11   BEYOND END-TO-END TESTING

I think BDD adds a level of complexity. It requires a lot of code that will only be used as "glue" between the test and the test implementation. BDD tests also can be difficult to debug, as you must find out which step was applied.

An alternative approach to that is **approval testing**. You can write your test as usual but then this test will produce human-readable results exported as a file. This file will serve as a reference for future test runs, and a support to exchange test results with business people. It can also be used as documentation.

The library `approvals` feature helps to generate reference files easily and make comparisons. But we have a much simpler one in our hands: Playwright's snapshot testing. In the Listing 11-4 example, we just leverage `toMatchSnapshot()` to write the reference file as plain old markdown.

Listing 11-4. Generating a document file as Given When Then

```
expect(`
Given a coupon of ${coupon.amount}$ with a minimum of ${coupon.
minimumPurchase}$ of purchase
When the shopping cart is of ${cartTotal}$
Then the amount billed is ${billedAmount}$ `).toMatchSnapshot('coupon.md');
```

This method has the advantage of being easy to set up. It can prove handy when working on legacy code and during a refactor.

REST API Testing

Playwright is great at end-to-end testing, but is not limited to that. For example, it also provides a comprehensive solution for API testing thanks to the request fixture. You can create an isolated context and test APIs directly with Node.js, without launching a browser.

Verifying API behavior with or in addition to end-to-end tests is a plus because REST APIs effectively act as a contract between frontend and backend. These parts should be tested together but also in isolation. APIs can be tested independently of the UI, in addition to the backend inner tests, by using what it exposes: the endpoints and methods specified by this contract.

Many REST APIs are accessed with CRUD operations on resources: Create, Read, Update, Delete. These operations are triggered with the corresponding HTTP methods. Playwright's request can perform all as seen in Table 11-1.

Table 11-1. CRUD operations

CRUD	HTTP	Playwright
Create	POST, PUT	await request.post(), await request.put()
Read	GET	await request.get()
Update	PATCH, PUT	await request.patch(), await request.put()
Delete	DELETE	await request.delete()

This part explores basic mechanisms to perform HTTP requests and validate data with Playwright. I will give you some example use cases for API tests, how to leverage HTTP requests to set up tests, and even how to combine API and UI testing seamlessly in the same test, sharing the same authentication and context.

Your First GET

The APIRequestContext is very simple to use. You will find it familiar if you already use the Fetch API, in browser or Node.js.

Listing 11-5. request.get()

```
test('basic GET', async ({ request }) => {
  const response = await request.get('https://dummyjson.com/quotes/1');

  expect(response.status()).toBe(200);
  const data = await response.json();
  expect(data.id).toBe(1);
  expect(data.quote).toBe(
    'Your heart is the size of an ocean. Go find yourself in its hidden
    depths.',
  );
  expect(data.author).toBe('Rumi');
});
```

Listing 11-5 performs a GET with the request fixture. Once we get the response to our request, we can check a few things:

1. The HTTP response code with `response.status()`

2. The data itself by inspecting `await response.body()`, `await response.text()`, or `await response.json()`

3. The headers with `response.headers()` or `response.headersArray()`. The first method returns an Object, while the second conveniently returns an Array.

Instead of expecting a response code 200, we can use the more robust `response.ok()`. This method determines whether the response was successful, i.e., with a status in the 2xx range.

Note HTTP response status codes at a glance:

1xx Informational – they indicate progress

2xx Successful

3xx Redirection

4xx Client error

5xx Server error

Simple Data Validation

Before adding a fancy schema validator library, consider that Playwright Test can make some data validation without adding any plugin or library.

Our applications usually communicate via JSON, so we want to check the corresponding JavaScript Object. For that, we can check each field like in Listing 11-5, or we can use `expect().toEqual()` to compare the whole Object. It's good but not perfect because that would mean that all fields should be equal.

`expect().toMatchObject()` is a better fit since it allows you to omit some fields and compare only what is important. For example, in Listing 11-6, we verify the `quote` and `author` but not the `id`.

CHAPTER 11　BEYOND END-TO-END TESTING

Listing 11-6. toMatchObject

```
test('toMatchObject', async ({ request }) => {
  const response = await request.get('https://dummyjson.com/quotes/1');

  expect(response.ok()).toBeTruthy();
  const data = await response.json();
  expect(data).toMatchObject({
    quote:
      'Your heart is the size of an ocean. Go find yourself in its hidden
      depths.',
    author: 'Rumi',
  });
});
```

Playwright will give you a clear diff if the comparison fails, both in the terminal and in HTML report.

```
→ 11-API git:(main)   npx playwright test get

Running 3 tests using 3 workers
  1) [chromium] › tests/get.spec.ts:16:7 › API › toMatchObject ─────────────────

    Error: expect(received).toMatchObject(expected)

    - Expected  - 1
    + Received  + 1

      Object {
        "author": "Rumi",
    -   "quote": "The heart is the size of an ocean. Go find yourself in its hidden depths.",
    +   "quote": "Your heart is the size of an ocean. Go find yourself in its hidden depths.",
      }

      19 |     expect(response.ok()).toBeTruthy();
      20 |     const data = await response.json();
    > 21 |     expect(data).toMatchObject({
         |                  ^
      22 |       quote:
      23 |         'The heart is the size of an ocean. Go find yourself in its hidden depths.',
      24 |       author: 'Rumi',
        at /home/jfgreffier/confidence-playwright-test/11-API/tests/get.spec.ts:21:18

  1 failed
    [chromium] › tests/get.spec.ts:16:7 › API › toMatchObject ─────────────────
  2 passed (647ms)

Serving HTML report at http://localhost:9323. Press Ctrl+C to quit.
```

Figure 11-2. *Diff in terminal*

Nice, we have a basic data validation!

But it only works with this one resource, given that it does not change its value in the future. It won't work with `https://dummyjson.com/quotes/random`. This API endpoint

243

will return a random quote every time it is called with a GET. So, maybe we don't want to validate the exact data of the API response, but rather the shape of the data. This is exactly what we can do with pattern matching (also known as asymmetric matchers).

Comparing with expect.anything() checks that there is a value (not undefined nor null). It must be used in an expect such as toEqual() or toMatchObject().

Listing 11-7. Pattern matching

```
expect(value).toEqual({ prop: expect.anything() });
```

expect.any() lets you match with a constructor or a primitive type (like Number, String, or Boolean). It is perfect with toMatchObject() to check the shape of data for API testing. In Listing 11-8, we verify the API response but not the exact values themselves. Anyway, they will change since the quote is random.

Listing 11-8. toMatchObject with pattern matching

```
test('toMatchObject with pattern', async ({ request }) => {
  const response = await request.get(
    'https://dummyjson.com/quotes/random',
  );
  expect(response.ok()).toBeTruthy();
  const data = await response.json();
  expect(data).toMatchObject({
    id: expect.any(Number),
    quote: expect.any(String),
    author: expect.any(String),
  });
});
```

Playwright Test offers interesting comparison capabilities: object matching, regex, number comparison (toBeGreaterThan, toBeLessThan, ...) or pattern matching. However, it might not fit everyone's needs for API testing. If this is the case, you should then consider schema validation libraries like Zod or Ajv, or even maybe a tool that supports OpenAPI.

Context Request

So far, we have used the `request` fixture to write tests in isolation. We also have the option to use `page.request` or `context.request`; they share cookies with the browser context.

It means that `page.request` will perform requests with the context's cookies, but will also set the browser cookies when responses have the `Set-Cookie` header. This allows a transparent use of cookies with API requests and browser. For example, you can log in as a user through the UI and perform API checks that require authentication. If the auth is based on cookies, that is.

Why Playwright for API Testing?

There are perfectly good tools dedicated to API testing, like Postman, so why use Playwright? Or more broadly, what does an end-to-end testing solution have to do with API testing?

Being able to perform actions in the browser and via APIs in the same flow makes many use cases possible:

- Leverage shared (cookie) authentication
- Prepare a test context with API: create a user, authenticate, flush data, ...
- Fast teardown with API instead of UI
- Golden master: you make actions in the browser, then compare an API data against a reference

I think the key here is Playwright's ability to mix and match API testing with browser testing at every step of the very same test.

Component Testing

Most test frameworks use jsdom or happy-dom to simulate a browser. This is sufficient in many if not most cases. But this is only a tradeoff between faster, easier-to-set-up tests and realism. In this part, we will detail solutions to have isolated component tests in a real browser environment.

Chapter 11 Beyond End-to-End Testing

First, let's see an example of why Component Testing gives you more confidence.

Listing 11-9. Fetch greeting

```
import { useState } from 'react';

function GreetingComponent({ url }: { url: string }) {
  const [buttonClicked, setButtonClicked] = useState(false);
  const [greeting, setGreeting] = useState('');

  const fetchGreeting = async (url: string) => {
    setButtonClicked(true);

    // ...

    setGreeting(result);
  };

  return (
    <div>
      <button onClick={() => fetchGreeting(url)} disabled={buttonClicked}>
        Load Greeting
      </button>
      {greeting && <h1>{greeting}</h1>}
    </div>
  );
}

export default GreetingComponent;
```

The GreetingComponent from Listing 11-9 works flawlessly: when the user clicks, it fetches a greeting and displays it. Yet, it does not work in production. This is because the component breaks when we apply the stylesheet.

Listing 11-10. Broken button

```
button {
  padding: 10px 20px;
  margin: 0 10px;
  font-size: 36px;
```

```
  border-radius: 5px;
  cursor: pointer;
  background-color: #99ccff;
  color: #333;
  border: none;
  transition: background-color 0.5s;
}
button, :disabled {
  opacity: 0.5;
  pointer-events: none;
}
button:hover {
  background-color: #77aaff;
}
```

Can you catch the typo?

On line 13 of Listing 11-10, the CSS selector is incorrect.

```
button, :disabled {
```

Instead of applying to a disabled button, it will apply to buttons and disabled Elements. Let's write an in-browser component test to detect that.

...with Playwright

We will create our project in the same way that we used the Command Line Interface to scaffold the end-to-end tests. We only need to add the `--ct` option.

```
npm init playwright -- --ct
```

The wizard first asks which language to use, TypeScript or JavaScript. Then the CLI asks which framework you are using. This information is crucial because, unlike Playwright Test, Playwright Component Testing is bound to the framework.

```
✓ Do you want to use TypeScript or JavaScript? · TypeScript
? Which framework do you use? (experimental) ...
▶ React 18
```

CHAPTER 11 BEYOND END-TO-END TESTING

React 17
Vue 3
Vue 2
Svelte
Solid

Let's take a look at what files the initialization script has added (Table 11-2).

Table 11-2. Files added by initialization script

File	
playwright/index.html	A harness for the components
playwright/index.tsx	Here you can add global code, import code, or apply a stylesheet
playwright-ct.config.ts	A configuration Playwright Test configuration file tailored for Component Testing
package.json	
.gitignore	

The CLI also added an npm script for convenience. It is simply launching a test with a specific configuration file.

```
{
  "scripts": {
    "test-ct": "playwright test -c playwright-ct.config.ts"
  }
}
```

This is interesting because it means that running component tests is only a matter of configuration file. You can run component tests and end-to-end tests on the same project, by using different configuration files.

We can now write our test. It consists of the Arrange Act Assert pattern:

1. Mount our component.

2. Click on the 'Load Greeting' button.

3. Check that the 'Hello there' message appears.

Listing 11-11. Greeting test

```
import { expect, test } from '@playwright/experimental-ct-react';
import GreetingComponent from './greeting';

test('loads and displays greeting', async ({ mount }) => {
  // Arrange
  const component = await mount(<GreetingComponent url="/greeting" />);
  const button = component.getByRole('button', { name: 'Load Greeting' });

  // Act
  await button.click();

  // Assert
  await expect(component.getByRole('heading')).toHaveText('hello there');
  await expect(button).toBeDisabled();
});
```

It is almost identical to an end-to-end test, with two notable differences:

- We import expect and test from the experimental component testing module. They have the exact same behavior as their regular counterparts.

- The component under test must be mounted. Actions and assertions will be on the mount result instead of page.

At first, the test is successful because we didn't load the global CSS yet. This can be performed in the playwright/index.tsx file as shown in Listing 11-12. This file is a global initialization and is ideal for global styling, for example.

Listing 11-12. index.tsx

```
// Import styles, initialize component theme here.
import '../src/common.css';
```

Now that once we've applied our global CSS, we can see the issue: obviously the button is not clickable when it should be.

Playwright Component Testing is using Vite in the background. First, it takes your components that are under test and bundles them into a simple application. It writes to the filesystem and Vite serves it back for Playwright to run the tests on.

CHAPTER 11   BEYOND END-TO-END TESTING

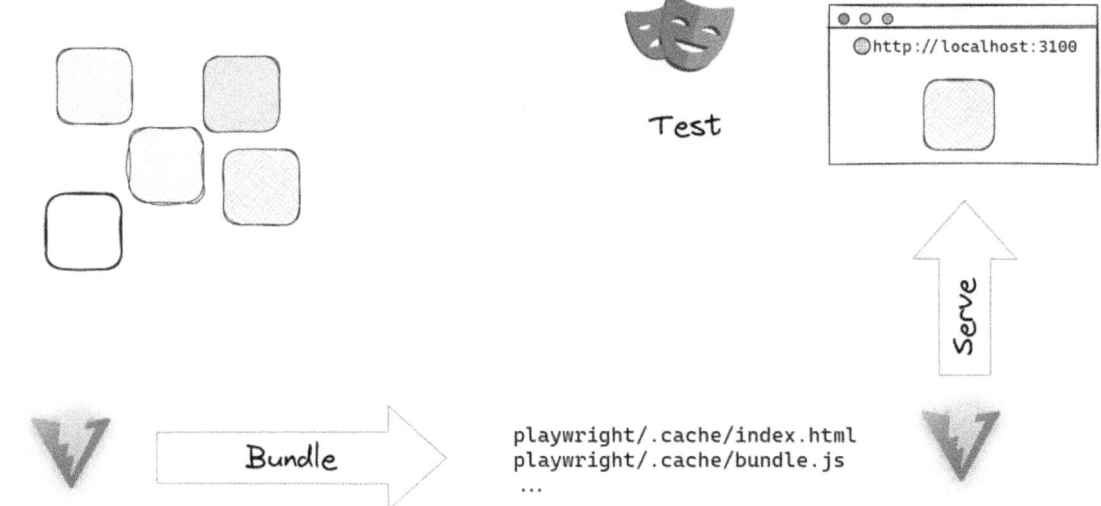

Figure 11-3. Playwright component testing

Basically, Playwright Component testing is a test harness with a framework-specific mount adapter + a dev server + Playwright Test. Because ultimately it's still Playwright Test, you can get the usual features:

- Web-first assertions
- Locators
- Auto-waiting
- Testing Library queries
- Debugging
- Trace viewer

On top of that, I use component testing as a workbench. Because the components are rendered in a browser, I can interact with and inspect components while I develop them.

CHAPTER 11   BEYOND END-TO-END TESTING

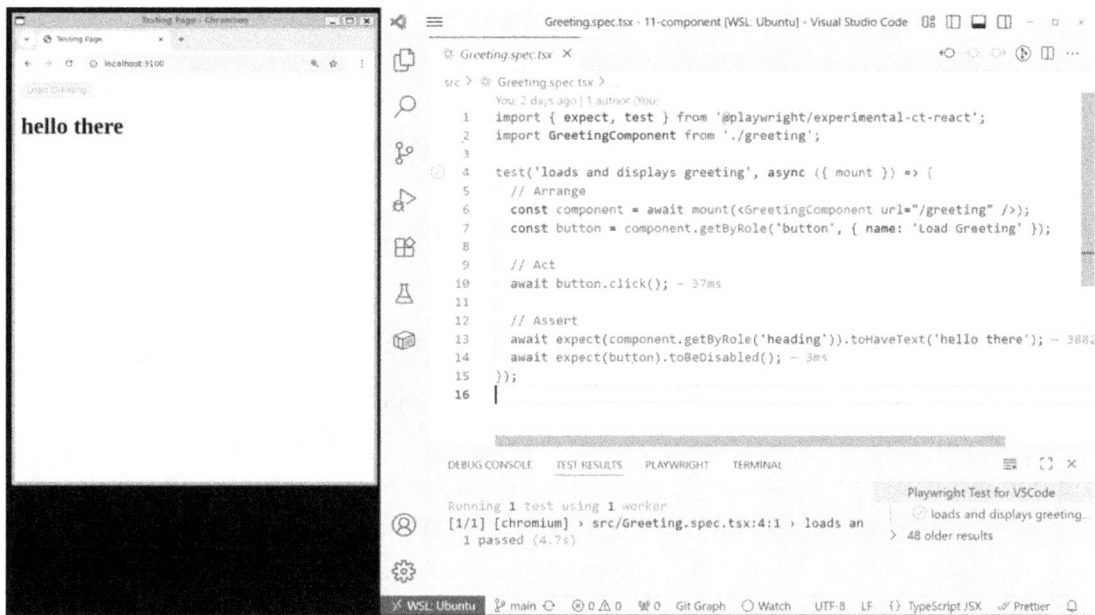

Figure 11-4. *Playwright component testing*

Playwright Component Testing supports React, Vue, Svelte, and Solid. But sadly, it does not support Angular, one of the most popular and used web application frameworks. While community-led alternatives exist,[1] this situation is not optimal.

Moreover, there is no plugin system to easily add a framework mount adapter. Other limitations include the following:

- This feature is experimental.

- Documentation is somehow lacking.

- Passing props has some tricky limitations that are not intuitive at first.

- To my liking, it's not quite fast enough for TDD. It's not as fast as unit tests, and will probably never be. That's the case for all in-browser component testing solutions that I've experimented with.

---

[1] https://github.com/sand4rt/playwright-ct-angular

251

Using an experimental feature has some risks; its API may change drastically or may be deprecated. This and the lack of proper Angular support are, in my opinion, the main drawbacks. The good news is that it is "just" setup. Apart from the test harness, the rest remains plain old Playwright Test. You can pivot from Playwright Component Test to something else, like Storybook.

...with Playwright and Storybook

Storybook is a popular tool that allows you to render your frontend components (and pages) in isolation to display them in a catalog. It's perfect if you are building and maintaining a design system, but it's also valuable if you don't. Storybook makes components easier to share and document the reusable components of your application.

Components run outside the full application, without the need for a backend or other dependencies, giving you more control. It is performed with code that describes uses cases of the component, called **story**. This isolation is precisely what is interesting for automated testing.

There are three main solutions to do component testing with Storybook:

- Storybook's test runner

  Based on Jest and Playwright, it will be superseded by the Vitest addon.

- Storybook's Vitest addon

  It is actually using Vitest Browser Mode, an experimental feature that uses a Playwright-like Locator library and drives browsers with Playwright or WebdriverIO.

- Use our favorite end-to-end testing framework against Storybook catalog

As of now, I personally prefer the last solution. Here is why: instead of introducing another test runner, or a deep integration between Storybook and Playwright, I just perform end-to-end against Storybook pages.

The main benefit is that you can leverage your knowledge of Playwright and its features, and you get Storybook's isolation, i.e., test components without the whole application.

Let's adapt our greeting test to Storybook.

Listing 11-13. Greeting test with Storybook

```
import { test, expect } from '@playwright/test';
test('loads and displays greeting - with Storybook', async ({ page }) => {
  await page.goto('http://localhost:6006/iframe.html?id=greetingcomponent--
  default&viewMode=story');
  const button = page.getByRole('button', { name: 'Load Greeting' });

  await button.click();

  await expect(page.getByRole('heading')).toHaveText('hello there');
  await expect(button).toBeDisabled();
});
```

Except for the targeted URL, there is nothing special in Listing 11-13. The test code looks like a regular Playwright end-to-end test.

Note Each Storybook story can be loaded in isolation via its canvas URL. To get the URL, look for the "Open canvas in new tab" or "Copy canvas link" icon (top-right of the preview panel).

My favorite use case is testing an already existing Storybook. A number of companies have a design system: a set of reusable UI components with consistent UX and branding. Some of them are public, like Google's Material Design or Shopify's Polaris.

Let's take Shopify's Polaris Storybook: `https://storybook.polaris.shopify.dev`

CHAPTER 11   BEYOND END-TO-END TESTING

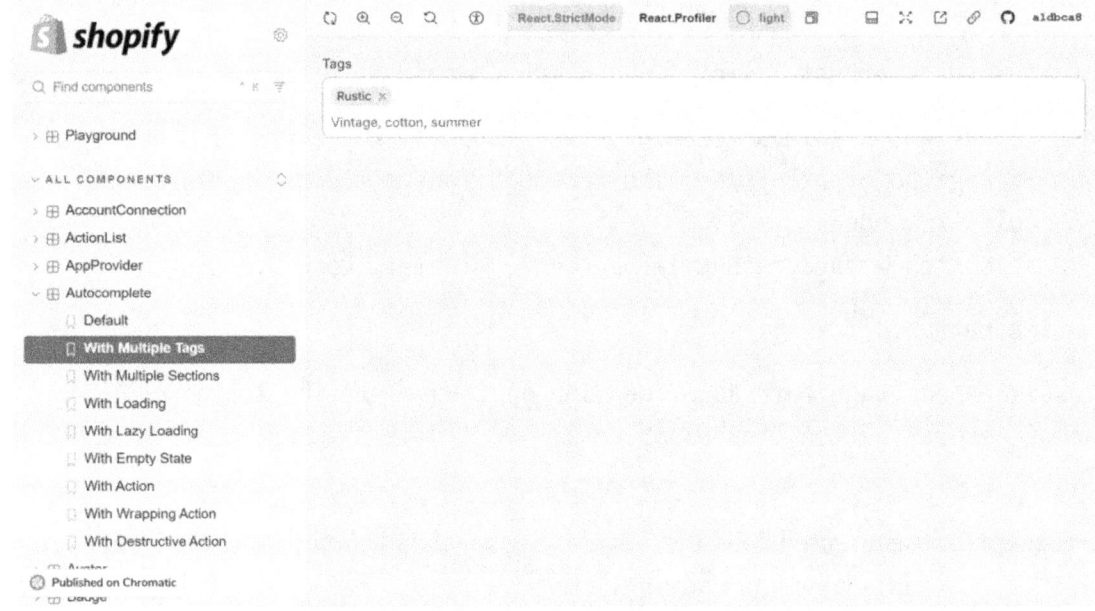

Figure 11-5. Autocomplete component in Storybook

To test the **Autocomplete** component, we need its canvas URL. It will display the component only and nothing else. The perfect entry point for Playwright Test.

In our case the canvas URL is https://storybook.polaris.shopify.dev/iframe.html?globals=&id=all-components-autocomplete--with-multiple-tags&viewMode=story

We can then create an end-to-end test on this URL to test the component. We can even generate the base of our test with the Playwright VS Code extension.

Listing 11-14. Shopify Autocomplete component

```
import { test, expect } from '@playwright/test';

test('Shopify Autocomplete component', async ({ page }) => {
  await page.goto(
    'https://storybook.polaris.shopify.dev/iframe.html?globals=&id=all-components-autocomplete--with-multiple-tags&viewMode=story'
  );

  await page.getByRole('button', { name: 'Remove Rustic' }).click();
  await page.getByRole('combobox', { name: 'Tags' }).click();
```

254

```
  await page.getByRole('option', { name: 'Antique' }).click();
  await page.getByRole('combobox', { name: 'Tags' }).fill('refurbished');
  await page.getByRole('combobox', { name: 'Tags' }).press('Enter');

  await expect(page.locator('#storybook-root')).toContainText(
    'AntiqueRefurbished'
  );
  await expect(page).toHaveScreenshot();
});
```

That's it! An end-to-end test against a public Storybook component. The main drawbacks of this technique are as follows:

- Storybook setup can be rather hard. You'll need to write stories (component descriptions) for each component you want to test.

- It's not possible to pass different props from the test itself. You should rely on Storybook stories to get different states of the component.

- Not quite fast enough for TDD.

My advice is to write tests with Storybook if you already have a catalog of components in place. If not, you may need to consider other solutions.

Summary

In this chapter, we've seen

- How to use **Behavior-Driven Development** and benefit from Playwright Test

- Not only testing API but having a **unified testing experience**

- **Component testing** with different technical solutions

We've seen that the experimental Playwright Component Testing has its limitations. The first one being that it might not support the web framework you are using, notably Angular. You should also take into account that as of now, it is not under active development.

Component testing with Playwright Test and Storybook is easy to set up. That is, if you already use Storybook.

Another alternative is Vitest Browser Mode, a promising feature that offers a similar Developer eXperience to Playwright Test.

Component testing in a browser is still relatively new, and evolving. It is definitely something to watch closely.

Beyond end-to-end testing and component testing, you might also wonder if it is possible to use Playwright's test framework for unit tests. It is possible, but maybe not the best choice as it lacks some key features. Mocking is missing, and this is especially troublesome if you want to mock module imports (i.e., `require()` or `import`). I only know of one code base that uses Playwright Test for unit testing: Playwright.

That's right, the team uses Playwright Test to test their tool. The practice of using their own product is called dogfooding. It is not that rare in the computer industry. For example, in 1980, Apple asked their employees to stop using typewriters in favor of personal computers.

In the next and final chapter, we will discuss the testing strategy and the frameworks that you can use for your testing needs.

CHAPTER 12

Solving the Test Frameworks Puzzle

We have come to the end of our learning journey. I hope that you learned things about Playwright Test, testing strategy, and how you can apply the content of this book in the future. We will see in this final chapter how end-to-end testing can fit in your testing strategy and how to integrate Playwright Test to a consistent testing technical stack.

Before exploring different testing strategies, let's talk about the different kinds of tests and testing activities. Obviously, that's a vast domain where quality engineers are experts. Static analysis, code review, pair-programming, mob-programming, Continuous Integration, exploratory testing, three amigos... You don't have to know it all, but as developers, we should take the responsibility of making well-crafted software. And for this, we need testing.

I personally tend to stick to the test dichotomy of Kent C. Dodds. If you don't know Kent, he theorized the Testing Trophy, is an educator, playwright, ambassador, and creator of Testing Library.

Here are different kinds of tests:[1]

- Static: These are not tests per se, but rather basic checks that will make potential errors visible and more difficult to create.

- Unit: Checks a "Unit," usually a function, a class, or a module.

- Integration: Test different components together, usually with some mocking. Narrow integration tests focus on a component and some of its dependencies, whereas broad integration tests may avoid mocks altogether.

---

[1] https://kentcdodds.com/blog/static-vs-unit-vs-integration-vs-e2e-tests has great definitions and examples focused on frontend.

- End-to-end: Well, I guess you know this one. This kind of test interacts with your application like your user would, with the entire system in place. It effectively means that it will test through every layer and component of your application, i.e., browser, REST API, cache, microservices, database, ...

Now, what test should we write and what should be the strategy for our tests?

The Test Pyramid Is a Wrong Model

The Test Pyramid is a way to organize automated tests that finds its origins around the year 2004. It was popularized by Mike Cohn who describes this way to distribute test effort in his book *Succeeding with Agile*. It basically states that you should have lots of unit tests, some integration tests, and a few end-to-end tests.

This recommendation is more than 20 years old, and while old doesn't mean outdated, the Test Pyramid is definitely a product of its time. I believe that it was created while taking into account assumptions that are now false or at least less relevant than in the 2000s.

Assumption 1: Unit tests are fast and cheap.

I think now there is a general agreement that unit tests are invaluable for development practices like TDD. However, nobody seems to agree on how big a unit should be. A function, a class, a JavaScript module are the most common answers but it can definitely be bigger and I think it should. While narrow unit tests can verify business logic easily, that's usually only one part of the problem. You must add integration test because the unit you are testing is not working in vacuum. Another default of unit tests is that they make you commit to the interface of what you are testing, i.e., you are testing a function with certain parameters. What happens when you refactor it and change the function signature, or move this function around, rename, and merge functions logic? Your unit tests cannot run as is during your refactoring if you change the interface. It means that you can't use these tests as a safety net during your refactoring. Integration tests can help.

Assumption 2: Integration tests are slow and difficult to debug.

Now we have lots of efficient tooling and patterns for mocking. In frontend, we'll often use component integration test, where we don't test code in vacuum but rather component in its natural environment: mainly DOM and API. jsdom or happy-dom will mock some parts of a browser; Mock Service Worker allows you to mock an API; we can also easily make module mocking, partial mocks, and so on. Narrow integration tests are way cheaper than before.

Assumption 3: End-to-end tests are brittle, expensive to write, and slow.

I think end-to-end tests being brittle was a major issue with Selenium-WebDriver when the Test Pyramid was theorized. I also experienced overnight tests that failed because of timing issues, WebDriver crashes, and poor selectors. We are now in a much better position (with Playwright and other end-to-end testing frameworks). With fixtures, helper functions, Testing Library queries, and a better test recorder, end-to-end tests are no more expensive to write than other types of tests. However, they remain expensive to maintain because of their very nature: they are testing the entire system, so changes in different application layers may have an impact on end-to-end tests. It is true that end-to-end tests are much slower than other kinds of tests, even with Playwright that is really fast. But two things balance this: end-to-end tests cover way more perimeter than other kinds of tests; one end-to-end test can cover functionalities that may otherwise require dozens of other tests. Second, our machines, physical or virtual, are much faster than before and we can parallelize them. It is not only a question of fast vs. slow, but also cheap vs. expensive and simple vs. complex testing setup (with only-changed, projects, …).

What I personally find useful:

- Tests that are fast enough and relatively narrow to make **TDD**. Unit test or narrow Integration test fits this definition. I tend to prefer integration tests with few mocks to have more coverage and not commit to implementation details.

- Tests that give me **confidence**. Only end-to-end tests can make me confident that my users can log in to an app with OAuth, redirect to the main app, search content through the backend and its database, and check that their favorite content is available. If this doesn't work, I know that users will not be happy.

- Tests that allow me to **refactor mercilessly**. An application code changes when we add new features, but we also improve it along the way. Tests are essential to be able to refactor without breaking things. Like a safety net.

Take some time to think about what kind of automated tests you want to write. Let's take a look at the available testing tools that will help you.

CHAPTER 12   SOLVING THE TEST FRAMEWORKS PUZZLE

State of JavaScript Testing

Keeping up with the latest techniques, languages or tools is essential to our work as developers. Participating to meetups and conferences, exchanging with colleagues and peers are probably the most efficient and rewarding ways to keep up to date. Reading articles, developers surveys, research papers, and books allows you to deepen your knowledge.

I have mapped out the existing testing tooling based on the different projects' GitHub repositories, my own experience, and the State of JavaScript 2024 developer survey. JetBrains' Developer Ecosystem report and Stack Overflow are interesting too, but not as detailed.

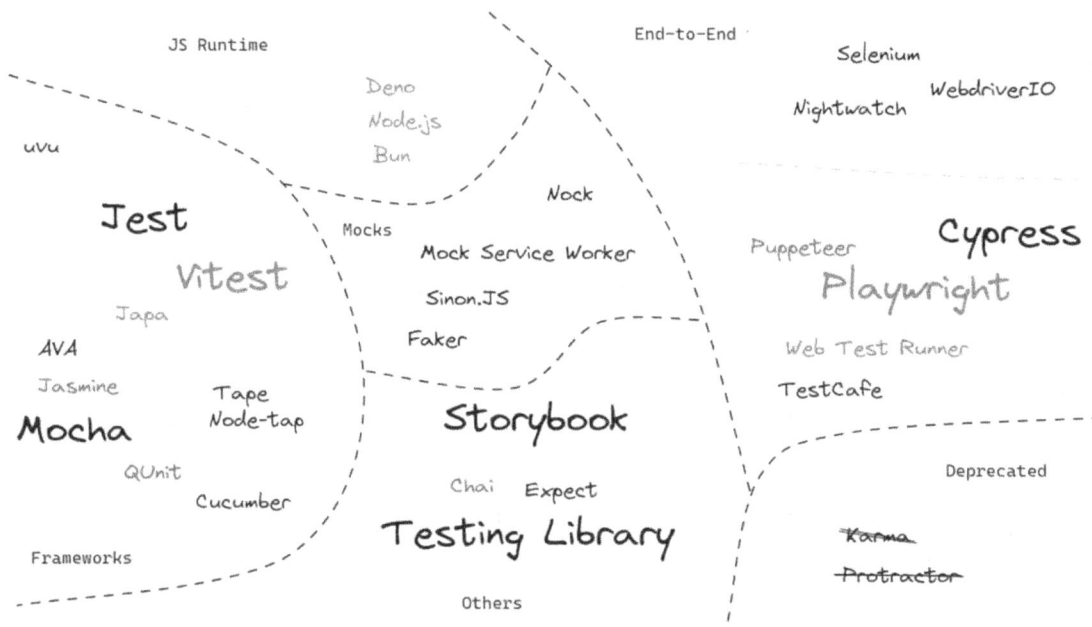

Figure 12-1. *Test map*

The biggest items in Figure 12-1 are the most popular testing solutions: Jest, Mocha, Vitest, Testing Library, and Cypress.

Among the newcomers, a few are worth noting. Firstly, the meteoric rise of Vitest. Also, we can see that all JavaScript runtimes now offer an integrated testing solution (Node.js since version 20). Finally, Playwright has established itself as a leading end-to-end testing framework. It has had more downloads than Cypress for some time and continues to gain popularity. It is also increasingly used as an automation library for other solutions built on it.

Frameworks

Jest remains the reference for unit testing: it is well-known, used massively, modular, actively maintained and it inspired modern test frameworks. Another advantage is the amount of plugins and reporters available for Jest.

The rise of **Vitest** is very impressive. It's the testing framework with the most traction, even if its usage in professional environments is not big yet.

Mocha is still popular but it is not exactly a framework, as you need to add a mocking and an assertion library. Its popularity and usage are slowly decreasing.

Japa is interesting as it focuses on Node.js backend, with features like contract-based testing. If you have an OpenAPI definition (aka Swagger), Japa can use it to test your API.

Note that **Cucumber** is the most popular solution for Behavior-Driven Development. Its usage is limited, as not everyone follows this practice. We've seen in the previous chapter that approval testing can also be useful and that there are alternative frameworks like Playwright-BDD.

JS Runtimes

Node.js, Deno, and Bun all offer an integrated testing solution. This is great if you don't need code transformation, like in frontend.

Everything is new, fast, and shiny with **Bun**, but imperfect.

End-to-End

There are two families of end-to-end testing solutions:

- Selenium WebDriver–based solutions like Selenium, Nightwatch, and WebdriverIO. WebDriver is a W3C recommendation that can drive pretty much any browser.

- Using the browser's DevTools Protocol. That's the approach of Cypress, Puppeteer, and Playwright. This has the reputation to be faster than WebDriver.

The most popular end-to-end test framework is still **Selenium**; it is widely used and has a ton of learning resources and tooling. However, **Cypress** is probably the most used solution among developers, with strong competition from **Playwright Test**.

Part of the **Puppeteer** team left Google to go build Playwright. While Puppeteer is actively maintained, I would advise migrating to Playwright as you will find similar APIs and many more functionalities. The first one being Playwright Test: Puppeteer does not have a test runner. It must be paired with Jest, for example. There is a guide in the official documentation to help you migrate from Puppeteer to Playwright.

Mocking

Mocks, spies, and other testing doubles are often provided by your test framework (such as Jest and Vitest). Still, **Mock Service Worker** is notable because it allows you to mock network requests easily.

As seen in Chapter 6, you should use **Faker** with Playwright. It integrates without issue with any other testing framework and gives you the benefit of better and more realistic tests.

And More

Testing Library is very popular for integration testing, or component testing. It allows checking the DOM easily. In this way, you can test the actual behavior of a front-end component, instead of testing its inner functions and implementation details.

Storybook is not a testing solution per se, but it is very interesting. Storybook allows you to create a catalog of isolated front-end components. This isolation makes it easy to test components in a browser, either manually or with browser automation. Check Chapter 11 on how to use Storybook with Playwright to perform in-browser component testing.

Now that we know what kind of tests we want to write and what tools are available to us, we can now put the pieces of the testing puzzle together.

A Homogenous Testing Stack

Now that we've seen different types of tests and the current state of JavaScript testing, we have everything to make our technological choices for our tests. In the following part, I give my personal recommendations of testing tools, based on my own criteria.

CHAPTER 12   SOLVING THE TEST FRAMEWORKS PUZZLE

Reliable *and* ***battle-tested*** *solutions*

Tools that are ***efficient***

Homogeneity *to reduce cognitive load*

I am conservative about the tooling I use and prefer reliable solutions rather than all-new ones. This means using tools with lots of usage, good maintenance, and a community to rely on when you have a question.

I need fast tests for a shorter feedback loop. First, in Continuous Integration, I'd like my builds to be under 10 minutes (an eXtreme Programming practice). If it's longer, I might switch to something else or go grab a coffee. This is inefficient because context-switching costs a lot in terms of focus. I also need fast tests to be able to make TDD, Test-Driven Development. TDD helps me a lot to develop. To be efficient, the (unit) tests should be as fast as possible.

I like having tools that share some similarities. Our job is complex enough as it is, that is why I propose a testing stack (shown in Figure 12-2) with consistent syntax and principles:

- Assertions are all Jest Expect-inspired
- Two closely related test runners (Vitest and Playwright Test)
- Fixtures
- Testing Library queries

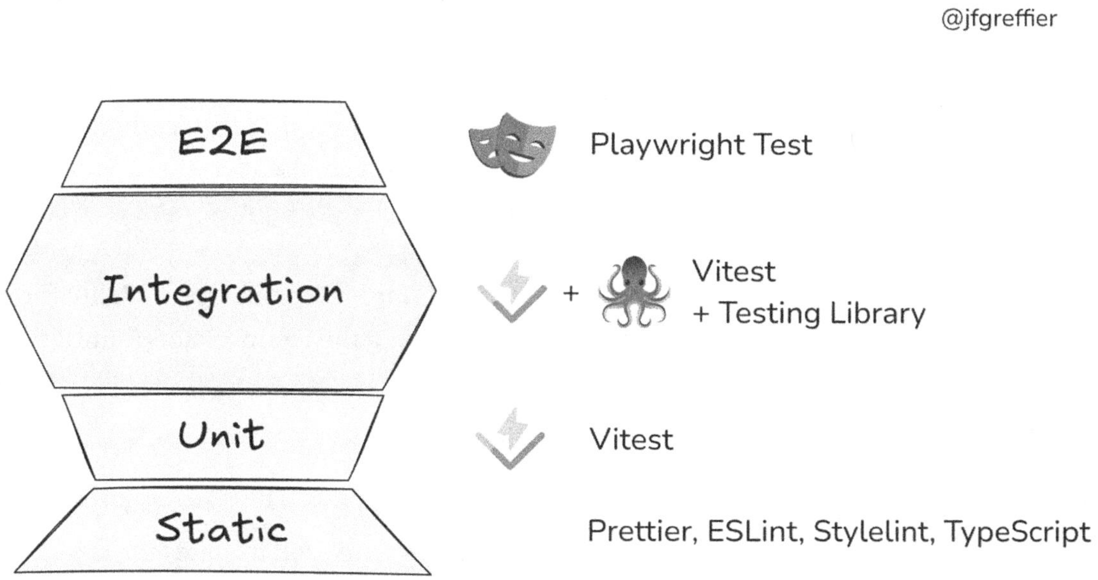

@jfgreffier

Figure 12-2. *My own trophy of tests*

In the end, it's all about Developer eXperience: having something that's useful and efficient on a daily basis. Good DX makes the developers' lives easier and makes them more prone to write tested, good-quality code.

Static – Prettier, ESLint, Stylelint, TypeScript

Prettier is a code formatter for JavaScript, TypeScript, HTML, CSS… It will help you reduce your cognitive load by working behind the scenes. By enforcing formatting, it will make diffs and merges easier and stop endless discussions about semicolons or indentation type. Prettier will also verify that your code is well formatted. It lets you concentrate on more important stuff.

ESlint performs static code analysis to find potential problems and bugs. The great thing is that this tool can be used via a script, but also directly in your IDE. Displaying problems directly ensures a short feedback loop. I like to add Prettier to ESLint to check formatting at the same time. To put it differently, checks must fail when the formatting is incorrect.

Stylelint is somehow similar to ESLint, except that it's for CSS and SASS/SCSS. It will check for syntax, rule precedence, formatting, but can also enforce concentric CSS or whatever good practice your team wants to use.

Biome is a great alternative to Prettier and ESLint. It can be set up with little to no configuration, will format and lint your code very quickly. It is not on par with ESLint, especially with TypeScript, but it's a great alternative overall that I really enjoy using.

TypeScript is a real plus as it makes your code more expressive, powers auto-completion, and will make potential issues more obvious. The TypeScript compiler can spot issues at build instead of at runtime. If you are not using it already, you can migrate to TypeScript gradually. The great thing is: you probably already know some TypeScript thanks to Playwright Test.

I strongly suggest installing extensions on your IDE for Prettier, ESLint, Stylelint (or Biome). It will give you feedback as you write code, making the feedback loop shorter.

Unit – Vitest

For unit tests, I advise Vitest. It's a test framework created in 2020 by Anthony Fu, from the Vite community. You can see it as a clone of Jest based on Vite: it shares the same assertions, similar syntax, and test runner; the CLI options are also familiar for a Jest user. There is something really cool called fixtures. As a matter of fact, it is inspired by Playwright Test's fixtures.

Vite + Jest = Vitest

The syntax is very familiar if you have ever written test in TypeScript or JavaScript, being with Jest, Playwright, or another test framework. It is very close to the Playwright syntax and usage, with similar principles. This makes it a great choice as it is a good testing solution by itself, but also you will feel at home when using Vitest.

Listing 12-1. vitest.spec.ts

```
test('adds 1 + 2 to equal 3', () => {
  expect(sum(1, 2)).toBe(3);
});
```

My main criterion to use Vitest instead of Jest is purely performance. It's just fast. Jest is a great tool, so it's a solid alternative in this proposed test stack. Keep in mind that most of the performance gap can be explained by the transformation process (i.e., preparing code to be tested). Babel will be slower than Vite, but esbuild can be on par.

Integration – Testing Library

For component Integration tests, I use Vitest together with Testing Library. This solution was created by Kent C. Dodds in 2018 and is particularly popular among React developers. Testing Library will help you to have tests that are less relying on the implementation details, but rather on the results in the DOM. This is great to test not only functions but whole components, or set of components, based on what they do. Testing Library works with anything: React, Vue, Angular, and so on with Jest, Vitest, Cypress…

Here are examples of the queries syntax, which Playwright Test shares.

Listing 12-2. vitest+testing-library.spec.ts

```
screen.getByLabel('User Name');
screen.getByLabel('Password');
screen.getByRole('button', { name: 'Sign in' });
screen.getByText('Welcome, John!');
```

CHAPTER 12   SOLVING THE TEST FRAMEWORKS PUZZLE

Using Testing Library encourages you to build more accessible and testable components. This works well with Playwright Test best practices, pushing good habits on both integration and end-to-end testing.

End-to-End – Playwright Test

This feels like the final piece of a puzzle. Playwright Test complements and fits the previous listed tooling, with the goal of testing applications as the user experiences it in a browser.

Playwright Test shares a lot with the previous recommendations we've seen: the assertions are like Jest expect and Vitest; the queries are like Testing Library. There is something really cool called fixtures, just like in Vitest!

Consider Playwright Test's syntax and how it shares similarities with the other recommended tools.

Listing 12-3. playwright.spec.ts

```
test('login', async ({ page }) => {
  await page.getByLabel('User Name').fill('John');
  await page.getByLabel('Password').fill('secret-password');
  await page.getByRole('button', { name: 'Sign in' }).click();

  await expect(
    page.getByText('Welcome, John!')
  ).toBeVisible();
});
```

Notice how

- `getByLabel()` is similar to Testing Library queries
- Assertions like `expect().toBeVisible()` are familiar if you already know Vitest or Jest
- The `test`, `describe`, test structure, and the Command Line Interface are similar to Jest

All of this makes Playwright Test learning curve rather low. However, because Playwright Test focuses on web testing on the main browser engines, you might consider other solutions in limit cases. For example, if you run tests on a real mobile device, an older browser, or a browser that is not based on Chromium, Firefox or WebKit.[2] In these cases, you'll need to look at Selenium WebDriver.

Conclusion

I believe that if you read this book thoroughly, you are serious about testing and Playwright Test. Still, let me warn you about Hype-Driven Development. No tool should be chosen solely because of its popularity, or because of its Developer eXperience, or because you read a book. Select a tool because it fits your needs and context.

If you are a professional developer, it's not only your choice but the team's. Show Playwright to your colleagues. Let them challenge it, try it, and discuss it. Write and automate a test on your application happy path, then make a live demo of it. Then finally, make an informed choice as a team.

We've seen how Playwright can easily be integrated into a consistent testing stack. My hope through this book is to help you set up, use, and customize Playwright Test so that it can fit your testing needs.

Start small but start now. A minimal setup with just one smoke test, in Continuous Integration, can provide a lot of value. Even a single test running regularly gives you more confidence, which I believe is the main goal of tests. You can later explore sharding, POM, and fancy mocking.

If you think about it, there were no Unit Tests before tooling. Or at least no widespread adoption of Unit Tests without xUnit. Test-Driven Development is only possible because of fast, reliable unit test framework. Automated end-to-end testing is only possible because there are technical solutions to achieve it. Moreover, testing so largely and often is only economically viable thanks to test automation. In this case, the usages change thanks to the progress in techniques and tooling. Not only does tooling make practices possible and viable: I believe that a breakthrough in tooling fosters practice changes.

By making end-to-end testing faster and more affordable, Playwright Test challenges the traditional test pyramid. I believe that it's more than a great tool. I think Playwright Test is about to create a major paradigm shift in software testing.

---

[2] This is probably very rare, except for IE and Ladybird. If you know another browser, let me know!

Index

A

Actions, 45, 78
    advanced
        accessibility and testability, 33
        addLocatorHandler, 33
        drag and drop, 31
        upload, 32
    check and focus, 31
    checkboxes, 29
    clear, 28
    click(), 27
    fill sets, 28
    forms, 28
    goto, 27
    HTML Elements, 26
    press and pressSequentially, 28
    selectoption, 30
    tap, and mouse hover, 27
    uncheck, 29
addInitScript, 195
Allure setup, 97, 98
Angular, 10, 251, 252
Annotations, 137–139
API testing, 245
Apple's dynamic island, 179
Approval testing, 240, 241
Aria snapshots, 40–43
Array.filter(), 73
Assertions, 78
    generic, 34
    library, 34
    snapshot, 38, 42
    toHaveScreenshot(), 38
    web-first, 36
    web-first assertions, 43
Asymmetric matchers, 35, 244
Authentication, 121–122
Autocomplete component, 254
Automated testing, 252
Automatic fixtures, 170, 171
Automation
    and Checkly, 232–235
    end-to-end testing, 223
    PDF generation, 230, 231
    with Playwright Library, 223–225
    screenshots, 228
    and testing, 223
    videos, 229, 230
    web scraping, 225–227
Auto-retrying assertions, 37, 202
Auto-waiting, 199–201, 217
Awesome Playwright, 14, 142
AWS Lambda functions, 128
Axe reporter, 142, 143

B

baseURL, 49, 154
BDD, *see* Behavior-driven development (BDD)
Behavior-driven development (BDD), 261
    approval testing, 240, 241
    Gherkin feature, 237
    Playwright-BDD, 238, 239

INDEX

Block content, 126, 127
Browser automation, 230
Browsers
    Playwright
        browser debug protocol, 4
        Chromium, 4
        drawback, 5
        Firefox, 4
        WebKit, 4
Building blocks, 17
    assertions, 18
    DOM and CSS, 17
    environments, 52
    locators, 17
    test.use(), 52
Built-in fixtures, 158, 164, 168, 176
Burn-in testing, 208–210

C

Callbacks, 44
CDP, *see* Chrome DevTools
    Protocol (CDP)
Chaos, 209, 210
Checkly
    benefits, 234, 235
    CI, 232
    configuration, 235
    peace of mind, 232, 233
    use with playwright, 233, 234
Chrome DevTools Protocol (CDP)
    CPU slowdown, 196
    Emulation.setCPUThrottlingRate, 197
    great resources, 197
    parameters, 197
Chromium, 4, 6, 12, 91
Chromium-based browser, 91
Chromium's DevTools, 195

CI agents, 111
CI runners, 111, 184
CI tests, 207
CLI, *see* Command Line Interface (CLI)
CLI wizard, 233
Clock API, 184–187
clock.fastForward(), 186
clock.runFor(), 186
Codegen, 3, 13, 54, 55, 70, 78, 224, 225
    toolbar, 54
Command Line Interface (CLI), 52, 85,
    230, 234, 247, 248, 264
Component testing
    broken button, 246, 247
    in browser environment, 245
    fetch greeting, 246
    ...with Playwright, 247–252
    ...with Playwright and
        Storybook, 252–255
Confidence
    automated tests, 199
    auto-waiting, 199–201
    Flaky tests (*see* Flaky tests)
    test framework, 199
    test retry, 204–206
    timeouts, 203, 204
    web-first assertions, 202, 203
Content generation, 223
Context request, 245
Context.route(), 189
context.setGeolocation(), 188
Continuous integration (CI), 212, 213, 216,
    218, 232, 263
    action/checkout, 83
    adding Trace, 95
    advantages, 83
    configuration, 95
    Docker, 89

end-to-end tests, 81
environment, 97
feedback loop, 108
GitHub Workflows, 83
gitlab-ci.yml, 88
parallelism, 94
pipeline, 81, 94, 98, 119, 124
playwright.yml, 83, 84
principles, 107
runner, 111, 127
slow(), 95
solutions, 82
timeout, 94, 95
toHaveScreenshot(), 92
CSS matcher creation, 133–135
CSV file, 148
Cucumber, 261
Custom expect
    composing matchers collection, 135, 136
    CSS matcher, 133–135
    extend expect, 132
    message, 131, 132
Cypress, 261

D

Data attributes, 69, 79
Data validation, 242–244
defaultBrowserType, 180
Dependency Injection, 18, 151
Developer eXperience, 106, 108, 256, 264
Device emulation
    isMobile, 180
    mobile device, 177, 178
    mobile testing, 182
    space and time
        clock API, 184–187

    geolocation, 188
    locale, 183
    permissions, 187
    timezones, 184
    usage, 180–182
    userAgent, 178
    screen, viewport and deviceScaleFactor, 179, 180
deviceScaleFactor, 179
DevTools Protocol, 261
Discord community, 15
Docker, 89, 92
    with GitHub Actions, 90
    image, 89, 91
    playwright.yml, 90
DOM snapshot, 104
Don't Repeat Yourself (DRY), 175
DRY, *see* Don't Repeat Yourself (DRY)

E

Endform, 128, 129
End-to-end test, 21, 102, 209, 247–249, 255, 258, 259, 266, 267
End-to-end testing, 1, 235, 257, 260–262, 266
    BDD, 237–240
    component testing, 245–255
    REST API testing, 240–245
Error Lens, 213
ESLint rule, 44, 45, 78, 213, 215, 264
expect() function, 133

F

Fail fast, 124
Fake clock, 186, 187
Faker, 145–148

INDEX

Faker.js, 147
Firefox, 1, 4–6, 12, 18, 91, 180
Fixture collection
    custom test, 174
    DRY *vs.* WET, 175, 176
    organizing helpers, 174, 175
    custom test, 173, 174
    third-party, 174
Fixtures, 18, 152
    advantages, 164
    composition, 163, 164
    decoupling setup and test, 159–163
    definition, 153
    improving tests, 154, 156, 157
    test hooks, 153
    wrap-up, 164
    writing, 157–159
Fixtures dependencies, 163
Fixtures usages, 176
    adding testing data, 168–170
    automatic fixtures, 170, 171
    test options, 171–173
Flakiness, 2
Flaky tests
    auto-waiting, 217
    burn-in, 208–210, 212
    chaos, 209, 210
    check explicitly, 217
    in CI, 207
    DOM, 217
    end-to-end tests, 218
    good practices, 215–218
    hydration, 217
    manual testing, 219
    quarantine, 215, 216
    statistics, 207
    test isolation, 218
    TODO app, 211, 212, 219–221
    toPass(), 218
    waitFor(), 217
    in workflows, 207
fullyParallel, 25, 47, 113–115, 218
Functions, 33, 44, 45, 60, 79, 123, 128

G

Generic assertions, 34, 35, 43, 44
Geolocation, 183, 187–189, 195
getByRole(), 62, 63, 65–68, 72, 76
Ghostery, 126
GitHub action, 86, 89, 96
GitHub Workflow, 83, 88
GitLab CI, 81, 88, 97, 117
Google's Material Design, 253
goto() method, 45, 125, 217
GreetingComponent, 249

H

Handle function, 190
home.spec.ts, 154, 160, 161
Homogenous testing
    CI, 263
    Developer eXperience, 264
    end-to-end, 266, 267
    integration tests, 265, 266
    static, 264
    TDD, 263
    unit tests, 264, 265
HTML report, 12, 95, 100, 102, 243
HTML snippets, 41
HTTP ARchive (HAR), 193
Hyperfine, 109, 112

I

ICU identifier, 184
iframe, 71, 72
IIFE, *see* Immediately Invoked Function Expression (IIFE)
Immediately Invoked Function Expression (IIFE), 224
Integration testing, 262
Integration tests, 257, 258, 265, 266
IntelliJ, 13
isMobile, 51, 180

J

Japa, 261
JavaScript, 10, 44, 247
JavaScript testing
    DOM, 262
    end-to-end, 261, 262
    framework, 261
    GitHub repositories, 260
    JetBrains' Developer Ecosystem, 260
    JS runtimes, 261
    mocking, 262
    test map, 260
jest-extended! library, 132
jest-extended.spec.ts, 132
JetBrains, 13, 260
JSON file, 83, 140, 148, 215

K

Kubernetes environment, 122

L

Large File Storage (LFS), 40
layout-matchers.ts, 134
Library, 59
    API discoverability, 62
    ARIA attributes, 67
    chrome accessibility, 66
    CSS selector, 59
    data-testid, 61
    getByAltText, 68
    getByLabel, 68
    getByPlaceholder, 69
    getByRole, 65
    getByTestId, 69
    getByText, 64
    getByTitle, 71
    testability and accessibility, 59
    text and data-testid, 61
    XPath, 62
Locale, 183
Locator handler, 127
Locator.innerText(), 227
Locator, 58, 60, 61, 63, 80, 98, 104, 134
    chaining, 74
    syntax, 75
    tier list, 77
Locator selector, 13
loggedInAdminPage fixture, 160, 163
loggedInPage fixture, 163

M

MatcherReturnType, 133
Matchers, 132–135
Math.random() behavior, 195
merge-report job, 118
Microsoft Playwright Testing, 128, 208
Mocha, 260, 261
Monitoring, 232–235
Multi-page PDFs, 230
Murphy's law, 207

INDEX

MyFixtures, 160, 169
my-test.ts, 150, 151

N

Network
    JavaScript injection, 194, 195
    record and replay HAR, 193, 194
    route, 189–191
    slow network emulation, 191–193
Network panel, 104
Non-retrying assertion, 202, 203
npm, 8
npm init playwright, 9, 10

O

The official Playwright documentation, 14
--only-changed option, 123, 124
Organizing tests
    applications, 23
    arrange act assert, 21
    describe and hooks, 22
    files and folders, 22
    playwright.config.ts files, 26
    projects, 24
    solutions, 20
    test files, 21

P

page.evaluate(), 194
Page Object Model, 67, 79
    advantages, 166
    class, 165–167
    definition, 164
    with fixture, 167, 168
page.route(), 126, 194
page.routeFromHAR() options, 193

Parallelism
    machine *vs.* CI agent, 111, 112
    number of workers, 108–110
    Operating System, 108
    options
        default, 112
        fullyParallel, 113, 114
        parallel, 112
        serial, 113
Parallelization, 128
PDF generation, 230, 231
Performance optimization, 120, 121
Permissions, 187
PhpStorm, 13
PIRequestContext, 241
Playwright
    Angular, 10
    auto-wait, 2
    browsers
        Chromium, 4
        debug protocol, 4
        drawback, 5
        Firefox, 4
        usage, 10
        WebKit, 4
    bun, 8, 9
    check prerequisites, 9
    Codegen, 3
    definition, 1
    dependencies to run the browsers, 6
    Discord community, 15
    end-to-end testing, 1
    example.spec.ts, 11
    Expect, 3
    flakiness, 2
    Get started with end-to-end testing, 14
    Host validation warning, 6
    IDE

INDEX

JetBrains test automation plugin, 13
Vim, 13
Visual Studio Code, 12
VS Code extension, 12, 13
initialization scrip, 10
JavaScript, 10
Library, 3
LTS version, Node.js, 5
Node.js application, 5
npm, yarn, pnpm..., 8, 9
nvm, Node.js, 5
the official Playwright
    documentation, 14
online resources, 14, 15
QA tips by Abi, 14
requirements, 5
selectors, types, 2
step-by-step tests, 2
solutions, 14
tests, 1–3, 9, 10
TL;DR, 8
trace viewer, 3
TypeScript, 10
unit and integration tests, 1
Playwright assertions system, 132
Playwright-BDD, 238, 239
playwright.config.ts, 22, 47, 140, 145,
    151, 180
Playwright configuration file, 24
Playwright documentation, 26, 46, 60,
    63, 86, 88
Playwright Inspector, 55, 106
Playwright Library, 223–226, 230, 235
Playwright snapshots, 40
Playwright's Traces, 102
Playwright team, 62
Playwright Test, 18, 20–22, 26, 47, 48, 70,
    82, 96, 105, 266, 267

Continuous Integration, 107
reputation, 107
Playwright Testing service, 128
@playwright/test package, 10
Playwright Test's fixtures, 20
playwright.yml, 85
Poka-yoke, 212
POM with fixture, 167, 168
Prettier, 264
Projects, 49
Promise, 44–46
Promise<MatcherReturnType>, 133
Puppeteer, 262

Q

QA tips by Abi, 14

R

Radio buttons, 30
Refactor mercilessly, 259
Reliability
    auto-waiting, 199–201
    test framework, 199
    test retry, 204–206
    timeouts, 203, 204
    web-first assertions, 202, 203
Reporter interface, 142
Reporters
    annotations, 137–139
    attach, 139, 140
    custom reporter writing, 142–145
    HTML report title, 140, 141
    importance, 137
    static URL, 137
    tags, 137
    third-party reporters, 141, 142

Reporting, 95
REST API testing
    context request, 245
    CRUD operations, 241
    data validation, 242–244
    GET, 241, 242
    HTTP methods, 241
    Node.js, 240
    Playwright, 245
    and UI, 241
route.fetch(), 190

S

Scraping, 223
Screen, 179
Screenshots, 228
Selectors
    Locator selector, 13
    types, 2
Selenium, 261
Semantic HTML, 75, 76
Serial, 113
Set-Cookie header, 245
setFixedTime, 184
settings.spec.ts, 156, 162
Sharding
    GitHub pipeline, 116, 117
    granularity, 115
    Playwright's startup time, 114
    reconstruct reports, 117–119
    test batches, 115
    third-party reporters, 119
Shopify's Polaris, 253
Snapshot files, 38
Snapshot testing, 38
Spread syntax (...), 51, 181
Standard GitHub-hosted runners, 111

Standard GitHub Linux runner, 111
Static code analyzer, 213
Static tests, 257, 264
Step-by-step tests, 2
strategy.job-index, 117
Stylelint, 264

T

Tags, 137
TDD, 251, 258, 259, 263
Ten-minute build, 107
Test data
    defining test cases, 148, 149
    Faker, 145–148
    parametrizing test, 149, 150
    TestOptions type, 150, 151
test.describe.configure(), 112
Test environment, 197
Test harness, 131
Testing Library, 257, 262, 265, 266
Testing strategy
    end-to-end, 258
    homogenous, 263–268
    integration, 257
    JavaScript testing, 260–262
    static, 257
    and testing activities, 257
    Test Pyramid, 258, 259
    unit, 257
Testing Trophy, 257
TestOptions type, 150, 151
Test Pyramid, 258, 259
Test retry, 204–206
Tests
    end-to-end, 1
    Playwright, 2
    step-by-step, 2

Tests lifecycle, 143
Time frame, 104
Timeouts, 203, 204
Timezones, 184
TODO App, 211, 212, 219–221
toHaveScreenshot(), 93
Trace viewer, 49, 102, 103
Tuple, 141
TypeScript, 10, 18, 213, 215, 247, 264

U

UI mode, 13, 56, 106
Unit tests, 257, 258, 264, 265
URLs glob pattern, 189, 190
User/admin dichotomy, 163
userData fixture, 169

V

vdouble-click, 27
Videos, 229, 230
Viewport, 179
Vim, 13
Visual Studio Code, 12
Vitest, 261, 264, 265

VS Code, 56, 105, 106
VS Code ESLint extension, 213
VS Code extension, 56

W

waitFor(), 227
Web application
   frameworks, 251
Web-first assertions, 37, 202, 203, 214
WebKit, 4
Web scraping, 225–227
webServer, 48
WebStorm, 13
WebViews, 182
WET, *see* Write Everything Twice (WET)
Write Everything Twice (WET), 176

X, Y

XHR request, 210
XPath, 61

Z

Zero-bug policy, 207

GPSR Compliance

The European Union's (EU) General Product Safety Regulation (GPSR) is a set of rules that requires consumer products to be safe and our obligations to ensure this.

If you have any concerns about our products, you can contact us on

ProductSafety@springernature.com

In case Publisher is established outside the EU, the EU authorized representative is:

Springer Nature Customer Service Center GmbH
Europaplatz 3
69115 Heidelberg, Germany

www.ingramcontent.com/pod-product-compliance
Lightning Source LLC
LaVergne TN
LVHW081347060526
838201LV00050B/1739